ROYAL HORTICULTURAL SOCIETY

how to grow
plants in pots

LONDON, NEW YORK, MUNICH,
MELBOURNE, DELHI

Project Editor Zia Allaway
Editors Sarah Ruddick, Christine Dyer
Project Art Editor Vicky Read
Jacket Designer Mark Cavanagh
Production Editor Joanna Byrne
DK Picture Library Jenny Baskaya,
Lucy Claxton
Managing Editor Esther Ripley
Managing Art Editor Alison Donovan
Associate Publisher Liz Wheeler
Art Director Peter Luff
Publisher Jonathan Metcalf

RHS Editors Simon Maughan,
James Armitage

Additional text Zia Allaway
Photography Peter Anderson

First published in Great Britain in 2011 by
Dorling Kindersley Limited
80 Strand, London WC2R ORL
Penguin Group (UK)

2 4 6 8 10 9 7 5 3 1
005-179522-May/11

A CIP catalogue record for this book is available
from the British Library

ISBN 978-1-4053-6228-3

Printed and bound in China
by Leo Paper Products Ltd

Discover more at
www.dk.com

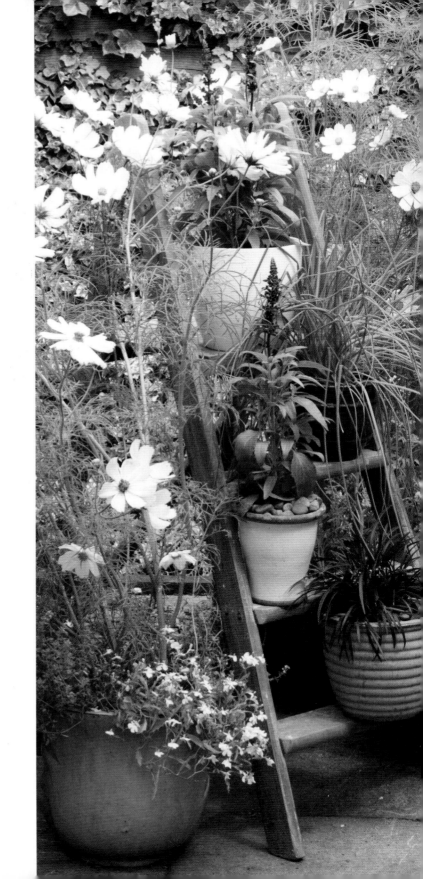

ROYAL HORTICULTURAL SOCIETY

how to grow
plants in pots

Martyn Cox

Contents

DESIGNING WITH CONTAINERS

Eco-friendly ideas	9
Contemporary designs	10
Modern materials	11
Old-world charm	12
Traditional materials	13
Perfect partners	14
Pots in gardens	16
Pots on patios	20
Balconies and roof terraces	24
Decorative windowsills	28
House warmers	30

FOLIAGE AND FLOWERS

Choosing ornamentals	34
Fragrant flowers	36
Tropical effects	48
Drama queens	64
Desert dwellers	78
Easy orchids	86
Plants for shade	94
High climbers	104
Spring spectacles	114
Summer blooms	126
Cold-season displays	142

FRUIT AND VEGETABLES

Planning crops in pots	154
Salads	156
Mediterranean mixes	164
Tasty greens	172
Perfect pods	176
Delicious roots	182
Cool-season crops	188
Herbs	192
Citrus fruit	204
Pudding fruit	208
Mediterranean fruit	212
Exotic fruit	216
Summer berries	218
Tree fruit	224
Unusual fruit	230

PLANTING GUIDE

Planting techniques	234
Caring for container plants	238
Sowing vegetable seeds	240
Pests and diseases	242
Index	250
Acknowledgments	255
Picture credits	256

 indicates that plant is generally grown as a house plant

A–Z OF PLANT ENTRIES

Foliage and Flowers

Abutilon x hybridum p.139
Acer palmatum pp.68-69
Acorus gramineus p.147
Aechmea p.63
Aeonium pp.78-79, 82-83
Agave p.80
Alocasia x amazonica p.60
Aloe p.81
Alpines p121, 134-135
Ananas comosus p.77
Anthurium pp.53, 96-97
Arisaema p.53
Asplenium pp.96-97
Aster species p.144
Astilboides tabularis p.71
Aubrieta p.120
Alopecurus pratensis p.120
Azalea pp.122-123
Bamboo species pp.54-55
Begonia pp.100-101
Blechnum gibbum p.103
Bougainvillea glabra p.113
Brugmansia p.47
Buxus sempervirens p.142
Cactus species pp.82-83
Calathea makoyana p.61
Callistephus p.144
Caltha palustris p.137
Canna pp.50-51

Carex pp.146-147
Chamaedorea elegans p.56
Chamaerops humilis p.73
Clematis pp.104-105
Clivia p.149
Codiaeum p.61
Convolvulus p.107
Cordyline australis p.67
Crassula pp.82-83
Cycas revoluta p.57
Cyclamen persicum p.125
Cymbidium pp.90-91
Dahlia pp.130-131
Daphne tangutica p.37
Dendrobium p.89
Dianthus p.41
Echeveria pp.78-79
Ensete ventricosum pp.48-49
Epipremnum aureum p.103
Equisetum hyemale p.137
Eragrostis elliotti pp.146-147
Eriobotrya japonica p.65
Erysimum p.120
Euphorbia trigona pp.82-83
Fatsia japonica pp.64-65
Ferns pp.96-97
Ficus elastica p.76
Fuchsia pp.94-95
Gaillardia p.132
Galanthus p.115
Gardenia augusta p.47
Gerbera p.132

Gloriosa p.112
Graptopetalum p.84
Gunnera manicata p.70
Hamamelis mollis pp.44-45
Hardenbergia violacea p.113
Hebe p.129
Hedera helix p.143
Hedychium densiflorum p.65
Helianthemum p.135
Heliotropium p.41
Heuchera p.99
Hibiscus rosa-sinensis p.138
Hibiscus syriacus p.129
Hippeastrum p.148
Hosta p.98
Hoya p.46
Hyacinthus p.36, pp.150-151
Hydrangea p.128, p.145
Hypericum p.145
Ilex crenata p.143
Ipomoea p.107
Iris laevigata p.137
Iris reticulata p.115
Jasminum polyanthum p.111
Juncus ensifolius p.137
Kalanchoe p.85
Lantana camara p.139
Lathyrus odoratus p.107
Laurus nobilis p.143
Lavandula pp.39-39
Lilium pp.42-43
Lobelia cardinalis p.137

Lobelia siphilitica p.137
Lonicera fragrantissima
  pp.44-45
Lonicera nitida p.143
Lotus berthelotii p.53
Malus p.119
Medinilla magnifica p.62
Melianthus major p.65
Monstera deliciosa p.59
Musa basjoo pp.48-49
Narcissus pp.114, 150-151
Nicotiana p.40
Nymphaea p.136
Oncidium p.88
Ophiopogon planiscapus
  'Nigrescens' p.147
Opuntia pp.82-83
Pachypodium pp.82-83
Paphiopedilum pp.92-93
Pelargonium p.133
Pericallis x hybrida p.125
Phalaenopsis pp.86-87
Philodendron p.59
Phlox subulata p.135
Phormium p.66
Polystichum pp.96-97
Prunus species p.119
Rhapis excelsa p.57
Rhodochiton p.106
Rhododendron pp.122-123
Rhododendron simsii p.124
Rodgersia pinnata p.71

Rosa pp.126-127
Saintpaulia p.141
Sansevieria p.102
Saxifraga stribrnyi p.121
Schefflera p.58
Sedum morganianum p.81
Sedum rupestre p.135
Sempervivum pp.134-135
Smithiantha p.75
Solanum p.149
Solenostemon
  scutellarioides p.52
Stephanotis p.110
Stipa tenuissima pp.146-147
Streptocarpus p.140
Stromanthe sanguinea p.77
Syringa p.118
Tacca p.74
Taxus baccata p.143
Tetrapanax p.65
Thunbergia alata p.107
Topiary pp.142-143
Trachelospermum p.108
Trachycarpus fortunei p.72
Tulipa pp.116-117
Viburnum tinus p.143
Viburnum x burkwoodii p.37
Viola p.120
Yucca filamentosa p.67
Zantedeschia p.137

Fruit and Vegetables

Apples pp.226-227
Apricots p.213
Aronia berries p.231
Aubergines p.166
Basil p.199
Bay p.196
Beetroot p.185
Blackberries p.220
Blackcurrants p.209
Blueberries pp.222-223
Buddha's hands p.207
Cabbages p.191
Calamondin p.206
Carrots pp.186-187
Chamomile p.194
Chard p.172

Cherries p.224
Chicory p.160
Chillies pp.168-169
Chives p.163
Citrus fruits pp.204-207
Clementines p.207
Coriander p.203
Courgettes p.167
Endive p.191
Fennel p.194
Figs p.214
French beans pp.176-177
Garlic pp.170-171
Ginger p.203
Goji berries p.230
Gooseberries p.211
Guavas p.217
Honeyberries p.222-223
Horseradish p.114

Kale p.174
Kohl rabi p.173
Kumquats p.207
Leeks p.190
Lemon balm p.195
Lemon grass p.202
Lemons p.204
Lettuces pp.156-157
Limes p.205
Loganberries p.221
Makrut limes p.205
Mandarines p.207
Mangetout p.181
Micro greens p.159
Mint pp.192-193
Mizuna p.158
Mustard p.158
Olives p.215
Onions pp.170-171

Orach p.161
Oranges p.207
Oregano p.201
Pak choi p.173
Parsley p.200
Peaches p.212
Pears pp.228-229
Peas p.180
Peppers pp.168-169
Pineapples p.216
Plums p.225
Potatoes pp.182-183
Pumpkins pp.188-189
Quinces p.217
Radishes p.162
Redcurrants p.208
Rhubarb p.210
Rocket p.159
Rosemary p.201

Runner beans pp.178-179
Sage p.197
Sorrel p.161
Spinach p.175
Spring onions p.163
Squash pp.188-189
Strawberries pp.218-219
Sugar snaps p.181
Tangerines p.207
Tayberries p.221
Thyme p.198
Tomatilloes p.231
Tomatoes pp.164-165
Whitecurrants p.209

DESIGNING WITH CONTAINERS

Large or small, contemporary or traditional, there's a container to suit every garden, interior, and design style. Select those that match your planting schemes, and combine pots in complementary materials and colours for a coordinated look. To make your home and garden stand out from the crowd, browse through this chapter for inspirational container designs and striking plant combinations.

Use bold pots of summer blooms for a modern scheme, or choose a vibrant dahlia to brighten up a border. Patterned foliage plants make exceptional specimens for the home, while herbs in crates lend a rustic note to country gardens.

Creating a design

The choice of containers for your prized plants is vast and varied. Recycled items can make quirky pots, while traditional shapes and materials suit informal and classical designs. Sleek cubes, cylinders, and conical pots made from metal, synthetics, or smooth stone are ideal for low-maintenance, contemporary gardens.

Plants have the potential to make stunning, highly valued features when teamed with the right containers, so it's well worth considering your choices carefully. By uniting plants and pots in perfect harmony, you can create a wealth of sensational displays using the myriad different styles, colours, shapes, and sizes on offer.

Materials for containers include plastic, fibreglass, terracotta, stone, glazed ceramic, metal, and wood, but with so many options, how do you make your choice? First, consider the overall design and style of your garden, and then think about the plants you want to display and try to match these with complementary pots. Place your plants in appropriate sites to ensure they thrive, but don't be afraid to experiment with unconventional schemes, as the beauty of container gardening is that mistakes are easily rectified.

Above **Plant up** Penstemon **and** Ligularia *in weathered wooden crates to create a rustic design for a country or informal-style garden. The crates can be stacked and arranged to create a well-proportioned display on different levels.*

Right **The brilliant red of** Acer palmatum **foliage** *creates a striking contrast with the cobalt blue of an old oil drum. Plant creatively to add height and structure to your design.*

Eco-friendly ideas

Creating your own containers by recycling items that may otherwise be consigned to the bin is good for the environment and good for your pocket, and will lend a personal touch to your garden. Just about anything that has space for compost can be turned into a plant pot, including old boots, tins, buckets, wine boxes, fruit trays, yoghurt cartons, colanders, and plastic cups. Food cans of all shapes and sizes also look effective; catering-sized tins, available from restaurants and delicatessens, are ideal. However, before turning any item into a home for plants, drill some drainage holes in the base, and make sure there is enough space inside for your chosen plants to grow comfortably.

Below **Grow salad crops in recycled drinks cartons** *or plastic tubs. These plants have shallow roots and are suitable for a wide range of containers, but remember to create drainage holes in the bottom before planting up.*

Below left **Transform decorative tins** *into beautiful displays by filling them with dainty daffodils.*

Below **These boots were made for planting** *compact flowers such as* Brachyscombe *and* Bidens.

Cool and contemporary designs

When creating displays for a modern patio garden or minimalist courtyard, opt for simple, elegant containers with a sculptural quality, or use angular shapes that complement sharp, geometrical designs. Avoid overly ornate or traditional pots, which will clash with a modern setting. Tall, rectangular containers look great teamed with contrasting spiky or feathery foliage, while low cubes make ideal homes for lollipop-shaped standard trees or the curved outline of a dome of clipped box. Use rectangular planters to raise vegetables, herbs, and other edibles, and try slim cylinders and tapering conical pots with trailing plants to create a striking asymmetric display. Most plants can be grown in contemporary containers, but architectural forms, crisp topiary, grasses, bamboos, and succulents suit them best.

Far right **Create a garden catwalk** *by lining a decked walkway with a row of tall polycarbonate containers. Grow spiky* Imperata cylindrica *'Red Baron' to add colourful pizazz.*

Right **Use a minimalist arrangement** *of box topiary and Japanese maples in large containers to frame an outside seating area and provide some stylish screening.*

Below **Choose a conical container**, *set into a metal plate for stability, to complement the colour and shape of spiky succulents and leafy trailers in a Japanese-inspired pebble garden.*

Right **For a contemporary look** *that will maximize your growing space, plant* Heuchera, *herbs, rosemary, violas, grasses, and ivy in wooden boxes fixed to slatted timber screens.*

Modern materials

Metal or synthetic materials are most commonly used to make contemporary containers, as they suit modern designs. These versatile pots tend to be long lasting, lighter, and easier to clean than those made from traditional materials.

METAL

Zinc, hammered aluminium, polished steel, galvanized steel, and heavy-duty Corten steel that ages to a beautiful rusted finish are just some of the metals used for plant containers. As metal heats up quickly, line your pots with bubble plastic before planting to prevent the roots being fried. In shady plots, use shiny metals to reflect light.

Right **Create a garden hall of mirrors** *using striking pots, such as this woven aluminium container. Use the spiky leaves of a cordyline as the main focus, above a skirt of colourful blooms.*

SYNTHETIC MATERIALS

Lightweight pots made from fibreglass or fibre clay are ideal for roof gardens, balconies, or other areas where weight is an issue. Modern plastic and polycarbonate pots can look very chic and are available in a wide range of styles and colours. Synthetics are also frost-proof and durable.

Left **Contrast finger-like fronds** *of ferns with the sleek, modern shape of a polycarbonate pot. This flexible material can be moulded into an infinite range of modern designs.*

Above **Invest in a unique designer container** *for a modern garden, such as this sleek metal pot that looks just like a silk bag.*

Left **Underplant standard olive trees** *with a fringe of feathery blue* Festuca glauca *in contrasting metal pots.*

Old-world charm

Set the scene in an informal or country garden with containers made from traditional materials and moulded into classic shapes, such as urns or bowls. In a country garden with deep borders, a tiny cottage-style garden enclosed by brick walls, or a plot with a simple lawn and small patio, try warm-coloured terracotta and clay containers to maintain the natural look. These materials offer the perfect foil for most plants, as their muted tones do not overpower either flowers or foliage, and their rustic appearance improves as they weather and age. Remember that many terracotta pots are not frostproof, so look for those with 10-year guarantees – they are usually more expensive but can be cost effective in the long run.

Alternatively, use distressed zinc containers to add a dash of old-world charm to your design, or wooden boxes, which look fabulous in naturalistic settings. Wicker baskets in all shapes and sizes are also charming; either line them with plastic punctured with drainage holes, or use them to hold plants potted up in plastic containers.

Grow ornamental grasses and compact alpines, *such as Saxifraga, in round clay pots. Larger plants, such as Mahonia, make strong sculptural displays in terracotta containers.*

Glazed containers work well in traditional settings *if you choose dark colours that complement your design. This pot lends a modern note, inspired by the graphic forms of Euphorbia characias Silver Swan ('Wilcott') and Ophiopogon.*

Left **The glossy scarlet spathes** *of Anthurium create a striking contrast with the matt texture and subtle colour of a wicker basket. Marry these opposites to make a bold statement in a period or traditional home.*

Below left **Plant up lush ferns** *and fiery cannas in a shallow copper bowl. Treat the copper to maintain its colour, or allow it to oxidize to form a patina of green-blue verdigris.*

Below **Create a striking silhouette** *in a formal garden with a Carex comans bronze form, with fountains of foliage spilling from a classic urn.*

The tight rosettes of foliage *and tiny, dark pink flowers of Saxifraga x arendsii are thrown into contrast by the sharp lines and cool colour of this weathered metal box, making a decorative feature for a patio display.*

Traditional materials

Containers for traditional gardens come in a wide range of natural materials, but three of the most popular are terracotta, stone, and wood, which blend perfectly into rustic and formal settings. Choose pots that suit the colour and form of your plants, garden style, and your available budget.

TERRACOTTA

This versatile material is used for a vast range of containers, from tiny pots to large urns, and in plain or intricately decorated styles. Terracotta is porous, and will crack in frosty conditions unless fired at high temperatures to make it weather-proof. Line these porous pots with bubble plastic to stop water leaching out.

STONE

Limestone, ironstone, granite and other types of stone make durable containers, ideal for planting up trees, shrubs, and perennials. For a pot with a weathered patina, check out architectural salvage yards. If budgets are tight, opt for Terrazzo or stone resin, which are cheaper, but have the look and feel of real stone.

WOOD AND BASKETRY

Versailles-style and wooden planters, and half barrels suit informal schemes, and a wide variety of plants. Line timber containers and baskets with plastic to prevent compost falling out of the gaps, and to protect softwood from rotting. Keep them under cover in winter and treat timber annually with preservative.

Perfect partners

Combining pots and plants to create a balanced display is often a case of trial and error. Those with less experience may find it easier to opt for a collection of containers made from the same material, which will make an harmonious design for a formal or modern garden. A random group of pots in a variety of shapes, sizes, and materials is ideal for a cottage-style garden or an informal space. Either set your containers out in height order in a formal fashion, or in a looser way to produce a more relaxed display.

Matching materials

A uniform group of plants growing in pots made from the same material can be a highly effective way of creating a focal point on a patio or terrace. For contemporary gardens, choose containers in colours and a design or finish that echoes your interior decoration to create a seamless flow from inside to out, or throw caution to the wind and use pots that contrast with your décor to create colourful punctuation points.

Confer a sense of unity on your design by placing similar containers throughout your space to help draw the eye from one part of the garden to another. Alternatively, set identical plants and containers in a row to divide or enclose a patio, or to frame a feature or gateway. Tall, elegant containers work well in this context, and ensure the materials complement your garden style.

Match galvanized containers of varying heights and widths in a contemporary space to create a raised vegetable patch of chives, peppers, leeks, strawberries, and tomatoes.

Mix the complementary hues of green Dasylirion longissimum *with a set of dark red contemporary containers.*

Make a feature for your home with decorative Echeveria 'Duchess of Nuremberg' *housed in small metal units.*

Mixing shapes and sizes

Groups of containers made from different materials, and in different shapes and sizes are ideal for a relaxed flower-filled space where a natural look is required. Add movement, scale, and a sense of perspective by grouping planters by height, or raise your game and create a collection on a table, bench, or even an old ladder, using the treads as a theatre to show off the plants. Mixed pots tend to look unbalanced when arranged in a row, so try a more staggered display instead. Also include a few similar elements to unify your collection, such as pot and plant colours, foliage shapes, or a pebble mulch.

Above **A limited colour palette** *of* Cosmos, Lobelia, *blue* Salvia, *white snapdragons, and* Ophiopogon *in mixed glazed pots creates a balanced display.*

Above left **Choose one material** *for your pots but then mix and match their sizes and shapes, and the colours of your flowers.*

Far left **Use similar shades and hues** *to integrate a diverse collection of plants, including cacti, dahlias,* Echeveria, *and fountain grass in a set of mixed, neutral containers.*

Left **Contrast plant forms** *to produce an exciting mixed display. Here,* Carex dipsacea, Skimmia japonica *'Rubella',* Euonymus fortunei *'Emerald 'n' Gold', and* Heuchera *'Silver Scrolls' make a dramatic foliage group.*

Pots in gardens

The great appeal of plants in pots is that they are versatile, adding pizazz to an urban chill-out zone, providing a decorative touch to a flower-filled cottage garden, and injecting a dash of colour into almost any plot. Use large containers as focal points in beds or borders, and tiny pots to help to dress up more intimate areas of the garden. Containers also allow you to ring the seasonal changes with spring bulbs, and summer and autumn bedding.

Traditional designs

Weathered and rustic containers lend themselves to traditional, formal, and period gardens. A large pot planted with a specimen shrub or grass makes a great focal point for the end of a turfed path or pergola, drawing the eye through the garden. Choose stone urns filled with a profusion of flowers and foliage to complement herbaceous borders or mixed beds, and raise them on plinths for added impact. Containers can also be set among plantings to heighten the sense of mystery and surprise as visitors discover them, and used to integrate seasonal colour into a parterre or knot garden.

Above **Make a stately feature** *of colourful flowers, such as pelargoniums and petunias, planted in ornate stone urns to frame the entrance to a grass walkway and long borders.*

Left **Plant variegated ivy** *in a terracotta urn and squeeze it between other plants to provide a subtle focal point in a woodland garden or fernery.*

Liven up a formal parterre *with large terracotta containers filled with a bright mix of pelargoniums. As autumn approaches, replace the summer flowers with spring bulbs and a selection of violas.*

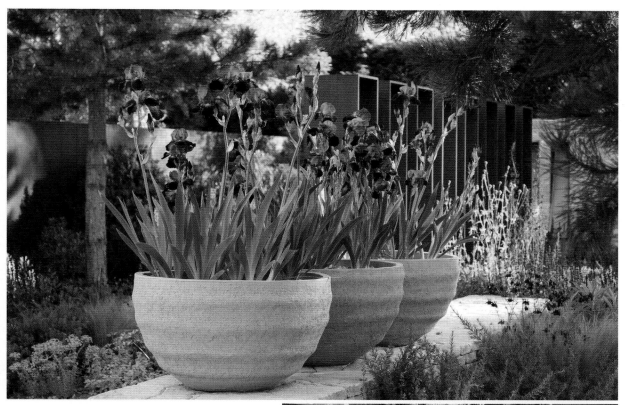

Above **Contrast the spiky foliage and delicate petals** *of traditonal cottage-garden irises with the bold permanence of contemporary containers in a fusion of old and new styles.*

Contemporary schemes

Containers with clean, simple designs complement the elegance of a modern garden. Choose a tall, slender pot made from contemporary materials, such as composite stone or metal, matched with an architectural plant and positioned in a prominent place to create an eye-catching sculpture. Minimalist planting schemes also work well in chic city gardens. Try similar plants grown in identical geometric-shaped containers to add structure and movement to your garden, and use them to flank a flight of steps, add height to a low wall, or edge a pathway. Bold foliage plants will help to enhance your design. Good choices include spiky phormiums, flowing grasses, and neatly clipped box balls or lollipop-shaped bay trees, which look fantastic in elegant containers standing like sentries on either side of a front door or entrance.

Above **Mix plants and planters** *in a range of geometric shapes to create a unified display.*

Left **Select slender columns** *topped with box topiary balls, and mirror these with small rectangular containers for a neat, minimalist look.*

Edible gardens

Many edible crops have attractive leaves, fruits, or an architectural form that will add an ornamental touch to a garden scheme, while also providing you with tasty pickings. Crops with showy fruits, such as aubergines, chilli peppers, tomatoes, and strawberries can hold their own in containers, while low-growing leafy crops like herbs are best grouped together for maximum impact. Many edibles are not ready to harvest until the end of the growing season, so provide some earlier interest by combining crops with flowers or foliage plants. Dot your fruit and vegetables among permanent schemes in a border or arrange them *en masse* for a spectacle that is definitely good enough to eat. While many edible plants will hog a container, you can use the empty space below standard fruit or bay trees by underplanting with trailing fruit or low-growing herbs that enjoy similar conditions.

Far left **Interplant your crops** *with colourful flowers, such as fuchsias, for a sumptuous display. Try tomato 'Minibel' and chilli pepper 'Hungarian Hot Wax'.*

Centre **Arrange your pots** *of strawberries, mint, parsley, and chives at different heights to make harvesting easy and to maximize their visual appeal.*

Left **Grow aubergines** *in pots in a hot spot for a display of colourful fruits. Try varieties 'Pingtung Long' (left), 'Fairy Tale' (rear), and 'Listada de Gandia' (right).*

Above **With creative planning and planting**, *a vegetable garden can be both elegant and productive. Underplant standard bay trees with lavender, and grow crops such as salads and cabbages in raised beds.*

Informal spaces

If you are aiming for an eclectic mix, just about anything goes. Plunge containers of seasonal flowers into bare patches in your borders – you could plant up a series of inexpensive plastic pots with plants that bloom in succession from spring to autumn to ensure there is never a gap in your display. Containers of sweet peas wound around an ornamental obelisk will bring height to a scheme in a cottage garden, or place pots on an old wooden stool or chair to create a vertical accent.

As well as recycled containers, which lend themselves to informal designs, wicker baskets, glazed urns, wooden wine crates, and distressed terracotta pots all complement informal spaces. You can also use walls, fences, and trees as props for your decorative designs.

Left **Elevate baskets** *by fixing them to sturdy wooden poles to create a dramatic scene-setter in an herbaceous border. Choose drought-tolerant pelargoniums and bacopa for small baskets.*

Below **Corten is weatherproof steel** *that forms a rusty patina; pots made from it blend perfectly into informal spaces, such as gravel gardens. Choose plants that reflect your garden design.*

Suspend small pots of pansies, *such as* Viola cornuta *'Gem Apricot Antique',
from tree branches with ribbon or twine.*

Use trailing begonias *and blue* Convolvulus *to tumble over the sides of a terracotta urn in a gravel garden.*

Pots on patios

Gardeners often feel constrained by small patios, but you can grow a wide range of plants on the tiniest of terraces. Choose carefully to ensure your plants won't take over all your available space and make it appear even smaller. Good choices include crisp topiary, scented bulbs, grasses, slimline architectural shrubs, flowering annuals, edibles, and herbs. On small patios, opt for just a few sculptural pots and use the walls and windowsills to increase your container collection.

Contemporary terraces

To create a modern look, clear your space of clutter and focus on elegant forms of both pots and plants. A minimalist approach works well; group similar pots, planted with topiary, bamboos, grasses, lavender, or regal lilies, along a boundary. Also use the vertical space to make your patio feel larger, training the eye up to the sky, rather than towards the boundaries. Select well-behaved climbers, such as *Trachelospermum* and clematis, and plant them in smart troughs next to a wall or fence. Avoid hanging baskets and opt instead for smart wall pots and simple windowboxes made from modern materials. Grow sun-loving architectural plants, such as cannas, in hot spots, and use ferns, hostas, and heucheras to brighten up shady areas.

Top right **Transform a dull, shady corner** *with Japanese-inspired clouds of box and privet topiary.*

Right **Tall slim pots** *are perfect for tight spaces. Use upright plants, such as cannas, dahlias, and blood grass, with a skirt of lively red busy Lizzies to form a head of colour at the top.*

Far right **Train scented star jasmine** *on a slatted fence and use chic black planters for a bang-on-trend look.*

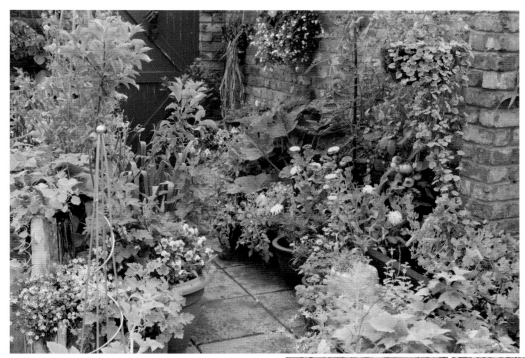

Left **Fill a productive patio** *with a range of pots and crops to extend your fruit and vegetable harvest. Interplant with violas, marigolds, and nasturtiums, which are also edible, and try tumbling tomatoes in hanging baskets to maximize your space.*

Edibles for small spaces

Long gone are the days when an allotment or kitchen garden were thought to be minimum requirements for growing fruit and vegetables. Today, a vast range of compact crops have been bred specifically for growing in containers, while many other edible plants are suitable for raising in large troughs or half barrels.

Plants on patios and terraces have to work hard to earn their keep, as they're visible whenever you step out of the door or look from your window. To address this, choose edibles with showy leaves, pretty flowers, or jewel-like fruit, such as kale, beetroot, frilly-leaved lettuces, strawberries, and peppers. Either arrange groups of containers alongside colourful annuals and other ornamentals, or fill large troughs with a selection of different crops. Make the most of vertical spaces, too, and plant up hanging baskets with tumbling tomatoes, strawberries, and chillies. Small pots of herbs set on a garden table allow diners to pick them fresh when eating al fresco, or plant a fruit tree in a big pot on a patio for sweet treats from late summer.

Above left **Bays with plaited stems** *provide an elegant addition to a patio, offering fresh leaves for the kitchen, and sophisticated focal points.*

Above **Dainty dianthus** *and flowering sages brighten up a kitchen-garden scheme of large galvanized containers filled with cabbages and artichokes.*

Left **Ruby-red strawberries** *hang from arched stems in a recycled colander, making a pretty display of tempting fruits ripening conveniently within reach.*

Relaxed plantings

If you don't have space for a well-filled border, or your garden is in need of a colourful lift, opt for a vibrant arrangement of plants grown cheek-by-jowl on your patio. Informal designs suit a confection of pots and plants with ornamental flowers and textural foliage. For a long season of interest grow heathers, evergreen grasses, and small shrubs as a backdrop to spring bulbs, summer bedding, and leafy autumn feature plants. On a large decked terrace adjacent to a suburban plot of lawn and shrubs, use a range of colourful pots and flowers. For a patio in a more muted woodland or shady garden, try wooden or terracotta pots filled with foliage specimens, and violas, tobacco plants, and busy Lizzies in pastel shades. Soften the edges of your pots with trailers that suit the aspect.

*Far right **Vibrant pots** filled with bright blooms produce a festive touch on a decked patio against a backdrop of foliage.*

*Right **Petunias in raspberry hues** enliven a glazed pot of Hakonechloa macra 'Aureola' and trailing Vinca minor.*

*Right **Colour up an autumn patio** with a medley of heathers, cyclamens, lavender, and Helichrysum italicum in a clay pot. Use hardy cyclamens that will not be cut down by frost.*

*Far right **Recreate a summer border** in a large glazed pot, with the blue grass, Leymus arenarius, scented pinks, Gaura, and trailing silvery Helichrysum petiolare.*

Left **Make a stylish urban outdoor room** *ultra cool with cylindrical containers that match your furniture and complement chic limestone paving.*

Urban sanctuaries

There are no hard and fast rules about containers for urban gardens – the choice really depends on the look you're trying to achieve. You can opt for a sophisticated scheme by matching your pots with patio furniture, or go for galvanized metal containers to reflect light into a shady courtyard. To enhance a minimalist scheme, choose plants that have a neat habit or architectural form, such as compact lavenders, grasses, bamboos, and hummock-forming hebes. Or create your own city forest with terrazzo cubes planted with multi-stemmed birch trees. These will be happy in large containers, as long as the compost is never allowed to dry out. If you want a refuge from the rigours of city life, create a cocoon of foliage by lining your patio or courtyard with a profusion of plants in tall containers. Not only will they keep your patio cool, but the foliage will help to baffle traffic noise too.

Scent your city plot *with a range of herbs, such as rosemary, marjoram, and thyme, in shiny metal pots. Use steps and walls to produce a multi-layered effect, and water small herb pots every couple of days in summer.*

Combine cool greens and soft pinks *on a small paved terrace, with hardy gerberas, dahlias, grasses, Phygelius, and the beautiful variegated shrub Aralia elata 'Variegata', for a relaxed performance of flowers and foliage.*

Balconies and roof terraces

Compact or slender plants are perfect for balconies, as they leave you with plenty of elbow room, while those who garden up on a rooftop should choose tough plants that can cope with strong winds and sun. Despite the limitations, there are plenty of options for these difficult spaces.

Balconies

Most balconies are tiny, with just a few square metres for plants and people. To make the most of your available space, fix windowboxes securely to railings, and consider installing shelving units made from treated wood or metal. Decorate your shelves with herbs, houseleeks, alpines, and a few house plants in summer. For year-round colour, use slender conifers, and box pyramids, spirals, and other topiary forms to add verdant tones. Also include a few fruits, such as strawberries and tomatoes, which will ripen quickly in a sunny spot.

Dazzle your neighbours with a bold Rhododendron yakushimanum in a glazed container. This compact form produces large clusters of pink flowers that smother the evergreen foliage to produce a spectacular feature.

Create a fruitful balcony, with a miniature allotment encased in a range of rustic pots. Tiny tomatoes, such as 'Minibel', and the fiery chilli pepper 'Medusa', together with some cut-and-come-again lettuces, will provide a feast for summer, while strawberries in windowboxes and a dwarf apple tree add sweet flavours.

Left **Create a shield of plants** *to shelter a private space, with summer bloomers vying with a range of leafy shrubs.*

Below **Tiers of elegant planters** *make a dramatic screen. Keep your scheme simple by repeating key plants, such as phormiums, grasses, ivies, and echeverias.*

Above **Keep your scheme cool** *with glaucous hostas, silvery* Stachys byzantina *and the graceful* Miscanthus sinensis *'Morning Light' in a metal pot.*

Up on the roof

Choose lightweight synthetic or metal containers for roof terraces where the total load-bearing weight is an issue, and make the most of any wall space by fixing pots or troughs to vertical surfaces to produce a layered effect.

High winds can cause problems, so install windbreaks to make your space more usable. Line the boundaries with tough plants, such as *Elaeagnus* x *ebbingei*, the bamboo *Phyllostachys*, *Viburnum tinus*, and *Prunus laurocerasus* to create a green shelterbelt, or use timber, woven bamboo, or metal screens, but ensure that they allow 40 to 50 per cent of the wind to pass through them to prevent turbulence. With more shelter, your planting options broaden and you can include a range of flowering annuals and perennials, as well as edibles.

Before buying plants, measure door widths and stairways to ensure you can move your plants up to the roof – you may need a crane for heavy containers and large trees.

Combine a collection of green foliage plants on a city roof terrace. Choose hostas, rhododendrons, and wind-tolerant shrubs, together with sculptural pines, and plant in decorative wooden and terracotta containers.

Edge a terrace with a garden of flowers and foliage in pots and raised beds. Select seasonal favourites, like chrysanthemums, salvias, and sedums, and use evergreen conifers to shield your space from neighbours' windows.

Above left **Use black-stemmed bamboo** *in three galvanised containers to create a living sculpture on a terrace. The evergreen foliage provides a year-round windbreak.*

Above **Secure timber trellis to a wall** *and suspend a series of metal troughs filled with Ophiopogon and strawberries to dress up a modern balcony.*

Left **High above the city** *the wind can make a roof terrace uncomfortable, but a range of grasses, such as Miscanthus, Anemanthele, and Calamagrostis, planted in large metal containers, will provide some shelter.*

Decorative windowsills

Give a windowsill an instant facelift with a collection of pots or a windowbox crammed with any compact plants that take your fancy. For a year-round display, try a selection of small shrubs or neat topiary as a backdrop to a supporting cast of ever-changing seasonal flowers and bulbs. Edibles are another possibility, with pots of herbs, salad leaves, and tomatoes taking pride of place on a sunny sill. Remember to fix pots firmly to high windowsills to prevent accidents.

Year-round displays

South-facing or in shade, you can use any windowsill space for plants and edibles. Foodies can grow their own vegetables, herbs, and fruit, while stylish box topiary will suit a period home. Alternatively, create a cottage garden in a windowbox using pinks, trailing campanulas, and a selection of herbs. The sheltered, relatively warm conditions will also allow you to experiment with tender plants that may not survive in the garden; in urban areas pelargoniums and other tender summer perennials may overwinter on a sunny sill.

Sun and shelter provide perfect conditions for ripening dwarf tomatoes, such as 'Balconi Red'. Terracotta pots mirror the warm tones of the tomatoes; water them daily for good results.

Group your favourite herbs on a sill so that you can just open the window to pick a few leaves. Sage, parsley, rosemary, basil, fennel, and tarragon will be happy in a warm sunny site, while lavender and pelargoniums add a splash of colour.

Above **Create an elegant picture** *by decorating the front of a period house with box pyramids, white pelargoniums, and ivy in a sleek black container.*

Far left **Celebrate spring with daffodils** *in a galvanised metal windowbox.*

Centre **Trailing ivy** *spilling from tiny pots suspended from meat hooks makes an elegant display.*

Above right **Create a simple scheme** *by mixing white and purple pansies.*

Left **Reflect summer's abundance** *with a large, deep window-box filled with petunias, Thunbergia, and Jamesbrittenia.*

House warmers

The easiest way to breathe life into your home is to introduce a few well-chosen house plants. Cheaper than a makeover and instantly rewarding, there's an option for almost every room – from elegant palms in a formal sitting room, to a riot of spring flowers on a sunny windowsill.

Perfect pairings

House plants make beautiful displays when paired with the right container, so take time to find the perfect pot. Elegant modern interiors are enhanced by sleek ceramics, metallic pots, neutral tones, and simple designs, while bright colours and sculptural shapes will contribute to a funky, contemporary décor. Match your pots with foliage plants, such as ferns, elephant's ears, and succulents. If you favour shabby chic or a cosy country style, try herbs and flowering house plants, such as primulas and African violets, in distressed galvanized pots, wicker baskets, rattan pots, or recycled containers.

Right A classic white ceramic pot complements the smooth lines and fresh green and white of the peace lily, Spathiphyllum.

Cook's favourites, such as basil and parsley, can be kept close to hand in the kitchen on a waterproof tray set into a rustic wooden planter.

For a splash of 60s chic, pair stripy, glazed ceramic pots with spiky-topped spider plants, Chlorophytum laxum.

Informal groups of Aeschynanthus, Begonia Hiemalis Group, Adiantum, Soleirolia, and Saintpaulia in mixed glazed pots create a flower garden on a windowsill.

Far left **Contrast the pink bracts** *and grassy foliage of zany* Tillandsia *with cool, elegant white pots.*

Left **Create an office setting** *for a group of echeverias and other succulents in mixed pots in an old metal cabinet drawer.*

Centre left **Team fiery bromeliads** *with ivy in rattan baskets on a well-lit windowsill out of direct sun.*

Far left, bottom **A trio of distressed ceramic pots** *add design magic to the flowing stems and tiny leaves of mind-your-own-business,* Soleirolia soleirolii.

Left **Bring spring indoors** *with a basket brimming with primulas,* Hyacinthus *'Pink Pearl',* Viola cornuta *'Sorbet Coconut Duet',* Narcissus *'Inbal' and ivy. Line the basket with plastic and set plants in small plastic pots inside.*

FOLIAGE AND FLOWERS

Whether you're looking for seasonal sensations or a container display to turn heads all year round, you'll find a wealth of ideas in this chapter. Choose bold house plants for modern containers to inject colour and texture into your home, and pots of ornamental trees, shrubs, perennials, and annuals to transform outdoor spaces with fabulous flowers and lush foliage.

Create focal points with trees in large pots, or convey a country-garden style with baskets of seasonal blooms. Orchids are a must for modern interiors, while tender foliage plants will brighten up windowsills.

Selecting ornamental plants

Grow your plants in the conditions they enjoy and you'll be rewarded with healthy, thriving specimens. Some prefer warm sunny sites, others do best in shade, while many are not too fussy and will cope with both. Use these checklists to help you choose plants that are best suited to your home or garden environment, and follow the page references for more details.

Pairing plants with sites

Plants evolve to cope with their natural environments, and you'll get the best from yours by providing similar conditions. In most cases, plants with small, silvery, or hairy leaves are from sunny areas, such as alpine regions or the Mediterranean, where their foliage provides protection from the sun. Those with large, dark leaves have evolved to trap as much sunlight as possible in the dimly lit conditions on a forest or woodland floor, and will be happiest in shade. Many flowering plants perfom best in sun, as they are more visible to the insects that pollinate them, while some with pale blooms become luminous in the evening because they are pollinated by nocturnal insects.

This sophisticated arrangement pairs Fatsia japonica, which thrives in partial shade, with Pelargonium 'Lady Plymouth', one of the few pelargoniums that can cope with some shade. Alocasia is also happy in filtered light, and completes the scheme.

Spring displays of violas, aubrietia, and wallflowers will bloom best in a sunny site, while grassy sedges tolerate sun and shade.

PLANTS FOR SUNNY SITES

- Aeonium pp.78–9
- Alpines p.121, pp.134–5
- Aster p.144
- Bamboo pp.54–5
- Bananas pp.48–9
- Caltha palustris p.137
- Canna pp.50–1
- Chamaerops humilis p.73
- Clematis pp.104–5
- Cordyline australis p.67
- Dahlia pp.130–1
- Dianthus p.41

- Echeveria pp.78–9
- Erysimum p.120
- Gaillardia p.133
- Gerbera p.132
- Graptopetalum p.84
- Grasses pp.146–7
- Hamamelis and Lonicera pp.44–5
- Hebe p.129
- Hedychium densiflorum p.65
- Heliotropium arborescens p.41
- Hibiscus p.129

- Ipomoea p.107
- Iris laevigata p.137
- Juncus ensifolius p.137
- Lathyrus odoratus p.109
- Lavender pp.38–39
- Lilium pp.42–3
- Lobelia p.137
- Lotus bertholelotii p.53
- Malus p.119
- Melianthus major p.65
- Nymphaea pp.136–7

- Pelargonium p.133
- Phormium p.66
- Prunus p.119
- Rhodochiton p.106
- Roses pp.126–7
- Solenostemon p.52
- Syringa p.118
- Tetrapanax p.65
- Thunbergia p.107
- Tulips pp.116–7
- Viola p.120
- Yucca p.67
- Zantedeschia p.137

PLANTS FOR SHADY OR PARTIALLY SHADY SITES

- Acer palmatum pp.68–9
- Arisaema p.53
- Astilboides p.71
- Azalea pp.122–3
- Cotoneaster p.145
- Daphne tangutica p.37
- Equisetum hyemale p.137
- Eriobotrya japonica p.65
- Fatsia japonica p.64
- Galanthus p.115
- Gunnera p.70
- Hardy ferns pp.96–7
- Hardy fuchsias pp.94–5
- Heliotropium arborescens p.41
- Heuchera p.40, p.99
- Hosta p.98
- Hyacinthus p.36
- Hydrangea p.128
- Iris reticulata p.115
- Narcissus p.114
- Nicotiana p.40
- Phormium p.66
- Rhododendron pp.122–3
- Rodgersia p.71
- Sedges p.147
- Tetrapanax p.65
- Topiary pp.142–3
- Trachelospermum p.108
- Trachycarpus fortunei p.72
- Viburnum x burkwoodii p.37
- Viola p.120
- Zantedeschia p.137

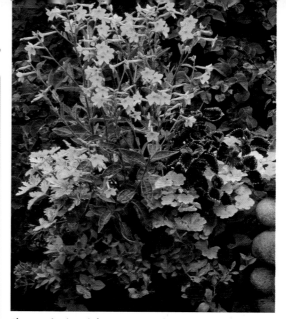

Elegant Nicotiana *is happy* in some shade, while petunias prefer sun but will flower in a site that's shaded for part of the day.

PLANTS THAT TOLERATE EXPOSED SITES

- Alpines p.121, pp.134–5
- Androsace villosa *var.* jacquemontii p.121
- Aubrieta p.121
- Cotoneaster p.145
- Daphne p.37
- Galanthus p.115
- Gentiana acaulis p.121
- Grasses pp.146–7
- Iris reticulata p.115
- Leontopodium alpinum p.121
- Narcissus p.114
- Saxifraga p.121
- Sedum rupestre p.135
- Sempervivum p.134
- Sedges p.147

Sempervivum tectorum

PLANTS THAT NEED A SHELTERED SITE

- Arisaema p.53
- Bamboos pp.54–5
- Canna pp.50–1
- Chamaerops humilis p.73
- Cordyline australis p.67
- Dahlia pp.130–1
- Echeveria *and* Aeonium pp.78–9
- Eriobotrya japonica p.65
- Gaillardia p.133
- Gerbera p.132
- Gunnera p.70
- Hardy fuchsias pp.94–5
- Hebe p.129
- Hedychium densiflorum p.65
- Hibiscus p.129
- Ipomoea p.107
- Kalanchoe p.85
- Lathyrus odoratus p.109
- Lotus bertholelotii p.53
- Melianthus major p.65
- Pelargonium p.133
- Petunia p.40
- Rhodochiton p.106
- Solenostemon p.52
- Tetrapanax p.65
- Thunbergia p.107
- Trachelospermum p.108
- Trachycarpus fortunei p.72
- Yucca filamentosa p.67

PLANTS FOR THE HOME

- Abutilon x hybridum p.139
- Aechmea p.63
- Agave p.81
- Aloe p.81
- Alocasia x amazonica p.60
- Ananas comosus p.77
- Anthurium p.63
- Begonia pp.100–1
- Blechnum gibbum p.103
- Bougainvillea p.113
- Brugmansia *and* Gardenia augusta p.47
- Cacti pp.82–3
- Calathea makoyana p.61
- Chamaedorea elegans p.56
- Clivia p.149
- Codiaeum p.61
- Cycas revoluta p.57
- Cyclamen persicum p.125
- Epipremnum aureum p.103
- Ficus elastica p.76
- Gloriosa p.112
- Hardenbergia p.113
- Hibiscus rosa-sinensis p.138
- Hippeastrum p.148
- Hoya p.46
- Jasminum polyanthum p.111
- Lantana camara p.139
- Medinilla p.62
- Monstera deliciosa p.59
- Narcissus *and* Hyacinthus pp.150–1
- Orchids pp.86–93
- Pericallis x hybrida p.125
- Philodendron p.59
- Rhapis excelsa p.57
- Saintpaulia p.141
- Sansevieria p.102
- Schefflera p.58
- Sedum morganianum p.81
- Smithiantha p.75
- Solanum p.149
- Stephanotis p.110
- Streptocarpus p.140
- Stromanthe p.77
- Tacca p.74

Spring fragrance

With the darkest days of winter at an end, the new season greets us with the arrival of spring bulbs and flowering shrubs. Pots planted with those noted for their fragrance will lift your spirits further as they fill the air with sweet perfume. Place them in a prominent spot close to the kitchen door, windows or seating areas, then breathe in and enjoy.

Spring bulbs

Plants used
Hyacinths, pussy willow stems

Height and spread
H 30cm (12in)
S 7cm (3in)

Aspect
Sun or partial shade

Temperature needs
Hardy to -15°C (5°F)

Suitable pot size
20cm (8in) or larger

Suitable container material
Terracotta, stone, ceramic, or plastic pots placed inside decorative outer containers

Compost type
Bulb fibre

Spring bulbs are among the easiest plants to grow – plant them in autumn and simply wait a few months for them to burst through the soil. While many provide colourful flowers, some offer even better value with a beautiful scent. Hyacinths are highly fragrant and available in a wide range of colours, including white, yellow, pink, purple, and red. Some muscari or grape hyacinths are also scented – choose the yellow *Muscari macrocarpum* 'Golden Fragrance' for the best perfume. To complete your fragrant displays, add scented daffodils, such as the small-cupped jonquils and tazettas, and pheasant eyes.

SITING YOUR PLANTS
Flank your front door with pots of scented bulbs so that their fragrance greets you each time you enter the house. In the back garden, place pots on patios, close to paths or by seating areas, raising them up on tables, chairs, or window ledges to intensify their effect.

Hyacinths have a strong fragrance and make a decorative display when planted en masse in a basket with stems of furry willow buds.

TOP TIP: CARE AFTER FLOWERING

Many people treat spring bulbs like annuals, and compost them once they have started to fade, but they can be retained for repeat performances year after year. To do this, remove the withered flowers, apply a liquid fertilizer to the leaves, and allow the foliage to die back naturally. Then lift the bulbs from the pot, knock off any excess compost, and allow them to dry. Store the bulbs in brown paper bags, label, and keep in a cool, dark place until autumn when you can plant them out again.

Scented shrubs

Plants used
Daphne tangutica;
Viburnum x
burkwoodii

Height and spread
Daphne tangutica:
H 1m (3ft) S 1m (3ft);
Viburnum x
burkwoodii: H 1.5m
(5ft) S 1.5m (5ft)

Aspect
Sun or partial shade

Temperature needs
Hardy to -15°C (5°F)

Suitable pot size
30–45cm (12–18in)

Suitable container material
Terracotta, stone, metal, wood

Suitable compost
Soil-based compost, eg, John Innes No 3

The spring shrub *Viburnum* x *burkwoodii* makes a fabulous centrepiece on a patio when grown in a contemporary grey stone pot. Evergreen in sheltered areas, its dense clusters of white, sweetly scented flowers will lift any container display. To prolong the interest, underplant with trailing plants, primroses, and evergreen grasses. Part of a large family of deciduous and evergreen shrubs, other viburnums worth growing for their scented spring flowers include *V. farreri, V.* x *juddii,* and *V. carlesii.*

FRAGRANT OPTIONS
Many daphnes are also renowned for their early scented blooms. Among the best are *Daphne tangutica*, which has pink tubular flowers, and *D.* x *burkwoodii*, whose white flowers appear for a few weeks from late spring. Other fragrant shrubs to consider include *Ribes odoratum, Osmanthus delavayi,* and *Euphorbia mellifera,* a large evergreen with honey-scented flowers.

Above: **The evergreen foliage** of Daphne tangutica provides a foil for the pale pink, scented flowers.

Large shrubs like this Viburnum x burkwoodii *need a soil-based compost, and balanced granular fertilizer each spring. Planted with primulas, ivy, and* Phalaris arundinacea *'Dwarf Garters', it creates a stunning effect.*

FRAGRANT FLOWERS

Lavender scents

Nothing is more evocative of a summer's day than the scent of lavender wafting across the garden on a gentle breeze. A magnet for bees and butterflies, the perfume is also used in aromatherapy to soothe the nerves and lower stress levels, making lavender the perfect plant for a relaxing seating area.

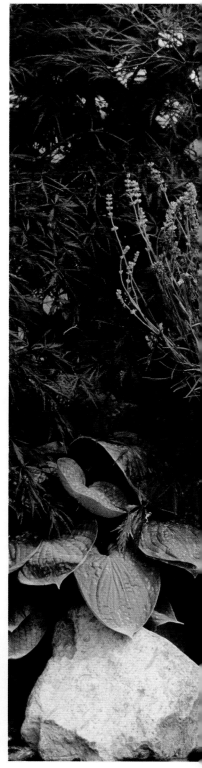

FRAGRANT FLOWERS

Plants used
Lavandula angustifolia 'Hidcote'

Height and spread
H 60cm (24in)
S 75cm (30in)

Aspect
Full sun

Temperature needs
Hardy to -15°C (5°F)

Suitable pot size
20–40cm (8–15in)

Suitable container material
Terracotta, stone, metal

Compost type
Loam-based compost, eg, John Innes No.3, with extra grit

Lavender is a welcome addition to a patio, balcony, or garden, with aromatic foliage that releases essential oils when warmed by the sun and scented flowers that buzz with wildlife. One of the best compact forms for a container is *Lavandula angustifolia* 'Hidcote', a traditional English lavender with dark, highly scented purple flowers and silver-grey leaves. Alternatively, choose one from the hundreds of other varieties, available in a range of sizes, colours, and flower shapes.

Native to the Mediterranean region, lavenders love a warm, sunny spot and do best in light, well-drained compost – they absolutely detest wet feet. Fill a large pot with a soil-based compost, such as John Innes No 3, mixed with some horticultural grit. Largely trouble-free, plants last for years with the right care, and are best planted on their own so that you can enjoy their hummock shape without distraction, or mix several cultivars to produce a combination of shades and long flowering season.

CARING FOR PLANTS

Mix some slow-release fertilizer granules into the surface of the compost each spring, and water plants frequently in summer. Lavenders hate cold, wet soil, so raise containers up on pot feet in winter to allow excess water to drain away. Although most forms can be left outside all year round, overwinter tender varieties in a frost-free place. Also keep a close eye out for metallic green and purple rosemary beetles, which strip the plants' leaves.

*Centre: **English lavender**, such as forms of* Lavandula angustifolia, *have the strongest scent of all the species. Choose a large rounded container to balance the mound of flowers and foliage.*

TOP TIP: PRUNING LAVENDER

If left unpruned lavender will develop a mass of leggy, woody, unattractive stems. To avoid this, keep plants compact, bushy, and floriferous by trimming off old flowerheads as they fade in summer. Prune plants harder in early spring, but don't cut into old, leafless wood as it won't reshoot.

Choosing lavenders

Lavandula angustifolia *'Hidcote'* is covered with spikes of heavily scented purple flowers in midsummer.

Lavandula stoechas *'Kew Red'* is a tender form with striking cerise flowers topped with pinky-white "ears".

Lavandula angustifolia *'Loddon Pink'* is a compact shrub with soft pink flowers and narrow grey foliage.

Lavandula angustifolia *'Munstead'* is slightly shorter than 'Hidcote', with bluish-purple blooms and grey foliage.

Lavandula *'Willow Vale'* is a French form with deep purple flowers topped by violet "ears". Likes a sheltered spot.

Lavandula *x* chaytoriae *'Sawyers'* has conical purple flowers on long spikes above a mass of silver foliage.

Lavandula angustifolia *'Nana Alba'* is a dwarf white form of English lavender, perfect for a small patio container.

Lavandula pinnata is a tender species with long stems of spear-shaped, purple flowerheads and hairy, white leaves.

FRAGRANT FLOWERS

Summer perfume

For a dazzling display of scented flowers, try a few annuals, such as the tobacco plant, *Nicotiana*, and richly perfumed cherry pie, *Heliotropium*. Ideal for mixed displays, combine these scented stars with other brightly coloured blooms as part of a summer scheme. Alternatively, where space is limited, pot up tiny alpine pinks, which have a delicious spicy fragrance.

Tobacco plant *Nicotiana*

Plants used
Nicotiana; Petunia; Solenostemon; Heuchera

Height and spread
Nicotiana: H 60cm (24in) S 25cm (10in); Trailing petunia: S 40cm (16in); *Solenostemon*: H 20cm (8in) S 30cm (12in); *Heuchera*: H 60cm (24in) S 30cm (12in)

Aspect
Sun or partial shade

Temperature needs
Plants not hardy below 0°C (32°F)

Suitable pot size
35cm (14in)

Suitable container material
Glazed ceramic, stone, terracotta

Compost type
Multi-purpose

Here's a smoking hot container recipe that won't damage your health. The flowering tobacco plant, *Nicotiana*, forms the centrepiece, its trumpet-shaped, scented flowers blooming until the frosts. The unusual acid-green flowers of this annual contrast dramatically with the red leaves of *Solenostemon,* or coleus, whose fiery shades echo those of the scarlet trailing petunia, which tumbles down the sides of the container. Plant up this group in late spring, starting with the tobacco plant in the centre, followed by the coleus, and green *Heuchera*, and finally dot the petunias in the remaining gaps. Set outside in a sunny spot when all danger of frost has passed.

COLOUR CHOICES

If lime-green flowers aren't to your taste, tobacco plants are available in many other colours, including white, red, lilac, pink, and purple. However, do check your seed or plant packs, since not all *Nicotiana* are heavily scented. You could also look out for dark purple petunias, most of which are fragrant.

TOP TIP: SOWING TOBACCO PLANTS FROM SEED

Nicotiana is easy to raise indoors from seed each spring. Fill small pots or cell trays with seed compost and sow seeds evenly on the surface. Do not cover. Water and place in a light spot to germinate. When seedlings are large enough to move, transfer them carefully into individual 7cm (3in) pots to grow on.

An elegant combination of greens and pinks, this display will bloom from early summer until the frosts.

Cherry pie *Heliotropium*

Plants used
Heliotropium arborescens

Height and spread
H 45cm (18in)
S 30cm (12in)

Aspect
Light shade or full sun

Temperature needs
Not hardy below 0°C (32°F)

Suitable pot size
20cm (8in)

Suitable container material
Stone, plastic, glazed ceramic, terracotta

Compost type
Multi-purpose

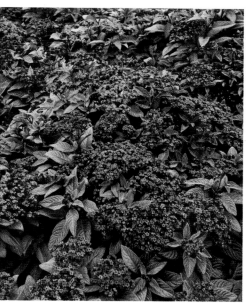

Some plants simply don't live up to their names, but cherry pie does not fail. A shrubby annual, its dark green leaves are topped with dense clusters of tiny purple flowers that pack a fruity punch which instantly reminds you of a freshly baked cherry pie. Perfect on their own in small pots or used as fillers around larger specimens, *Heliotropium* is easy to grow from seed sown indoors in early spring (*follow advice for tobacco plants in Top Tip box opposite*).

SIZE OPTIONS
One of the most popular forms, *Heliotropium* 'Dwarf Marine', reaches 35cm (14in), while 'Baby Blue Improved' grows to just 20cm (8in) making it perfect for window boxes. For larger plants, try *H.* x Hybrid Marine, which reaches 45cm (18in).

Heliotropium x Hybrid Marine

Pretty pinks *Dianthus*

Plants used
Dianthus 'Devon Flores' (syn. 'Starry Night'); *Frankenia thymifolia*

Height and spread
Dianthus: H 17cm (7in) S 17cm (7in); *Frankenia:* H 20cm (8in) S 30cm (12in)

Aspect
Full sun

Temperature needs
Hardy to -15°C (5°F)

Suitable pot size
25cm (10in)

Suitable container material
Terracotta, stone

Compost type
Well-drained, soil-based compost, eg, John Innes No 2, with added grit

Alpine pinks make great container plants, offering dainty clove-scented flowers on sturdy stems above a mat of grey leaves. Partner them with other alpines, such as the creeping *Frankenia*, whose stems of rose-pink flowers will tumble loosely down the sides of a pot. *Dianthus* 'Devon Flores' has bright magenta, double flowers that echo the warm shade of the *Frankenia* blooms.

COLOUR SELECTIONS
Pinks come in many colours, from white to pink and purple, with striped, flecked, or bicoloured flowers, as well as single and double blooms.

Easy to maintain, *Dianthus* are drought tolerant and need little attention, apart from watering a couple of times a week in summer, and an application of slow-release granular fertilizer worked into the compost in spring. Protect plants from winter rain, and remove fading blooms to encourage more to form.

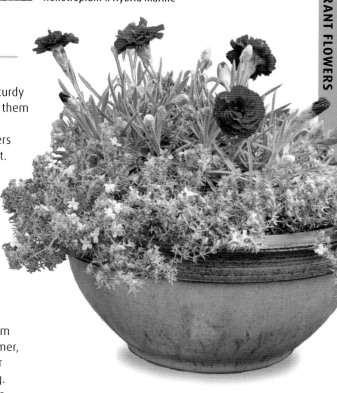

Perfect partners, Dianthus *'Devon Flores'* and Frankenia thymifolia *combine well in a small terracotta bowl.*

Elegant lilies *Lilium*

Large, dramatic flowers in an array of colours make lilies a favourite for both garden and home, but those with the added bonus of scent are most prized. The intoxicating perfume of the Oriental hybrids will fill the air of a large garden, while the delicate flowers of some species have a more subtle fragrance.

FRAGRANT FLOWERS

Plants used
Lilium formosanum var. pricei; *Ipomoea batatas* 'Margarita'; *Gerbera* Garvinea 'Nikki'

Height and spread
Lilium: H 30cm (12in); *Ipomoea*: H 15cm (6in), S 1m (3ft); *Gerbera*: H & S 45cm (18in)

Aspect
Sun or dappled shade

Temperature needs
These lilies are hardy down to -5°C (23°F)

Suitable pot size
30cm (12in)

Suitable container material
Glazed ceramic, terracotta, stone

Compost type
Soil-based compost, eg, John Innes No. 2, with extra grit

*Centre: **Mix-and-match scented lilies**, such as this* Lilium formosanum *var.* pricei, *with summer flowers like gerberas, and trailing foliage, such as the sweet potato vine.*

Many lilies are towering beasts best suited to the border, but the species *Lilium formosanum* var. *pricei* is a knee-high beauty with large flowers that match those of a regal lily for size and scent. Although this compact plant looks good on its own in a container, where it will happily spread to provide a bigger and better display each summer, it is also perfect for combining with other flowers and foliage to produce a long-lasting summer scheme.

The blooms are the main feature of the lily, while its uninspiring foliage can be disguised with the leaves and daisy-like flowers of a hardy gerbera, and the lime-green sweet potato vine, *Ipomoea batatas* 'Margarita'. This bushy, trailing plant produces masses of lush growth throughout summer and early autumn until stopped in its tracks by frost.

CARING FOR LILIES

Its compact habit means that *Lilium formosanum* var. *pricei* doesn't need staking, but taller lilies will require canes to support their flower stems. Water pots a few times a week in the summer, and in autumn remove and compost the frosted *Ipomoea*. Garvinea gerberas are hardy down to about -5°C (23°F), as is the lily, and if the pot is set close to the house in a sheltered position and protected from excessive rain, it should survive the winter outside. However, if temperatures threaten to fall below -5°C (23°F), bring the pot inside. In spring, feed with a slow-release granular fertilizer worked into the top layer of compost.

TOP TIP: PLANTING LILY BULBS

Lily bulbs are best planted in the autumn or spring. Fill the bottom third of a pot with compost and add 3cm (1¼in) of horticultural grit. Lay the bulbs on the grit on their sides; this allows water to drain from their scales, preventing them from rotting. Finally, top up the container with more compost.

Choosing lilies

Lilium *'Journey's End'* is not for the faint-hearted, with large, blowsy, pink, scented flowers with white markings.

Lilium nepalense is ideal for a shady container. This graceful species has green flowers with swept-back petals.

Lilium medeoloides has short stems, ideal for pots, that bear clusters of small orange flowers. Prefers light shade.

Lilium speciosum *var.* rubrum has highly fragrant, recurved blooms flushed pink with crimson spots.

Lilium martagon, the common Turk's cap lily, is happy in sun or partial shade and has dark pink, speckled flowers.

Lilium pyrenaicum is grown for its scented, nodding, yellow Turk's cap flowers. Ideal for sun or dappled shade.

Lilium *'Star Gazer'* is tall and looks best in a big pot. Its large, red, upward-facing flowers emit a powerful scent.

Lilium *'Sterling Star'* is a compact lily perfect for pots, with upward-facing snow-white, slightly fragrant flowers.

FRAGRANT FLOWERS

Winter surprise
Hamamelis and *Lonicera*

You don't need large borders to enjoy winter-flowering shrubs. Blooming when the rest of the garden is gloomy and lacklustre, witch hazel, *Hamamelis mollis*, and winter honeysuckle, *Lonicera fragrantissima*, will bring it back to life. Grow them in large pots in pride of place on a patio; you can then use their leafy growth later as a backdrop to spring and summer flower displays.

FRAGRANT FLOWERS

Plants used
Hamamelis mollis; *Lonicera fragrantissima*

Height and spread
Hamamelis: H 1.8m (6ft) S 1.2m (4ft); *Lonicera*: H 1.2m (4ft) S 1.2m (4ft).

Aspect
Sunny and sheltered

Temperature needs
Plants hardy to -15°C (5°F).

Suitable pot size
45cm (18in).or larger

Suitable container material
Stone, terracotta, plastic

Compost type
Hamamelis: John Innes ericaceous compost; *Lonicera*: soil-based compost

Winter-flowering shrubs are a luxury in a small garden where every plant must earn its keep, but you can still make space for these seasonal stars. Plants like Chinese witch hazel, *Hamamelis mollis*, can be grown in a pot on a patio or balcony and then placed in a prominent spot when the heavily scented, spidery yellow flowers appear on the naked stems. Choose a witch hazel from a palette of yellow, orange, red, or purple flowers, and look out for those with twisted or crimped petals. The winter honeysuckle, *Lonicera fragrantissima*, is another prized plant, with highly fragrant, creamy-yellow flowers, which are produced in greater numbers when it is grown in a sheltered spot.

PLANTING LARGE SHRUBS IN POTS

To prevent shrubs becoming waterlogged, add a layer of broken clay pot pieces to the bottom of the container so that the drainage holes do not clog up with compost. Add a layer of compost and place your shrub on it to check that the top of the rootball is 5cm (2in) beneath the lip of the pot. Then slip the shrub out of its pot, place the pot on the compost and fill in around it with more soil. Remove the pot to leave a hole exactly the right size for the shrub's rootball. Place the shrub in the hole, firm around the roots with compost, water well and add a mulch (*see p.238*).

TOP TIP: PRUNING WITCH HAZELS

These shrubs can be pruned when the flowers start to fade in early spring. First, remove dead or diseased wood, and any branches that spoil the shape or crossing stems that are rubbing against one another. *Hamamelis* are very slow growing, so avoid cutting back very hard or too frequently. Prune back shoot tips to keep plants within bounds and to encourage bushy growth.

Bring witch hazel stems indoors to enjoy their scent inside and out. Cut stems that won't ruin the overall shape of the shrub when removed.

Choosing scented shrubs

Hamamelis virginiana *produces small flowers in autumn, just as the leaves are falling. Tolerant of urban pollution.*

Hamamelis x intermedia *'Pallida'* *has clusters of fragrant, sulphur-yellow flowers from mid- to late winter.*

Hamamelis x intermedia *'Jelena'* *decorates pots with large, coppery orange blooms from early to midwinter.*

Lonicera fragrantissima *is a shrubby semi-evergreen. Its highly scented, creamy white flowers appear in winter.*

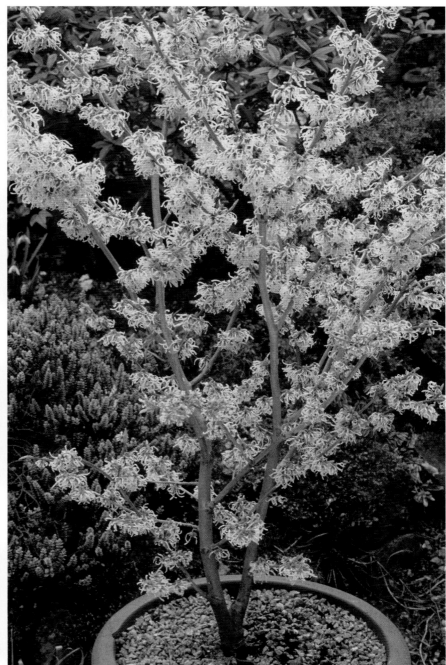

Hamamelis x intermedia *'Arnold Promise'* *produces large, bright yellow flowers throughout winter and makes a spectacular display in a large, frost-proof terracotta pot.*

Fragrant home

Breathe new life into your interior space with a selection of scented house plants. Perfect for a light airy room, such as a conservatory, these tender beauties produce gorgeous flowers that provide interest from the start of summer through to early autumn. With care, they will repeat their perfumed performance year after year.

Wax flower *Hoya*

Plant used
Hoya lanceolata
subsp. *bella*

Height and spread
H & S 45cm (18in)

Aspect
Bright spot indoors

Temperature needs
Min. 5°C (41°F)

Suitable pot size
20cm (8in)

Suitable container material
Glazed ceramic, plastic

Compost type
Soil-based compost. If possible, improve drainage by adding equal parts leaf mould, horticultural sand, charcoal and crushed bark to the compost

Native to a large area from the Himalayas to northern Burma, the wax flower, *Hoya lanceolata* subsp. *bella*, is a shrubby evergreen that features clusters of star-shaped, white summer flowers with red centres. Although their scent is noticeable during the day, the perfume is particularly potent when night falls. The pendulous stems make it perfect for a hanging basket, or tie them to slim stakes in a pot. Another popular wax flower, *Hoya carnosa*, has long climbing stems that can be trained up trellis or a similar support. It flowers for slightly longer, from late spring until autumn. Both plants can be grown outdoors in the summer in a sheltered, sunny spot, with some protection from the midday sun.

WATERING NEEDS
Water wax flowers regularly while in growth in spring and summer, and feed every four weeks with a balanced, liquid house-plant fertilizer. Occasionally mist the leaves to increase humidity around the plant. Reduce the amount of water given in winter.

TOP TIP: PRUNING AND TRAINING

Shrubby wax flowers need supporting with frames or canes to prevent the stems flopping over. Climbers potentially grow up to 4m (12ft) or more, but can be kept in check by training them up spiral supports or trellis that fits within your space. Simply tie the flexible stems onto their supports with soft twine and train them to fill out the trellis. If necessary, lightly prune *Hoya* plants after flowering to keep growth within bounds.

Simple ceramic containers contrast well with the Hoya's busy foliage and heads of small flowers.

Angel's trumpet *Brugmansia*

Plant used
Brugmansia x *candida* 'Grand Marnier'

Height and spread
H 1.8m (6ft)
S 90cm (3ft)

Aspect
Light spot in direct sun

Temperature needs
Min. 7°C (45°F)

Suitable pot size
30cm (12in)

Suitable container material
Glazed ceramic, plastic, metal

Compost type
Well-drained, loam-based compost

Brugmansia x *candida* 'Grand Marnier'

Angel's trumpet is a large dramatic plant, ideal as a focal point in a conservatory or sunny room. Often grown as a standard, the form 'Grand Marnier' produces a bushy head of green leaves that provide a foil for the heavily scented, pale peach, trumpet-shaped flowers that drip from its stems from summer until autumn. You can display *Brugmansia* outdoors in summer, but bring it back inside when night temperatures start to fall. Also keep it away from children and pets, as both the plant and its blooms are poisonous.

ANNUAL CARE
Keep the compost on the dry side over winter, then increase watering when the plant is in growth. *Brugmansia* is a heavy feeder and responds well to a liquid fertilizer every two weeks in summer. In late spring, prune to keep it in shape, and trim off dead or spindly growth.

Cape jasmine *Gardenia augusta*

Plant used
Gardenia augusta

Height and spread
H 60cm (24in)
S 45cm (18in)

Aspect
Bright, but not in direct sun

Temperature needs
Summer:
Daytime: 21–24°C (70–75°F)
Nighttime: 15–18°C (59–65°F)
Winter: 16°C (61°F)

Suitable pot size
20cm (8in)

Suitable container material
Glazed ceramic, plastic

Compost type
Soil-based ericaceous compost

Not for the beginner, the Cape jasmine requires a lot of care and attention, but get its growing conditions right and you'll be rewarded with large, waxy, white, heavily scented flowers from summer until autumn, held against a backdrop of glossy green leaves. *Gardenia* dislikes direct sunlight, so place plants on a west-facing windowsill during the summer and a south-facing windowsill over winter.

TEMPERATURE REGULATION
The Cape jasmine is a bit of a diva and conditions must be right for it to perform. To guarantee a flower display, plants need a nighttime temperature of 15–18°C (59–65°F) and daytime temperature of 21–24°C (70–75°F). In winter, plants prefer cooler conditions of around 16°C (61°F). Fluctuations between temperatures can upset flowering and plants should not be moved when in bud, as this may cause them to drop prematurely.

Use soft or rain water to prevent Gardenia leaves from yellowing, and apply fertilizer for lime haters.

FRAGRANT FLOWERS

Go bananas

Create your own leafy jungle with pots of bananas. The plants boast huge leaves that unfurl majestically from spring until autumn, and they are ideal for large containers. If you site them in a sunny, sheltered position, and feed and water them regularly, bananas will put on an exotic display for many years. Plants will also need protection from frost over winter.

Plant used
Ensete ventricosum
'Maurelii'
(Abyssinian banana)

Height and spread
H up to 2.2m (7ft)
S up to 2m (6ft)

Aspect
Full sun

Temperature needs
Not hardy below 0°C
(32°F)

Suitable pot size
Min. 45cm (18in)

Suitable container material
Stone, terracotta

Compost type
Soil-based compost,
eg, John Innes No 3

Although these ornamental bananas won't produce edible fruit if you grow them outside in your garden, the foliage more than makes up for it. Huge paddle-shaped leaves unfurl during the growing season from the top of a stout trunk to form a leafy, palm-like canopy. Natives of China, Japan, and other parts of Asia, bananas fall into three groups: *Musa, Ensete,* and *Musella.* Most have plain, jade-green foliage, but the leaves of some are attractively blushed or striped red, or variegated.

To prevent them from blowing over in strong winds, bananas are best grown in large, heavy containers filled with soil-based compost. Place pots in a warm, sunny, sheltered spot – the leaves of bananas shred easily if they are in a wind tunnel. Water plants regularly, but guard against waterlogged compost.

FEEDING PLANTS
Bananas are greedy plants and will grow taller and produce more leaves when given copious applications of fertilizer. Get the plant off to a flying start in spring by applying a general fertilizer, and then add a liquid feed every time it is watered. Supplement this every month during the growing season by sprinkling blood, fish, and bone over the compost surface, and water it in well.

**TOP TIP:
OVERWINTERING**

If you have the space, bring bananas into a heated greenhouse, cool room indoors, or conservatory. If you have no space indoors, the hardier types can remain outside if you cover the compost with a layer of bark mulch, and wrap the pot with bubble plastic or hessian. Cut off all the leaves, then stack lengths of flue liner on top of each other around the stem, filling the gap with straw. Cover the top with plastic or a tile to keep rain out.

The Abyssinian banana produces magnificent, paddle-shaped, green and maroon leaves. Site it in a sheltered spot to protect the leaves from wind.

Banana choices

Ensete ventricosum *is the green form of Abyssinian banana. Its long leaves are held upright like a shuttlecock.*

Some hybridized bananas *are attractively variegated – ideal for adding interest to a foliage display.*

Ensete ventricosum *'Tandarra Red' is a choice plant that carries huge red-flushed foliage.*

Musa basjoo *is the Japanese root-hardy banana. Widely available, it grows quickly and has massive green leaves.*

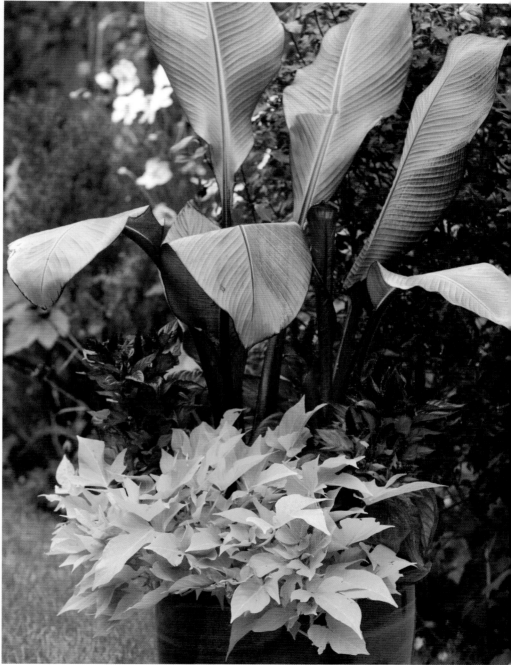

Team a colourful banana *with an underplanting of lime-green Ipomoea and Celosia argentea var. plumosa, which has dark red foliage to match the Ensete, and pinky-red, furry flowerheads.*

Colourful cannas

Turn up the heat in summer with tropical cannas. These sizzling sun-lovers flower continuously from midsummer until autumn, but their foliage provides a spectacular feature long before the blooms unfold. Both leaves and flowers come in many fiery shades reminiscent of carnival costumes from their native Brazil.

Plant used
Canna 'Durban'

Height and spread
H 1.5m (5ft)
S 50cm (16in)

Aspect
Full sun

Temperature needs
Not hardy below
0°C (32°F)

Suitable pot size
30cm (12in) or larger

Suitable container material
Stone, terracotta, glazed ceramic, plastic

Compost type
Soil-based compost, eg, John Innes No 3

Ideal in the centre of a display of annual bedding plants, cannas look equally effective in pots on their own, and combined with containers of *Crocosmia*, *Colocasia*, and bananas to create a leafy, colourful, tropical scheme. Cannas are frost-tender perennials grown from rhizomes and produce tall stems of magnificent iris-like flowers in hot reds, oranges, and yellows. The blooms are often paired with equally flamboyant brightly coloured or variegated foliage. *Canna* 'Durban' is one of the best, and features a combination of large, luminous orange flowers and dark red foliage with flame-like markings in red, pink, and orange. Others are grown for their dark leaves. *C.* 'Black Knight', for example, has sultry burgundy foliage that makes a great foil for its own deep red flowers and other summer blooms.

PROMOTING FLOWERING

Given a warm sheltered site where they can bask in full sun, cannas provide a long-lasting display, blooming from mid- to late summer, depending on the variety, and continuing to send out new flower shoots until the middle of autumn. However, if you attempt to grow them in even light shade, they are unlikely to bloom. As well as heat, plants enjoy moist conditions and must be watered frequently from spring to autumn and never allowed to dry out. They are also extremely greedy, so for robust growth and optimum flower production, feed them every fortnight during the growing season with a balanced liquid feed. Also remove fading blooms, which helps to promote more to form.

*Centre: **Flickering like flames** from an ornate pot, the leaves of Canna 'Durban' are set ablaze with an underplanting of fiery red busy Lizzies and Cuphea.*

TOP TIP: OVERWINTERING AND DIVIDING CANNAS

To protect your plants over winter, before the first frosts in autumn cut back the leaves and flower stems to 3cm (1¼in) from the soil surface and move the pot to a frost-free shed or greenhouse. Keep the compost damp, but not overly wet, in winter and then move plants back outside in late spring or early summer. Spring is also the time to divide rhizomes to make new plants. Clean the rhizomes of compost, then, using a clean sharp knife, cut them into sections, each with a bud, or eye. Pot up the rhizome sections in fresh compost.

Canna choices

Canna *'Assaut'* *is a tall plant, bearing dusky purple foliage and long stems of scarlet flowers from midsummer.*

Canna *'Richard Wallace'* *(syn. 'King Midas') is a robust plant with dark green leaves and golden yellow blooms.*

Canna *'Black Knight'* *has deep red flowers which stand out dramatically against a foil of dark burgundy foliage.*

Canna *'Rosemond Coles'* *produces vibrant red flowers with golden yellow margins above dark green leaves.*

Canna *'Striata'* *bears blazing orange flowers that sit above broad, oval, green leaves with bright yellow stripes.*

Canna speciosa *'Tropical Rose'* *is a dwarf form, with green leaves and pink flowers on knee-high stems.*

Canna *'Durban'* *produces bright orange flowers above bronze leaves with red, orange, and pink stripes.*

Canna *'Cleopatra'* *is a compact plant with green leaves and flashy red and yellow flowers with contrasting flecks.*

TROPICAL EFFECTS

Bright highlights

If your garden is in need of a lift, inject some colour with tropical-looking flowers and foliage plants. Flame nettles are perfect for plugging gaps in borders when spring or summer flowers have faded, or use them in a mixed container display. Parrot's beak provides interest at head height in baskets or trailing over the sides of tall pots, while *Arisaema* will brighten up shady areas.

Flame nettles *Solenostemon scutellarioides*

Plant used
Solenostemon
(mixed)

Height and spread
H 20cm (8in)
S 20cm (8in)

Aspect
Sun or partial shade

Temperature needs
Min. 15°C (60°F)

Suitable pot size
10cm (4in)

Suitable container material
Plastic, metal, stone, terracotta, baskets

Compost type
Multi-purpose compost

Known to generations of gardeners as coleus, and often sold as such, these leafy plants were long considered outdated, but are now back in vogue thanks to striking new forms with colourful and patterned foliage. Their vibrancy gives patio displays a lift, or use them to add colour to border schemes. Another idea is to use pots of flame nettles as underplanting around the stems of trees or shrubs in large containers.

Easy to grow from seed, young plants are also available from nurseries. Keep them well watered and repot young plants several times during the growing season. Prune stems to maintain a bushy shape and remove flowers, as the foliage loses intensity when plants bloom.

TOP TIP: PROTECTING PLANTS

In early autumn, place plants in a light, frost-free place where the temperature does not fall below 15°C (60°F). A warm windowsill or heated greenhouse is ideal. Cut back stems by about half and allow compost to almost dry out between waterings; too much moisture at this time of year can lead to fungal diseases.

Buy young plants in **spring** *and pot them on in larger containers for a long display of vibrant foliage from summer to autumn.*

Parrot's beak *Lotus berthelotii*

Plant used
Lotus berthelotii

Height and spread
H 20cm (8in)
S indefinite

Aspect
Full sun

Temperature needs
Not hardy below 0°C
(32°F)

Suitable pot size
30cm (12in)

Suitable container material
Plastic, terracotta, baskets

Compost type
Soil-based compost, eg, John Innes No 2

Lotus berthelotii **filling a large hanging basket.**

A close look at the red flowers that cover this evergreen plant immediately reveal how the parrot's beak got its common name. The other feature that makes it so popular is the trailing stems of grey ferny foliage, which are ideal for a hanging basket display or tumbling over the sides of a large container. Although it needs protection from frost over winter, Parrot's beak is perfectly happy outside in summer.

FLOWERING NEEDS

For maximum flower power, plants need around six to eight hours of sunlight each day, so place them in a warm, bright spot. Water plants regularly during spring and summer, and feed with a liquid fertilizer every couple of weeks during spring. Keep plants frost-free over winter and reduce watering (*follow advice for Flame nettles in the Top Tip box opposite*).

Arisaema *Arisaema candidissimum*

Plant used
Arisaema candidissimum

Height and spread
H 40cm (16in)
S 15cm (6in)

Aspect
Dappled shade

Temperature needs
Hardy down to -5°C
(23°F)

Suitable pot size
20cm (8in)

Suitable Container material
Plastic, terracotta

Compost type
Soil-based compost, eg, John Innes No 3

A group of tuberous spring- and summer-flowering perennials originating from China, Japan, North America and the Himalayas, arisaemas have curious flowers that in some species resemble the head of cobra about to strike. The flowers are generally held on long stems and are often teamed with large leaves. Their sinister appearance is perhaps a hint that the plants are poisonous, but not all look quite so gruesome. *Arisaema candidissimum* appears more like whipped ice cream, with its pink and white flowerheads, which are also delightfully scented.

SITING PLANTS

Arisaemas prefer the shade, and are perfect for small, sheltered, urban gardens where they can survive the winter outside. Either display a group of plants together or use them to plug gaps in a bed or border. You can then whip the pots out of the border when they've finished flowering and the leaves have died back. Water regularly during the growing season, but keep compost just moist when plants are dormant in winter.

Elegants spathes in ice-cream colours protect
the tiny flowers of Arisaema candidissimum.

TROPICAL EFFECTS

Graceful bamboos

Bamboos instantly add a lush, tropical effect to gardens, patios, and balconies, and include many different varieties, with tall, airy types suitable for large containers and more compact forms ideal for small spaces. Easy to look after and reliably hardy, these elegant evergreens provide interest all year round.

Plant used
Pseudosasa japonica

Height and spread
H 3m (10ft)
S 1.2m (4ft)

Aspect
Full sun or partial shade

Temperature needs
Hardy down to
-15°C (5°F)

Suitable pot size
45cm – 60cm
(18in – 24in)

Suitable container material
Metal, plastic, glazed ceramic

Compost type
Soil-based compost, eg, John Innes No 3

Bamboos are versatile plants and suit a range of garden styles and uses, whether you're looking for a focal point, backdrop, specimen to disguise an eyesore, or a screen to divide your space. Their main attractions are their decorative stems, which come in a range of colours, including golden yellow, black, green, and striped. Thriving in soil-based compost, such as John Innes No. 3, the larger bamboos, including *Pseudosasa, Sasa, Fargesia,* and *Phyllostachys,* need roomy pots that provide space for plants to spread. Containers made from metal, plastic, or with glazed finishes are ideal, but avoid terracotta, as this permeable material sucks moisture from the compost which can cause bamboo foliage to dry out and turn yellow. Although some bamboos are rampant thugs in the garden, spreading via underground root systems, when grown in pots even vigorous species won't turn into unwanted guests. However, it is still wise to avoid plants that grow very quickly and require frequent repotting or dividing; all of those shown here are well behaved, requiring the minimum of maintenance, apart from watering.

CARING FOR BAMBOOS
Bamboos are thirsty plants and need watering regularly to prevent the loss of foliage. If you have a number in pots, consider installing an automatic irrigation system to maintain moisture levels. Also apply a balanced fertilizer in spring or early summer to promote a mass of new canes and healthy leaves. As plants mature, thin out heavily congested clumps by removing some of the thinner canes or older shoots that look tatty. Stripping leaves from the bottom third of plants also helps to show off the canes.

TOP TIP: APPLY A DECORATIVE FINISH

Add interest to your container display and prevent weeds from growing on the compost around bamboos by covering the surface with an ornamental mulch. Choose a material that contrasts with the container and sets off the bamboo, such as pebbles, slate, coloured gravel, or glass beads.

Tall and graceful, Phyllostachys bambusoides *'Castillonii' makes a beautiful screen if given a large container and plenty of water.*

Choosing a bamboo

Fargesia murielae *produces masses of elegant, slim canes covered with lush green foliage. It also tolerates dry soils.*

Sasa veitchii *is a bushy bamboo with purple canes and variegated leaves that bleach to pale brown in winter.*

Phyllostachys vivax *f.* aureocaulis *is a tall plant with bright yellow canes occasionally striped green.*

Pleioblastus variegatus *is happy in sun or shade. It forms knee-high stems of creamy-white and green foliage.*

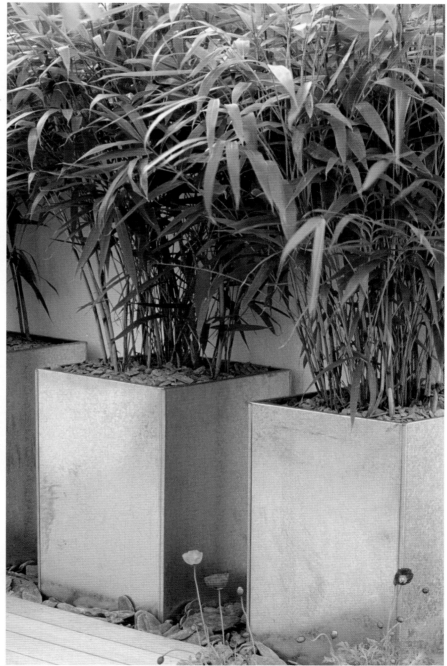

Contemporary galvanized containers *filled with the arrow bamboo,* Pseudosasa japonica, *and topped with a grey slate mulch, make a sophisticated boundary for a modern city garden.*

Potted palms

Elegant, happy in low light and easy to look after, tropical palms make great specimens for clean, simple containers that show off their architectural forms and beautiful fronds. Use them as focal plants or as the backdrop for a group of indoor pots. Palms also make a good foil for exotic blooms and most are happy to spend the summer outside on a warm, sheltered patio.

Parlour palm *Chamaedorea elegans*

Plant used
Chamaedorea elegans

Height and spread
H 2.4m (8ft)
S 1.5m (5ft)

Aspect
Bright, but away from direct sunlight

Temperature needs
Min. 18°C (64°F)

Suitable pot size
30cm (12in)

Suitable container material
Glazed ceramic, stone, plastic

Compost type
Well-drained, multi-purpose compost

Popular in homes since Victorian times, and known by a number of common names, including parlour and table-top palm, this bushy plant is still widely grown for its exotic appearance and long fronds of shiny green leaves. Small specimens can be used to brighten up shelves or gaps in bookcases, while larger plants are ideal for livening up a shady corner or as focal points where their attractive fronds are on show. Plants are fairly slow growing, so buy a plant of a size that matches your space.

CARING FOR PARLOUR PALMS
One of this plant's charms is that it is relatively undemanding. Water it regularly while in growth, keeping the compost on the moist side, but allow it to dry out between each watering in winter. Feed your parlour palm every month during spring and summer with a balanced liquid feed to keep the foliage lush and healthy. It will also enjoy a holiday outside on the patio in summer and makes a great foil for colourful bedding and tropical blooms.

TOP TIP: KEEPING FRONDS HEALTHY
If the tips of fronds turn brown you probably need to raise the humidity around the palm. Spray plants regularly with a mister or sponge the leaves – the latter also helps to remove any dirt. Conversely, this type of damage can be caused by root rot due to overwatering, so check that the bottom of the container is not filled with water. Brown leaves are sometimes the result of scorching; keep parlour palms in a cool, shady spot away from the midday sun.

Fronds of tropical-looking foliage *lighten gloomy corners and lend a touch of class to a minimal interior décor.*

Sago palm *Cycas revoluta*

Plant used
Cycas revoluta

Height and spread
H & S 1.5m (5ft)

Aspect
Bright, but out of
direct sunlight

Temperature needs
Min. 10°C (50°F)

Suitable pot size
30–45cm

**Suitable container
material**
Terracotta, stone,
plastic, ceramic

Compost type
Soil-based compost,
eg, John Innes No 3

Despite its ferny appearance, this slow-growing palm has tough fronds with spine-tipped leaves, and is best placed where you will not accidentally snag your clothes as you brush past. It likes bright light but not direct sun, making it ideal for a partially shaded area in a conservatory. Young plants have a bushy appearance, but over time the sago palm forms a distinctive trunk, lending it a passing resemblance to a tree fern.

WATERING AND AFTERCARE

Although these palms like moist compost, take care not to overwater or the leaves may turn yellow, and reduce watering in winter when temperatures fall. Avoid moving sago palms when new growth appears in spring; as the fronds unfurl they follow the sun, so moving plants at this time can result in crooked stems and an unbalanced shape.

A container made from bamboo makes the ideal partner for this exotic-looking palm.

Fan palm *Rhapis excelsa*

Plant used
Rhapis excelsa

Height and spread
H & S 1.5m (5ft)

Aspect
Partial shade

Temperature needs
Min. 15°C (59°F)

Suitable pot size
15–20cm (6–8in)

**Suitable container
material**
Metal, glazed
ceramic, terracotta

Compost type
Multi-purpose
compost

Dramatic fans of glossy leaves carried on upright stems make this clump-forming palm a real eye-catcher. It hails from subtropical East Asia, and looks stunning in an ornate, Oriental-style container. Really easy to grow, fan palms thrive in the shade of a north-facing room and enjoy a sojourn outdoors over summer, as long as they are brought in again long before the first frosts. Keep plants well watered during the growing season, but reduce moisture levels in winter. Also, mist the foliage every week to increase humidity.

FAN PALM OPTIONS

There are dozens of cultivars of *Rhapis excelsa* that are highly prized by collectors. Many are attractively variegated, including 'Taiheinishiki', which has boldly striped yellow and green leaves, and 'Variegata' with white-striped foliage. For a smaller form, try 'Zuikonishiki', which grows to just 60cm (24in) in height and has yellow variegated leaves.

Forest-floor dwellers, fan palms prefer shade and a fortnightly dose of fertilizer when in growth.

Foolproof foliage

Some house plants need careful cosseting and attention to detail to thrive, but these foliage species are almost foolproof. Their bold leaves may look exotic, adding a tropical touch to interiors, but umbrella plants, philodendrons and Swiss cheese plants are tough and resilient, putting on a show even when they have been neglected for a while.

Umbrella plant *Schefflera*

Plants used
Schefflera arboricola 'Gold Capella'; *Ficus pumila* 'Sunny'

Height and spread
Schefflera: H (1.5m) 5ft S (1m) 3ft; *Ficus:* S up to 1m (3ft)

Aspect
Good light, but not in direct sun

Temperature needs
Min. 13°C (55°F) in winter

Suitable pot size
30cm (12in) or larger

Suitable container material
Any

Compost type
Multi-purpose compost

Handsome specimens grown for their glossy leaves held aloft on slender stalks, umbrella plants are widely available and require very little care. You can buy green forms, but the variegated types are much showier and add more interest to a room. *Schefflera arboricola* 'Gold Capella' is one of the best and can reach 3m (10ft) high, with a similar spread, in warm climates. However, it is unlikely to scale such heights in a pot and can be kept within its designated area by pruning in spring. The main stem is quite weak, so provide a suitable support, such as a moss stick.

WATERING REQUIREMENTS
Keep the compost damp during the growing season, from spring to early autumn, but avoid overwatering, which may result in root rot. Reduce the watering frequency in winter, allowing the compost to dry out completely between each application. Feed umbrella plants every few weeks during the growing season with a balanced liquid fertilizer.

A frill of the trailing fig, Ficus pumila 'Sonny', softens the edge of the pot and contrasts well with the umbrella plant.

TOP TIP: RETAINING VARIEGATION

Growing variegated plants in poor light often results in sparce growth and loss of variegation. In addition, colourful *Schefflera* may revert to the parent plant's colouring and produce plain green leaves. These tend to be more vigorous than the variegated shoots and should be cut out completely when you see them.

Swiss cheese plant *Monstera deliciosa*

Plant used
Monstera deliciosa

Height and spread
H 1.8m (6ft)
S 60cm (24in)

Aspect
Light, but not in
direct sunlight

Temperature needs
Min. 15°C (59°F)

Suitable pot size
30cm (12in) or larger

**Suitable container
material**
Any

Compost type
Multi-purpose
compost

A tropical climber, the Swiss cheese plant produces
massive glossy green leaves, which sometimes
grow up to 90cm (36in) in length. The foliage
is deeply lobed and often punctured with
elliptical holes that increase in size as the
leaves expand. Train plants up a moss pole
or other form of support, and feed regularly
in summer with a balanced liquid fertilizer.

WATER AND LIGHT NEEDS
Water plants regularly, but allow the compost
to almost dry out between applications, and
reduce the frequency in winter. Clean the leaves
to remove dust, spray to increase humidity levels,
and prune plants to keep them within bounds. Although
Swiss cheese plants will cope with dark corners, plants
may sulk, producing tiny leaves on leggy shoots. To perform
well, they require some light but not direct sun, and you may need
to move plants to a brighter spot in winter when light levels are lower.

Monstera deliciosa

Philodendron

Plant used
*Philodendron
bipinnatifidum*

Height and spread
H & S up to 1.5m
(5ft)

Aspect
Light, but not in
direct sunlight

Temperature needs
Min. 15°C (59°F)

Suitable pot size
45cm (18in) or larger

**Suitable container
material**
Plastic, placed in a
decorative container

Compost type
Multi-purpose
compost

Provide this stately tropical shrub with plenty of
space in a light room and it will make a striking
specimen. A large architectural plant, it
produces huge, deeply lobed leaves that
provide glossy, verdant colour all year round.
Water and feed plants regularly during
the growing season, and allow the
compost to dry out between waterings
in winter. Clean the leaves with a soft,
damp cloth, and spray them occasionally
to raise humidity levels.

CHOOSING VARIETIES
There are many other types of philodendron
on offer. Among the best are *P. hederaceum*,
which has glossy heart-shaped leaves, and
P. angustisectum, with its deeply divided
foliage similar to a palm. *P. melanochrysum*
produces dark green, arrow-shaped leaves that have a velvety
texture. All of these are climbers and need a moss pole support.

Philodendron bipinnatifidum has magnificent foliage.

TROPICAL EFFECTS

Dramatic hot-house foliage

If you're fed up with the monotony of a neutral room, inject a dash of dazzling colour with tropical foliage plants grown in contemporary containers. Their flamboyant good looks make them eye-catching focal points, and they are best displayed in pots on their own, rather than in mixed groups where they will fight others for the limelight.

TROPICAL EFFECTS

Elephant's ear *Alocasia x amazonica*

Plant used
Alocasia x amazonica

Height and spread
H & S 60cm (24in)

Aspect
Light, but not
in direct sun

Temperature needs
Min. 15°C (59°F)

Suitable pot size
20cm (8in)

**Suitable container
material**
Plastic, stone,
ceramic, metal

Compost type
Multi-purpose
compost with added
bark or perlite

With leaves that measure a whopping 45cm (18in) long, this plant's common name is no exaggeration. Held on stout stems, the arrow-shaped, glossy, dark green foliage is truly spectacular, with its bright silver veins creating a beautiful pattern. Ideal for a bright position indoors away from full sun; it will be miserable and start to lose its intense colour in a gloomy corner. It also requires heat to thrive and will drop its leaves in cool conditions, but if you restore warm temperatures within a day or two, the plant will recover and produce new foliage.

PLANT CARE
Keep the compost moist at all times, but avoid overwatering as this could lead to root rot. Over winter, allow the compost to dry out completely before watering again. Spray plants regularly in the growing season to raise humidity levels, and during the same period feed every month with a balanced liquid fertilizer. Prevent the plant from looking unsightly by snipping off dead, dying, or damaged leaves.

TOP TIP: MAINTAINING HEALTHY FOLIAGE

Misting leaves with a hand-held spray to raise humidity levels will help to prevent dust settling on the foliage, but you will still need to clean the leaves occasionally to ensure they retain their lustre. Wipe the surface with a soft, damp cloth, and take care not to press too hard or you may bruise the leaves.

A bright bathroom is the ideal location for an elephant's ear, which will appreciate the warmth and humidity.

Peacock plant *Calathea makoyana*

Plant used
Calathea makoyana

Height and spread
H 45cm (18in)
S 22cm (9in)

Aspect
Bright, but not
in direct sunlight

Temperature needs
Min. 16°C (61°F)

Suitable pot size
15cm (6in)

**Suitable container
material**
Ceramic, glazed
terracotta, stone,
metal

Compost type
Multi-purpose
compost

For a spectacular display of variegated foliage, try the peacock plant. Native to Brazil, it makes a bushy clump of paddle-shaped leaves with dark green margins and ovals of dark green marking the surface. Turn the leaf over and the same pattern is repeated in purple, while the silvery effect is produced by net-like, see-through areas on the foliage. Plants are shown off to their best advantage in a neutral or light-coloured pot, and will enjoy a sheltered, bright spot, away from draughts, with high humidity.

CARING FOR PEACOCK PLANTS
Water plants regularly, but allow the compost to almost dry out between each application, and reduce watering even further in winter. Spray the leaves during the summer to raise humidity levels, and feed monthly with a balanced liquid fertilizer to boost growth.

Calathea makoyana **has peacock-patterned foliage.**

Croton *Codiaeum*

Plant used
*Codiaeum
variegatum* var.
pictum 'Gold Star'

Height and spread
H 1m (3ft)
S 60cm (24in)

Aspect
Full light, shaded
from hot sun

Temperature needs
Min. 15°C (59°F)

Suitable pot size
20cm (8in)

**Suitable container
material**
Stone, ceramic,
metal, plastic

Compost type
Soil-based compost,
eg, John Innes No 2

Codiaeum variegatum var. *pictum* 'Gold Star'.

Among the most spectacular foliage plants you can grow in the home, crotons come in a range of colours and leaf forms. Originating from Malaysia and the islands of the East Pacific, they are grown for their leathery leaves, which are splashed, dotted, or flushed with the bright colours you find in a child's paintbox.

In their native environment they grow into large trees, but they make compact plants when grown in containers in the home. To thrive, water plants regularly, reducing the frequency in winter. Mist leaves with a hand-held spray, and feed every month or so during the growing season with a balanced liquid fertilizer.

CHOOSING CROTONS
C. variegatum var. *pictum* 'Petra' has spear-shaped green leaves with dramatic yellow veins, while 'Gold Star' produces gold-splashed foliage. For bolder colours, try 'Excellent', which has large, forked leaves marked with green, yellow, and red patterns.

TROPICAL EFFECTS

Tropical blooms

Create a tropical paradise in your home with some exotic blooms. If you can provide the conditions that these plants enjoy, you will be rewarded with an enviable display. Medinillas are stately queens, with large leaves and spectacular flowers, while the flamingo flower is adorned with eye-catching waxy blooms. The vase plant's sculptural leaves and flowers are also guaranteed to turn heads.

Medinilla *Medinilla magnifica*

Plant used
Medinilla magnifica

Height and spread
H & S 1.2m (4ft)

Aspect
Bright, but not direct sun

Temperature needs
Min 15–20°C (59–68°F)

Suitable pot size
20cm (8in)

Suitable container material
Ceramic, stone, metal

Compost type
Orchid compost

A magnificent plant, *Medinilla* is worth growing for its large, glossy leaves with attractive veins, but it really comes into its own during spring and summer when long stems bend under the weight of blowsy, deep pink blooms. A native of the Philippines, this plant prefers a warm, bright environment, such as a heated conservatory or greenhouse, but shelter it from direct sun. Don't allow the compost to dry out while in growth and mist the leaves frequently to provide the humidity it needs to thrive. Also, wipe the foliage occasionally with a soft cloth to remove dust.

As flower buds appear, feed Medinilla every couple of weeks with a liquid fertilizer to ensure they fulfil their promise and open to reveal the exotic blooms.

TOP TIP: PROMOTING NEW BLOOMS

Plants may be shy to flower, but you can encourage them to bloom by lowering the temperature slightly in winter, and reducing the amount of water you apply. Wait until the compost is almost dry and give the plant just enough to prevent it from flagging. In spring, resume more frequent watering, feed fortnightly with a liquid fertilizer, and raise the humidity by misting the foliage.

TROPICAL EFFECTS

Vase plant *Aechmea*

Plant used
Aechmea fasciata

Height and spread
H & S 50cm (20in)

Aspect
Bright, but not
in full sun

Temperature needs
Min. 15°C (59°F)

Suitable pot size
15cm (6in)

**Suitable container
material**
Plastic, set inside
a decorative outer
container

Compost type
Well-drained,
multi-purpose
compost

Showy bracts last for up to two months.

Known as the vase or urn plant, *Aechmea
fasciata* is a native of South America. It is
admired for its upright rosette of leaves, which
are attractively marked with silver bands and
provide a feature in themselves. However, when
mature it performs its star turn, as a stem rises
from the centre of the foliage carrying a large
head of pink bracts and small blue flowers.

WATERING NEEDS

As well as keeping the compost damp around
the plant, use fresh rainwater to fill up the
"vase" that forms in the centre of the leafy
rosette. If you live in an area with soft tap water
this will be fine, but hard water leaves deposits
that spoil the foliage effect. Empty the "vase"
and refill with fresh water every month or so
to prevent the plant rotting and producing an
unpleasant smell.

Flamingo flower *Anthurium*

Plant used
Anthurium
andraeanum

Height and spread
H & S 50cm (20in)

Aspect
Bright. Avoid
south-facing
windowsills
in summer

Temperature needs
Min. 15°C (59°F)

Suitable pot size
15cm (6in)

**Suitable container
material**
Plastic, set inside
a decorative outer
container

Compost type
Use a mix of 1 part
soil-based compost,
1 part sharp sand,
and 3 parts
leafmould.

Reminiscent of the elaborate headgear you
might see at a Mardi Gras festival, the
decorative flowers of *Anthurium* bloom from
spring until late summer, providing a long season
of interest. Rising above spear-shaped glossy
leaves, the "flowers" are actually the finger-like
spadix that emerges from a waxy spathe. The
spathes come in a range of colours, including white,
yellow, green, pink, orange, and red.

Flamingo flowers like bright conditions out of
direct sunlight and away from draughts, although
when the sun is weaker in winter, move them to
a sunnier position. Ensure the compost never dries out,
but guard against waterlogging, which can damage the roots.

*Spray flamingo
flowers regularly
to create the humid
conditions they enjoy.*

REPOTTING FLAMINGO FLOWERS

Plants will need repotting every couple of years into slightly
larger containers. Position the rootball so that the roots that
grow above the surface of the compost are exposed. Cover
these with a layer of damp moss. Mix sharp sand and
leafmould with the compost to improve drainage and
provide the acidic conditions that these plants prefer.

Sculptural leaves

Foliage plants with leaves of different shapes, sizes, and colours create long-lasting, dramatic container displays. Many are perfect for a shady position, and suit small urban gardens and contemporary designs, but there are plenty to choose from for any aspect. Some of the most dazzling foliage plants are tender and will require winter protection.

Plants used
Fatsia japonica;
Alocasia sanderiana;
Pelargonium 'Lady Plymouth'

Height and spread
Fatsia H & S 1.5m (5ft); *Alocasia* H & S 1m (3ft); *Pelargonium* H 40cm (16in) S 20cm (8in)

Aspect
Dappled shade

Temperature needs
Protect from frost over winter

Suitable pot size
45cm (18in)

Suitable container material
Stone, metal, glazed terracotta

Compost type
Mix of multi-purpose and soil-based compost

The bright green, glossy leaves of *Fatsia japonica*, or false castor-oil plant, provide a striking focal point for a jungle-inspired container scheme, either as a single specimen or matched with other tropical-looking plants, such as *Alocasia sanderiana*, (*see also p.60*). Most frequently grown as a house plant, *Alocasia* will also add pizzazz to outdoor summer schemes with its dark green, arrow-shaped leaves and bold silver veins, while variegated pelargoniums provide contrast and scented foliage.

Fatsia prefers a shaded spot and is hardy down to -5°C (23°F), but if you grow it in a container with tender plants, bring the display indoors over winter. It can then be taken outside again after all danger of frost has passed in spring. Add some slow-release granular fertilizer to the compost in early spring, and keep the container well watered during the growing season, but allow the compost to dry out between waterings in winter.

RESTRICTING GROWTH

If your *Fatsia* becomes too tall for its container, prune it in spring or summer. Cut the main stem down to a more desirable height so that it balances the size of your pot. Lower branches can stifle plants grown beneath, so raise the canopy by removing a few stems to give plants at the base space to flourish.

TOP TIP: WRAPPING UP TENDER PLANTS

If you are growing a false castor oil plant in a pot on its own you can protect it from the worst winter weather by moving it to a shelted area, wrapping the container with hessian or bubble plastic, and then covering the plant with fleece when very low temperatures are forecast. Other plants that can be treated in this way include the loquat, *Eriobotrya japonica*, the ginger plant, *Hedychium densiflorum*, and *Tetrapanax*. *Alocasia*, pelargoniums, and *Melianthus* are all too tender to survive the winter outside and must be moved to a light, frost-free place indoors until late spring.

Fatsia *has glossy dark green leaves, accompanied in autumn by white, spherical flowerheads followed by shiny black fruits.*

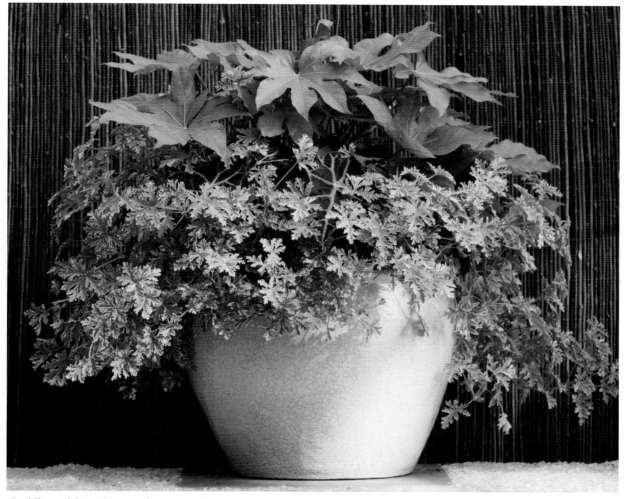

The different foliage shapes and textures in this combination are shown off to perfection in a white stone container.

OTHER LARGE-LEAVED OPTIONS

Melianthus major, *known as the honey bush, has large, glaucous-blue, serrated leaves that smell like peanut butter. Protect the pot and plant from frost over winter.*

Eriobotrya japonica *will produce fruit if grown in the ground, but in a pot enjoy this small tree for its architectural shape and deeply ribbed, large, dark green leaves.*

Hedychium densiflorum, *or perennial ginger, makes a large clump of long, lance-shaped leaves topped by perfumed orange flowers at the end of summer.*

Tetrapanax *has huge evergreen leaves carried on long stalks, and can be grown outside in mild areas with some winter protection. The cultivar 'Rex' is one of the hardiest.*

Spiked statements

There's not a flamboyant flower in sight, but these eye-catching plants still demand attention, thanks to their vibrant, spiky foliage. Single plants make fantastic living sculptures or they can be mixed together with a selection of other architectural plants in pots to create an arresting display of contrasting textures, colours, and shapes.

DRAMA QUEENS

New Zealand flax *Phormium*

Plant used
Phormium 'Jester'

Height and spread
H & S 1m (3ft)

Aspect
Full sun or partial shade

Temperature needs
Hardy to -5°C (23°F)

Suitable pot size
30cm (12in)

Suitable container material
Terracotta, stone, metal

Compost type
Soil-based compost, eg, John Innes No 3, with extra drainage material

New Zealand flaxes are easy-to-grow architectural plants with striking sword-shaped leaves that provide colourful focal points in tall containers. All these evergreen, clump-forming perennials need to thrive is free-draining, moisture-retentive compost, a sunny position, and regular watering, especially during hot, dry summers. Apply a slow-release granular fertilizer in late spring. Although most are hardy down to -5°C (23°F), in harsh winters you'll need to protect pots with bubble plastic and cover plants with horticultural fleece.

PLANT CHOICES

Phormium varieties related to *P. cookianum* have cascading foliage, while those bred from *P. tenax* have a more upright habit. *P.* 'Platt's Black' has deep purple leaves, *P.* 'Jester' produces pink leaves with green margins, and the foliage of *P.* 'Pink Panther' has red edges with a pink stripe; the cascading habit of all three suits tall pots.

TOP TIP: MAINTAINING HEALTHY FOLIAGE

To keep *Phormium* foliage at its best, remove any dead or dying leaves, as well as those around the base of plants that have become tatty. Thin leaves are easy to snip off with secateurs, but thicker plant material may need to be cut off with a sharp gardening knife. Keep the compost moist. Avoid splashing plants with water on hot, sunny days or you may scorch the foliage.

New Zealand flax *makes an attention-grabbing statement plant for a sunny spot in your garden.*

Cabbage palm *Cordyline australis*

Plants used
Cordyline australis
Purpurea Group

Height and spread
H 1.5m (5ft)
S 60cm (24in)

Aspect
Full sun

Temperature needs
Not reliably hardy
below 0°C (32°F)

Suitable pot size
30cm (12in)

Suitable container material
Terracotta,
stone, metal

Compost type
Soil-based compost,
eg, John Innes No 3

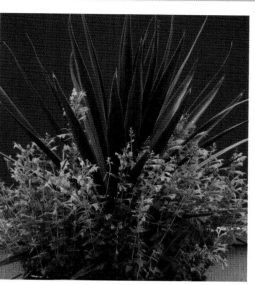

***Try pairing a* Cordyline** *with colourful flowering plants such as* Agastache *for a pleasing contrast to its spiky foliage.*

Cordyline makes a great focal point with its upright rosette of spear-shaped leaves. Tough and easy-going, plants can easily cope with a salty blast in a seaside garden and do best in full sun. There are many different coloured plants to choose from; all are happy in pots for a few years, but will eventually need to be planted in the garden, since they are very fast-growing and will start to sulk if their roots are restricted for too long. Set plants in a light area in a cool room indoors, or in a frost-free greenhouse over winter.

PLANTING PARTNERS

Cabbage palms produce a bare trunk that can be hidden by careful underplanting. Here, a mass of orange *Agastache* softens the architectural leaves of the *Cordyline*, alongside a lavender's purple flowers and silver-grey foliage.

Yucca *Yucca filamentosa*

Plant used
Yucca filamentosa
'Bright Edge'

Height and spread
H 90cm (3ft)
S 1.5m (5ft)

Aspect
Full sun

Temperature needs
Fully hardy

Suitable pot size
45cm (18in)

Suitable container material
Plastic, stone, metal,
terracotta

Compost type
Soil-based compost,
eg, John Innes No 2

The stiff rosette of sword-shaped leaves on this ornamental evergreen shrub will provide stunning year-round interest in a sunny part of the garden or on a south-facing patio or balcony. Masses of pendulous cream flowers appear on a 3m- (10ft-) tall flower stem in early summer. Although it makes a great statement plant on its own, its structural shape looks fantastic when displayed alongside other spiky plants, such as *Agave* and cabbage palms, in a summer display.

PLANT CARE

Keep plants looking good by watering regularly and feeding monthly during the growing season with a liquid feed. Remove any dead, diseased, or damaged leaves from the base of plants, and cut off the flower stalks as blooms start to fade. A large group of plants, some yuccas are hardy, but others will need to be given a sheltered site or be brought indoors to survive the winter.

Yucca filamentosa 'Bright Edge'

DRAMA QUEENS

Magnificent maples
Acer palmatum

Grown for their graceful foliage, Japanese maples create a sophisticated statement on a patio or in a garden. These compact trees are ideal for pots, where they provide a decorative canopy in spring and summer, followed by a spectacular autumn display of sparkling yellow, orange, and red leaves.

Plant used
Acer palmatum

Height and spread
H 2m (6ft)
S 1.5m (5ft)

Aspect
Best in sheltered, dappled shade

Temperature needs
Hardy to -15°C (5°F)

Suitable pot size
30–45cm (12–18in)

Suitable container material
Terracotta, stone, Oriental-style pot, plastic

Compost type
50/50 mix of soil-based compost, eg, John Innes No. 3, and ericaceous compost

Many trees are too vigorous or grow too large for pots, but most Japanese maples are either slow-growing or naturally compact and make beautiful container specimens. Japanese maples or acers comprise a large group of plants, but most coveted are forms of *Acer palmatum* which create low hummocks or rounded domes of arched branches clothed in elegant lobed foliage. While maples are undoubtedly prized for their blazing autumn tints, plants provide interest all year round. Stripped of foliage, they create architectural shapes in the winter garden and some also feature colourful stems. Spring foliage is often bright and changes colour as the leaves mature in summer.

Maples can be used as focal points, specimens on a lawn, or as features next to a pond. Their Asian origins make them perfect companions for bamboos, Oriental grasses, pebbles, and Japanese ornaments in a Zen-inspired patio or garden display.

PREVENTING SCORCHING

Although Japanese maples are quite hardy, their foliage is vulnerable to frost, wind, and strong sun, any of which can cause it to scorch, shrivel, desiccate at the edges and fall prematurely. To prevent problems, do not place pots in frost pockets, wind tunnels, or open, south-facing positions. Their ideal home is in a sheltered spot in dappled shade.

Centre: **Maples with red summer foliage** *add drama to a patio setting, and combine well with foliage plants and colourful seasonal flowers.*

> **TOP TIP: KEEPING MAPLES HEALTHY**
>
> Japanese maples require very little pruning. In spring, remove the top layer of compost and replace it with fresh compost mixed with slow-release fertilizer granules. Add a mulch to the surface to retain moisture. Keep well watered, and in winter cover the pot with bubble plastic.

Maple options

Acer palmatum var. *dissectum* **'Filigree'** *has feathery green foliage that changes to yellow in autumn.*

Acer palmatum **'Chitose-yama'** *has deeply lobed green leaves that start turning deep red in late summer.*

Acer palmatum **'Sango-kaku'** *has bright pink shoots and pink autumn leaves that then turn yellow.*

Acer palmatum var. *dissectum* **'Garnet'** *has finely divided, dark red leaves that turn scarlet in autumn.*

Acer palmatum **'Bloodgood'**, *a bushy tree with dark purple leaves, turns a dramatic shade of scarlet in autumn.*

Acer palmatum **'Linearilobum'** *has deeply cut leaves that turn from bronze to orange, then yellow before falling.*

Acer palmatum **'Nicholsonii'** *has olive green, lobed leaves that brighten up autumn pots with shades of orange.*

Acer palmatum **'Katsura'** *has red-edged, orange new leaves that fade to green, then turn yellow, red, and orange.*

DRAMA QUEENS

Big and bold bog plants

Not for the faint hearted, these moisture-loving perennials are guaranteed to create impact, with giant jungly leaves that would look at home on the set of a dinosaur movie. Despite their potential to grow into large beasts, these monsters can be tamed in containers if you are prepared to water them regularly during the growing season and never let them dry out.

Massive sculptural leaves *create an arresting focal point in a contemporary design with other foliage plants.*

DRAMA QUEENS

Gunnera

Plant used
Gunnera manicata

Height and spread
H 1.5m (5ft)
S 1.8m (6ft)

Aspect
Partial shade

Temperature needs
Hardy to -15°C (5°F), but vulnerable during prolonged cold periods

Suitable pot size
45cm (18in) or wider

Suitable container material
Plastic and other non-porous materials

Compost type
Soil-based compost with added leafmould

Prized for its huge leaves that can reach 2m (6ft) in diameter, *Gunnera* makes large clumps when grown in moist soil by a pond, but its ambitions are severely curtailed when confined to a pot. Happy in a shady spot, it can be used as a focal point, or a backdrop to other containerized, shade-loving foliage plants on a patio or terrace. In early summer, a long, cone-like spike of tiny red flowers rises from the centre of the clump, adding to the dramatic effect. The smaller species, *G. tinctoria,* is a great choice for a more confined spot. Feed *Gunnera* plants with a slow-release granular fertilizer in spring and apply a liquid feed every month in summer. Never allow the compost to dry out.

PRUNING PLANTS
An overly wide *Gunnera* will soon outgrow its welcome in a small garden, while top-heavy plants can cause their pots to topple over. Remove wayward leaves to keep plants in check, and don't be afraid to prune hard, as this treatment will not affect the plant's health.

TOP TIP: OVERWINTERING PLANTS
Gunnera is fully hardy, but the crown of the plant (where the stems meet the root system at ground level) is vulnerable to damage when temperatures are below freezing for prolonged periods. When frost cuts down the top growth, remove and place the leaves over the crown to provide some insulation. Alternatively, cover the top of the pot with a layer of straw pinned down with wire pegs. Remove these layers in spring when the worst frosts are over.

Rodgersia

Plants used
Rodgersia pinnata
'Superba'

Height and spread
H 1.2m (4ft)
S 75cm (30in)

Aspect
Partial shade

Temperature needs
Hardy to -15°C (5°F)

Suitable pot size
30–45cm (12–18in)

Suitable container material
Plastic, and other non-porous materials

Compost type
Soil-based compost with added leafmould

The *Rodgersia*'s tall plumes of white or pink flowers are beautiful in summer, but even before they appear, the plant's architectural shape and handsome palmate leaves make it an impressive feature. Up to 90cm (36in) long, the leaves are flushed bronze when young and then darken to a deep green. They are also heavily textured and beg to be touched. Plants add a stately form to container arrangements of ferns, lilies, and hostas, which enjoy similar cool, shady conditions and regular watering.

CONTROLLING PESTS
Although this plant is rarely troubled by pests, it is vulnerable to slug and snail damage when new leaves appear in spring. Protect plants with copper rings, organic pellets, or take other measures to prevent the plant being harmed at this critical stage.

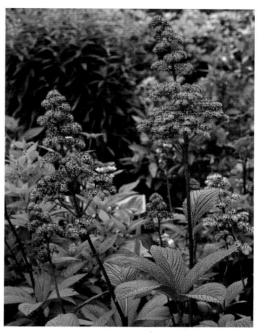

Tall spikes of pink frothy flowers appear in summer.

Astilboides

Plants used
Astilboides tabularis

Height and spread
H 1.2m (4ft)
S 90cm (36in)

Aspect
Partial shade

Temperature needs
Hardy to -15°C (5°F)

Suitable pot size
30–45cm (12–18in)

Suitable container material
Plastic, and other non-porous materials

Compost type
Soil-based compost with added leafmould

Leaves the size of a small table top create drama.

If you're looking for a more unusual foliage plant, try this shade-lover; its huge round leaves with scalloped edges sometimes reach 90cm (36in) across and are perfectly supported on strong stems. Worth growing for its foliage alone, *Astilboides* has the added bonus of small white flowers which appear on arching stems in midsummer. A native of boggy areas, use it in containers close to water features, and mix with other moisture-lovers, such as feathery-plumed *Astilbe* and purple loosestrife, *Lythrum salicaria*.

WATERING NEEDS
Astilboides is very sensitive to drought and does not tolerate dry soil conditions, which will quickly cause a check on growth and brown leaves. To keep compost moist, line a pot with plastic and perforate it around the sides, about 3cm (1½in) from the base of the container. This will create a reservoir, while allowing excess moisture to drain out. Alternatively, install an automatic watering system.

Palms for the garden

If you need a quick and easy way to add an exotic touch to your garden, pot up a palm. Architectural and evergreen, their spiky fronds make great partners for a contemporary container in a minimalist scheme, or use them to dress up a display of vibrant blooms and luxuriant foliage to transform your patio into a tropical paradise.

Chusan palm *Trachycarpus fortunei*

Plant used
Trachycarpus fortunei

Height and spread
H 1.8m (6ft)
S 1m (3ft)

Aspect
Sun or dappled shade

Temperature needs
Hardy to -15°C (5°F)

Suitable pot size
45cm (18in)

Suitable container material
Plastic, stone, terracotta

Compost type
Soil-based compost, eg, John Innes No 2

You would expect such an exotic-looking plant to need careful cosseting, but the Chusan palm is remarkably easy to look after in cool climates, requiring virtually no maintenance apart from watering, feeding while it's actively growing, and the occasional trim with secateurs. Best of all, it's tough and can cope with temperatures down to -15°C (5°F).

Although it's a robust plant, the Chusan palm performs best when grown in a sheltered situation, as it needs protection from strong winds, which batter the leaves, giving them a ragged appearance. Choose a large, sturdy container filled with soil-based compost, such as John Innes No 2, and feed plants annually in spring with a slow-release granular fertilizer. Water your palms regularly in summer, but ensure the compost does not become waterlogged in winter by raising pots on "feet".

Use plants as focal points on a sunny or partially shaded patio or in a garden; they look particularly effective as part of an Islamic or tropical scheme.

KEEPING PLANTS NEAT

To maintain the appearance of your palms, remove the lower fronds as they start to turn brown and die, which is a natural ageing process and not usually a sign of disease or stress. Cut back the stems so that the stumps are as flat as possible to the trunk. Although not strictly necessary, you can also strip the hairy growth from the trunk if you want a clear stem. To do this, remove the hairy fibre at the base with your hands and then cut it off, together with any old leaf stumps. Continue like this up the rest of the trunk.

Spiky fans of glossy green leaves look impressive when silhouetted against a plain backdrop.

TOP TIP: OVERWINTERING PALMS

Although hardy, the Chusan palm benefits from extra care to get it through the winter. Its worst enemy is soggy compost, so move it to a sheltered spot close to a house wall where rain will not drench the soil, and do not water your palm when temperatures fall in winter. You may also need to protect the pot, especially if it is made from porous terracotta. Wrap it up in a sheet of bubble plastic or hessian and secure with string.

Dwarf fan palm *Chamaerops humilis*

Plant used
Chamaerops humilis

Height and spread
H & S 1.2m (4ft)

Aspect
Full sun

Temperature needs
Hardy to -9°C (16°F)

Suitable pot size
30–45cm (12–18in)

Suitable container material
Terracotta, plastic, stone

Compost type
Well-drained, soil-based compost, eg, John Innes No 2 with added grit

This very slow-growing palm with fans of stiff leaves may eventually grow to 1.2m (4ft), but it can take several decades to achieve this height, so buy a plant of the size you require. Fairly low growing, it makes a bushy specimen when young, eventually forming a distinct trunk as it matures and the lower leaves die back.

Although not as hardy as the Chusan palm, its robust, dense growth is better equipped to cope with wind, and it even thrives in pots in coastal areas. The palm's compact size also makes it easy to move indoors when extremely low temperatures are forecast.

WHEN TO WATER
Water your palm regularly in summer and while in active growth until it is well established, when you should allow the compost to dry out between waterings. In winter, do not water plants grown outside, and move containers to a sheltered spot protected from heavy rain.

Three palms in a row produce a contemporary effect.

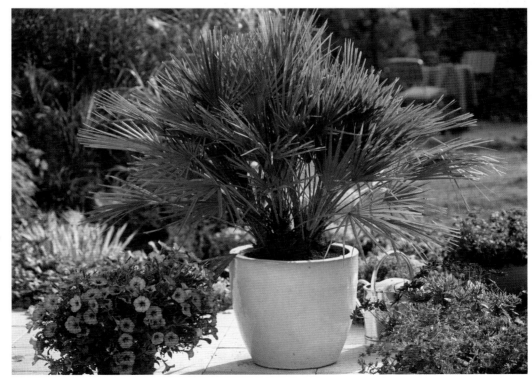

Positioned in pride of place on a patio, the dwarf fan palm makes an elegant feature in a clean, white ceramic pot.

Striking flowers

These indoor plants require a little more care and attention to detail than most, but you'll be amply rewarded for your efforts. Nurture them well, and they will produce breathtaking flowers that make stunning indoor features. Use them to add drama to a modern interior and choose colourful glazed containers to match, or provide a striking contrast to, the blooms.

DRAMA QUEENS

Bat flower *Tacca*

Plant used
Tacca chantrieri

Height and spread
H & S 1m (3ft)

Aspect
A bright spot, out of direct sunlight

Temperature needs
Min. 13°C (55°F)

Suitable pot size
20cm (8in)

Suitable container material
Plastic, metal, glazed terracotta

Compost type
Multi-purpose compost with added soil-based compost, eg, John Innes No 2

There are lots of unusual-looking flowers you can grow, but *Tacca chantrieri* is perhaps the most peculiar. A native of India and parts of south-east Asia, it's commonly known as the bat flower thanks to its nodding maroon blooms and thread-like "whiskers" that hang from large, wing-like bracts. The flowers are held on lofty stalks that rise above a cluster of lush, corrugated, green leaves. The bat flower likes a warm spot indoors, but can be placed outside in a sheltered position for several weeks over summer.

GROWING FROM SEED
Ready-grown plants are available from garden centres, but it's satisfying to raise your own from seed. Sow seeds 5mm (¼in) deep into small pots filled with seed compost, water them, and place in a heated propagator. After germination, which can take anything from one to nine months, move seedlings into 7.5cm (3in) pots when large enough to handle; you should have a flowering plant within three years.

TOP TIP: LONG-TERM CARE
To keep the bat flower looking good, ensure the compost never dries out and mist the leaves regularly to raise humidity in summer. It's a hungry plant, so feed monthly by spraying with a foliar liquid feed. When your plants fill their original containers, move them into larger pots, or divide plants in spring. The plants will enter a dormant period in the autumn, and should be kept dry and warm until spring, when you can resume watering.

The unique flowers of Tacca chantrieri *are held on tall stems and provide a dramatic focal point in a bright room.*

Temple bells *Smithiantha*

Plant used
Smithiantha 'Little One'

Height and spread
H 20cm (8in)
S 10cm (4in)

Aspect
Bright, but out of direct sunlight

Temperature needs
Min. 15°C (59°F)

Suitable pot size
15cm (6in)

Suitable container material
Plastic, ceramic, glazed terracotta

Compost type
Multi-purpose compost

A close inspection of the flowers of this Mexican perennial reveal why it is often called "temple bells" – the brightly coloured, pendulous blooms that drip from long stems in summer and autumn are perfectly bell-shaped. These delicate house plants prefer a bright position away from direct sunlight, and enjoy humid conditions. While they are growing, water the plants well, but allow the compost to dry out completely before watering again. Add a liquid feed with every watering, but don't overdo it – a quarter-strength dilution is ideal.

PLANT CHOICES

There are several named varieties of *Smithiantha* that are worth tracking down. 'Little One' is a dwarf form, and produces sprays of bright orange flowers and velvety purple leaves, while 'Extra Sassy' has pink flowers that rise above large red leaves. *Smithiantha cinnabarina* grows to about 60cm (24in) and has hairy red leaves and red flowers.

The dark velvety leaves of Smithiana plants need high humidity levels to thrive. Set pots in a tray of moist gravel to create the right conditions.

TOP TIP: OVERWINTERING

In winter, *Smithiantha* plants become completely dormant and the leaves and flowers die back. Remove the dead growth from the plant and allow the compost to completely dry out. Do not water the plants again until spring, at which time move them into a larger container of compost, and water lightly until the plant is back in full growth.

DRAMA QUEENS

Dramatic foliage

If you're searching for a house plant that blends into the background, look away now. These leafy lovelies are most definitely not shrinking violets; their bold, colourful foliage cries out for attention and will provide a talking point all year round. Try combining a few of them in a group for a dramatic display of foliage shapes and forms.

Rubber plant *Ficus elastica*

Plant used
Ficus elastica
'Tineke'

Height and spread
H 1.8m (6ft)
S 90cm (36in)

Aspect
Bright, but not in direct sunlight

Temperature needs
Min. 15°C (59°F)

Suitable pot size
30cm (12in)

Suitable container material
Plastic, ceramic, glazed terracotta, metal

Suitable compost
Soil-based compost, eg, John Innes No 2

When grown in a sleek, dark purple, contemporary container this well-known, easy-to-grow house plant is given a new lease of life and brought bang up to date – no longer a throwback to the interiors of the 1960s and 70s. Many attractive rubber plant cultivars are now available, in addition to the commonly found green form of *Ficus elastica*. 'Doescheri' produces large, elliptical leaves with grey patches and creamy edges, 'Tineke' has a similar camouflaged leaf pattern overlaid with pinkish-red, and 'Decora' bears dark green, broad leaves that are flushed bronze when young.

WATERING AND FEEDING

Water rubber plants all year round, but allow the compost to dry out between waterings. For plenty of healthy growth, apply a liquid feed that is high in nitrogen every month. If plants become too tall or leggy, keep them in check by pruning.

TOP TIP: CLEANING FOLIAGE

The smooth leaves of *Ficus elastica* attract dust like a magnet, so clean them regularly. This helps to keep the foliage healthy by allowing maximum light penetration, and improves its appearance. There are many commercially produced sprays and wipes, but these are not necessary unless you really want to add an artificial shine to the surface of the leaves. Simply wipe them with a soft damp cloth to remove dust, and add a little milk to make the leaves shine.

Variegated rubber plants, such as 'Tineke', thrive in good natural light with a monthly dose of liquid fertilizer.

Stromanthe *Stromanthe sanguinea*

Plant used
Stromanthe sanguinea 'Triostar'

Height and spread
H 50cm (20in)
S 45cm (18in)

Aspect
Bright, filtered light

Temperature needs
Min. of 15°C (59°F)

Suitable pot size
20cm (8in)

Suitable container material
Plastic, glazed terracotta, ceramic, metal

Compost type
Multi-purpose with added soil-based compost, eg, John Innes No 2

Vibrantly coloured 'Triostar' produces green, cream, and red variegated leaves, given a bright spot out of direct sunlight.

Perfect for adding a touch of the tropics, this exotic plant makes a clump of technicoloured leaves that can be used to brighten up a shady spot indoors. The long, lance-shaped, variegated leaves are smooth and glossy, and are splashed with green, pink, dark pink, burgundy, and white brush strokes. As an added bonus, the plant boasts clusters of tiny pink flowers in spring.

MAINTENANCE TIPS
Keep the compost moist at all times, as the leaves will start to curl if it's allowed to dry out. However, guard against overwatering as this may cause the stems to rot. In hot summers, mist the leaves to raise humidity levels and prevent them browning. Give plants a boost with a soluble fertilizer every four weeks in spring and summer. Congested plants can be divided before new growth starts in spring.

Pineapple plant *Ananas comosus*

Plant used
Ananas comosus var. *variegatus*

Height and spread
H 1m (3ft)
S 50cm (20in)

Aspect
Light spot in sun

Temperature needs
Min. 15°C (59°F).
Above 24°C (75°F) is best for flower formation

Suitable pot size
20cm (8in)

Suitable container material
Plastic, glazed terracotta, ceramic, metal

Compost type
Orchid compost

Closely related to the edible pineapple, this large, showy plant from South America makes a rosette of brightly coloured, variegated, arching leaves edged with spines. In summer the plant is topped by a flower followed by a small, bright red fruit that perches on a stout stem. The fruit can remain on the plant for around ten months. If you have the space for it, the pineapple plant makes a striking addition to a mixed display of bromeliads.

CARING FOR PINEAPPLES
This plant likes a sunny position, ideally in a conservatory, and needs high humidity to do well. Mist leaves regularly with a hand spray and keep the "well" at the centre of the rosette topped up with water. However, the compost should not be too wet – a free-draining orchid compost should help to provide the right conditions. Pineapples also require heat to flower, and when buds appear, feed every couple of weeks with a liquid plant food.

The pineapple plant grows all year round, and can reach a spectacular size in the right conditions.

DRAMA QUEENS

Easy-going drought busters
Echeveria and *Aeonium*

Some plants need lots of care, but *Aeonium* and *Echeveria* are easy going and trouble free. Native to dry, sunny climes, they are drought tolerant, slow growing and require virtually no pruning, making them perfect for those short of time. Their sculpted leaves and unusual flowers also make decorative displays.

Plants used
Mixed *Aeonium* and *Echeveria*

Height and spread
H 4cm–2m (1½in–6ft)
S 13cm–2m (5in–6ft)

Aspect
Aeonium: partial shade to full sun; variegated forms need good light for best colour
Echeveria: full sun

Temperature needs
Aeonium: 10°C (50°F)
Echeveria: 7°C (45°F)

Suitable pot size
7.5–22cm (3–9in)

Suitable container material
Terracotta, glazed ceramic, plastic

Compost type
Soil-based compost, eg, John Innes No 2, with added grit

In the past *Echeveria* and *Aeonium* would have been seen gathering dust on window ledges indoors, but these attractive tender plants are perfect for garden displays from late spring to the first frosts in autumn, after which they'll need some protection to survive the cold months ahead.

These decorative succulents encompass a great range of sizes and habits. Some make large multi-branched shrubs grown for their purple, bronze, green, blue, or variegated rosettes; others produce cascading stems, or form a single flat rosette. A number have leafy rosettes as large as dinner plates, while diminutive types are the size of a thumbnail. Despite their diversity, all thrive in gritty, soil-based compost and look particularly effective in terracotta or glazed containers. Water plants every two weeks in summer and shelter them from long wet periods. Top-heavy plants or those that produce a single main stem may need staking to prevent them toppling over.

GROUPING PLANTS
Although solitary specimens can look good, you can create a more striking display by grouping them together. Combine different colours, shapes, and sizes, placing larger succulents in the centre and low-growing ones towards the outside of the group to achieve a 3D effect. Top-dress pots with gravel or an ornamental mulch to complete the effect.

*Centre: **Create a striking display** by grouping succulents en masse on a simple wooden table on a sunny patio.*

TOP TIP: WINTER CARE

Protect these succulents from frost damage by placing them on a light windowsill indoors or by draping a sheet or two of horticultural fleece over the containers and storing them in a heated greenhouse over winter. Apply a small quantity of water when the compost dries out completely, and remove any dead or diseased leaves as soon as you see them. Control mealybug where necessary (*see p.243*).

Echeveria and *Aeonium* options

Echeveria agavoides *is a clump-forming succulent with tight rosettes of narrow, tapering leaves with red tips.*

Echeveria gibbiflora var. metallica *produces short spikes of red flowers in summer above huge purple rosettes.*

Echeveria secunda var. glauca *is a clumping-forming plant with small rosettes and red and yellow flowers.*

Aeonium haworthii 'Variegatum' *has bright, light new leaves, with yellow and green variegation, edged with red.*

Aeonium 'Zwartkop', *a multi-branching succulent, adds a dramatic note with its near-black rosettes.*

Aeonium arboreum *is a fast-growing shrub valued for its architectural shape and numerous pale green rosettes.*

Aeonium 'Ballerina' *forms a neat mound of rosettes, with narrow, greyish-green leaves with white edges.*

Aeonium haworthii *forms masses of small glaucous-blue rosettes that cover the wiry branches of this compact shrub.*

Textured sun-lovers

Whether armed with spines, edged with teeth or clothed in masses of small rounded leaves, these succulents offer exciting texture and form, which can be heightened further with contrasting smooth or simple containers. Traditionally these plants have been displayed indoors, but all can be grown outdoors in summer on a sunny sheltered patio, balcony, or terrace.

Agave

Plant used
Agave americana 'Mediopicta Alba'

Height and spread
H & S up to 1.5m (5ft)

Aspect
Full sun. Light position indoors

Temperature needs
Min. 5°C (41°F)

Suitable pot size
20–60cm (8–24in), depending on size of plant

Suitable container material
Terracotta, stone, plastic, metal, ceramic

Compost type
Well-drained, soil-based compost, eg, John Innes No 2

Prized for their architectural rosettes, *Agave* are low-maintenance plants that complement contemporary containers and modern designs. Best displayed individually, select a contrasting pot, such as a cool, white ceramic container with a white-striped form like 'Mediopicta Alba'.

Agave make excellent house plants, but site them carefully to prevent clothes catching on the tooth-edged leaves. Allow the compost to dry out between waterings, and keep plants even drier in winter. Vigorous species will need moving into larger pots every few years, or remove young offsets to keep them in check.

AGAVE OPTIONS

There are many *Agave* varieties to choose from. *Agave parryi* var. *truncata* has neat blue rosettes with wide leaves, while *A. stricta* is a dangerous-looking plant that forms a sphere of slender spiky leaves. *A. schidigera* is compact, and produces upright leaves edged with wispy white filaments, while *A. victoriae-reginae* is small and tender, with stiff, white-edged, green leaves.

TOP TIP: GROWING AGAVES OUTSIDE

Agave are ideal for growing in a sunny spot outdoors over the summer months, but most need to be moved to a light, frost-free place indoors for the winter. Large specimens of *Agave americana* that are too large to bring indoors will survive winters outside if you live in a mild area or have a sheltered garden. To increase survival rates, bring plants up close to the house, cover with fleece and tip the containers on their sides to keep the compost dry.

Agave americana 'Mediopicta Alba' *produces rosettes of striking white-and-green-striped leaves.*

Donkey's tail *Sedum morganianum*

Plant used
Sedum morganianum

Height and spread
H 30cm (12in)
S 60cm (24in)

Aspect
Light position

Temperature needs
Min. 5–7°C (41–45°F)

Suitable pot size
10–15cm (4–6in)

Suitable container material
Terracotta, plastic, ceramic

Compost type
Well drained, soil-based compost, eg, John Innes No 2

With its pendulous stems heavily weighed down by cylindrical grey-green leaves, this sedum is a curious sight. In spring and summer, small pink flowers may appear at the end of stems. Other than watering and repotting from time to time, donkey's tail needs very little attention, but take care not to break off the delicate leaves. Allow the compost to almost dry out before watering, and water even less in winter.

PLANTING IDEAS

While the plant is young it can be grown in a small, decorative pot, but once the stems have reached their full extent, it needs to be raised off the ground to prevent the leaves being damaged. It's ideally suited to a hanging basket or wall-mounted pot, or set a container on a bookcase or shelf where you can appreciate its cascading stems of bead-like leaves.

The leaves of Donkey's tail resemble strings of beads.

Aloe

Plant used
Aloe ferox

Height and spread
H & S up to 1m (3ft) in a pot

Aspect
A light position indoors, full sun in the garden

Temperature needs
Min. 10°C (50°F)

Suitable pot size
10–60cm (4–24in), depending on size of plant

Suitable container material
Terracotta, stone, plastic, metal, ceramic

Compost type
Gritty, soil-based compost, eg, John Innes No 2

Everyone has heard of *Aloe vera*, a plant famed for the healing properties of its sap, but there are many others worth growing too. Most come from Africa, and encompass a huge and varied range of plants, including dwarf, smooth-leaved varieties suitable for a south-facing windowsill indoors, and large plants, such as the heavily armoured *Aloe ferox*. Many can be placed in a sunny position outdoors in summer, as long as they are moved back inside before the frosts return. Keep the compost just moist in summer, and take care not to water the leafy rosettes. In winter, keep the compost almost dry.

ALOE SELECTIONS

Indoors, grow smooth-leaved *A. vera* or the partridge-breasted aloe, *A. variegata*, which boasts rosettes of green leaves decorated with white bands. *A. ferox* is an architectural plant with steely-blue leaves edged with red teeth, while *A. arborescens* 'Variegata' is a large plant with sword-shaped, yellow-striped leaves.

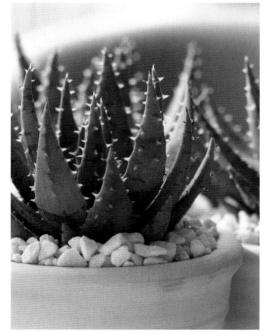

Aloe ferox's spiny foliage has architectural appeal.

DESERT DWELLERS

Prickly partners

A well-lit spot in a warm house is the perfect place for a low-maintenance display of prickly plants. Fascinating, architectural, and virtually indestructible, they look stylish in modern ceramic containers, and you can choose from a wide range of species to create a decorative group of colours and textures.

DESERT DWELLERS

Plant used
Euphorbia trigona;
Crassula;
Aeonium;
Pachypodium;
Opuntia

Height and spread
Euphorbia trigona:
H 1.5m (5ft) S 75cm
(30in); *Crassula:* H &
S 1m (3ft); *Aeonium:*
H & S 60cm (24in);
Pachypodium:
H 1.5m (5ft) S 45cm
(18in); *Opuntia:*
H & S 1m (3ft)

Aspect
Sunny, warm
position

Temperature needs
Min. 15°C (59°F)

Suitable pot size
Large cactus or
succulents 30–45cm
(12–18in)

**Suitable container
material**
Stone, ceramic,
plastic

Compost type
Well-drained,
soil-based compost,
eg, John Innes No 1,
with added grit

*Centre: **Ideal for
a centrally heated
home**, this group of
cacti and succulents
thrives in a warm,
sunny environment.*

If you're looking to add sculptural interest to a modern interior, forget about ornaments and snap up some architectural plants. Great choices include *Euphorbia trigona*, a statuesque, South African succulent whose tall, green, columnar stems have attractive black spines and small leaves. Add to this an *Opuntia,* with its classic cactus shape and spines, the dramatic tree-like *Pachypodium,* armed with a vicious-looking stem, and a bushy *Crassula* to provide a visual contrast.

When putting a display like this together, choose plants of different heights and shapes, with compact and clump-forming types set against tall and slender specimens. Include enough plants to make an impact, but ensure that the room does not feel cluttered. Also, give your cacti and succulents plenty of space so that each is displayed to full advantage, and place them where they won't be in your way or catch your clothes when you walk past. Remember, too, that they like a bright, airy position, so avoid pushing them back into dark corners.

WATERING NEEDS

They may hail from some of the most parched landscapes in the world, but this does not mean that you can completely ignore cacti. In summer, allow the compost to completely dry out between waterings, and for the rest of the year, water less frequently, but enough to prevent plants from withering. Succulents need just a little more water (*see plants on pp. 80–81*).

TOP TIP: PAIN-FREE PLANTING

The tiny hair-like spines on cacti can be very painful if you get them on your hands, so wear a pair of tough leather gloves when planting. In addition, handle plants by wrapping them in folded strips of newspaper or thin card, but don't squeeze too tightly or you will damage the delicate spines.

Choosing cacti

Notocactus magnificus *(syn.* Parodia magnifica*) is a compact, glaucous-blue, spherical cactus with golden yellow spines on pronounced ridges. It readily produces offsets to form large clumps and suits a large shallow bowl.*

Mammillaria zeilmanniana *is a clump-forming cactus armed with a combination of small spines and those that look like fishing hooks. Its barbed good looks are softened in summer by a profusion of bright pink flowers.*

Echinocereus *encompasses a large group of column-forming or cylindrical cacti, renowned for the rich colours of their bright, showy flowers which appear in spring and summer. Most are low-growing and suit small spaces.*

Opuntia microdasys *var.* albispina *is related to the large, imposing prickly pear, but this dwarf* Opuntia *is perfect for small pots in the home. It has oval-shaped, dark green pads studded with groups of white spines.*

Rebutia krainziana *produces dark green stems that resemble flattened spheres, and provide a great backdrop to tiny silver spines that are arranged in a spiral pattern on the surface. Scarlet flowers appear in summer.*

Schlumbergera truncata, *commonly known as the Christmas cactus, is perfect for a tall pot or a hanging basket, where the long, bright green stems terminating in pink flowers can rain down in autumn and winter.*

Flowering succulents

Most succulents are grown for their architectural foliage, but there's a group that sports equally eye-catching flowers. Easy to grow, these drought-loving plants thrive in sunny areas, and produce richly coloured blooms over many weeks. The flowers of *Graptopetalum bellum* look like tiny shooting stars while *Kalanchoe* comes in many different forms.

Graptopetalum

Plant used
Graptopetalum bellum

Height and spread
H 23cm (9in)
S 15cm (6in)

Aspect
Sunny windowsill

Temperature needs
Min. 5–10°C
(41–50°F)

Suitable pot size
10–20cm (4–8in)

Suitable container material
Terracotta, ceramic

Compost type
Well-drained, soil-based compost, eg, John Innes No 1, with added grit

At first glance, the flat rosette of leaves formed by this succulent are attractive, yet fairly unremarkable, but the plant undergoes a transformation when short spikes of flowers rise up in summer. The star-shaped blooms are shocking pink, instantly bringing to mind the colour of a 1950s Cadillac. Native to Mexico, this plant gives its best performance in a bright, sunny spot indoors.

Graptopetalum is drought tolerant and you should allow the compost to dry out between waterings in summer and water sparingly in winter, giving plants just enough moisture to prevent them drying out. Overwatering can result in root rot, so check that the plant is not standing in a pot of water. Plants spread easily and over time form a cluster of white-edged rosettes. When the original pot has been filled, either move the plant into a larger container or divide the rosettes up and replant them in small pots.

PLANTING PARTNERS

Graptopetalum makes a decorative feature on its own, but can look a little underwhelming when not in flower. To maintain interest, group a few plants together or combine *Graptopetalum* in a bowl with other succulents that require similar growing conditions. Team it up with *Crassula*, *Echeveria* or a small *Aloe*. Alternatively, combine it with trailing *Graptopetalum paraguayense*, alongside the reddish rosettes of *Graptopetalum rusbyi*. Add a decorative mulch to the surface of the compost (*see p.239*).

Graptopetalum bellum *flowers more profusely when grown in bright, sunny conditions. Feed plants monthly with a half-diluted cactus fertilizer to keep it thriving.*

Kalanchoe

Plant used
Kalanchoe pumila

Height and spread
H & S 45cm (18in)

Aspect
Bright, sunny spot

Temperature needs
Min. 10°C (50°F)

Suitable pot size
15cm (6in)

Suitable container material
Terracotta, plastic, ceramic

Compost type
Well-drained, soil-based compost, eg, John Innes No 1, with added grit

The powdery-grey, scalloped leaves of *Kalanchoe pumila* provide an excellent foil for the pale pink flowers that appear on slender stems during spring and summer. Its spreading habit makes this succulent an ideal candidate for a hanging basket or wall-mounted container, and *Kalanchoe* will be happy outside on a warm, sunny sheltered patio or terrace in summer.

Kalanchoe is a large family of succulents, and includes a range of plant sizes and habits. Others to try include forms of *K. manginii,* which have large, bell-shaped, pendent blooms held on long stems, and varieties of *Kalanchoe blossfeldiana,* or Flaming Katy, the most popular and widely available species, with green leaves and upward-facing blooms.

CARING FOR KALANCHOE
Keep plants on the dry side and take care not to water the leaves. Allow the compost to dry out between waterings and water sparingly in winter. Selections of *Kalanchoe* will flower happily on a sunny windowsill, but they need encouragement to bloom again after their initial burst. When the flowers start to fade, cut off the stalks at the base and move the plant to a shady windowsill for four weeks. Don't water during this time, then bring the plant back to a sunny sill and water as normal. Feed plants fortnightly in spring and summer with a liquid fertilizer.

Delicate pink flowers and pale grey leaves suit a pastel-coloured, glazed container that won't overpower them.

CHOOSING VARIETIES OF KALANCHOE

Kalanchoe 'Tessa' *has dark green, fleshy foliage that provides a contrasting backdrop for masses of orangey-scarlet, tubular flowers held on pendulous stems in spring.*

Kalanchoe 'Wendy' *produces scalloped leaves and wiry stalks topped with dramatic flowerheads of up to 15 pink, bell-shaped blooms edged with yellow ruffles.*

Kalanchoe blossfeldiana 'Calandiva White Monroe' *has white flowers that resemble rosebuds. They open from greenish buds above large glossy leaves.*

Kalanchoe blossfeldiana Pink Form *is one of the most widely available varieties, with large heads of tiny, star-shaped, pink flowers that appear in spring.*

Moth orchids *Phalaenopsis*

This orchid's popularity is well deserved. Plants bear lots of elegant flowers on branched stems that last for months, and will often produce several flushes of blooms throughout the year. Best of all, they are not fussy about temperatures and will flourish in the average centrally heated sitting room.

EASY ORCHIDS

Plant used
Phalaenopsis hybrid

Height and spread
H & S 30cm (12in)

Aspect
Light, but not in direct sun

Temperature needs
20°C (68°F) or higher in daytime;
16°C (61°F) or higher at night

Flowering time
Any

Suitable pot size
15cm (6in)

Suitable container material
Plastic, placed inside a decorative pot

Compost type
Orchid compost

With exotic blooms in just about every colour imaginable, which remain on the plants for months and will often reward you with repeat flowering during the year, you'd expect there to be a catch, but there isn't one. *Phalaenopsis*, or moth orchids, will perform well in any room that is unheated in summer and kept warm by a central-heating system during winter.

Flowers usually appear on multi-branched stems that will need supporting with small stakes. Plants bloom at any time of year, and by selecting a few varieties you can enjoy a continuous floral display. Moth orchids are ideally placed on an east-facing windowsill or in another bright spot out of direct sunlight. To ensure they perform well, water regularly to keep the compost damp, but avoid overwatering to prevent roots rotting. They enjoy high humidity, so stand pots on a shallow pebble tray half filled with water, or mist leaves with a hand-held spray. Do this in the morning so the moisture can dry before evening. A layer of moss placed on top of the compost will help to retain moisture, as well as giving your arrangement an attractive finish.

ENCOURAGE REPEAT FLOWERING
After the flowers start to fade, cut the stalk back to the second leaf joint from the bottom. A further stalk should form from this point and carry more buds to give you another show of flowers. Use a liquid orchid fertilizer when you water your plants (following the instructions) to encourage flower production.

Centre: **Phalaenopsis** *hybrids* *are widely available at reasonable prices. Group several plants together to create an elegant arrangement.*

TOP TIP: TRY PHALAENOPSIS HYBRIDS

If you can grow *Phalaenopsis* you can't fail with *Doritaenopsis* orchids, a cross between *Phalaenopsis* and *Doritis*. There is a huge range of colourful hybrids, such as the striking *Doritaenopsis* Taida Sweet Berry (left), and they're grown in exactly the same way as *Phalaenopsis*.

Moth orchid varieties

P. cornu-cervi *is a beautiful species that will fill a room with scent from its speckled, star-shaped flowers.*

P. *Brother Little Amaglad* *is a compact moth orchid with subtle, pale pink flowers with a pale orange lip.*

P. violacea *is a compact, fragrant beauty with star-shaped flowers, vividly marked purple, in spring and summer.*

P. *I-Hsin Black Tulip* *is a very desirable orchid thanks to its beetroot-red flowers that are edged with white.*

P. stuartiana *produces white flowers, with a lower lip that is attractively speckled red, on tall stems in winter.*

P. *Doris* *is grown for its large pink flowers that appear throughout the year on 30cm (12in) stalks.*

P. *Brother Pico Sweetheart 'K&P'* *is a diminutive orchid topped with masses of pale pink, red-lipped flowers.*

P. *Lundy* *is a compact orchid, growing to 15cm (6in), with spectacular greenish-yellow flowers with red veining.*

Intricate blooms

An orchid covered with flowers is an impressive sight, but get up close and personal with these plants and you'll see the beauty of their individual blooms, which are elaborately patterned or flushed with other shades, producing a breathtaking display. *Dendrobium* likes cool temperatures, while different *Oncidium* suit a range of conditions.

Oncidium

Plant used
Oncidium
Sharry Baby

Height and spread
H 60cm (24in)
S 30cm (12in)

Aspect
Light, but not
in direct sun

Temperature needs
18-24°C (64-75°F) in
the day and 13-16°C
(55-61°F) at night

Flowering time
Several times during
the year

Suitable pot size
15cm (6in)

**Suitable container
material**
Plastic, placed inside
a decorative
container

Compost type
Orchid compost

Although famed for their dazzling yellow flowers, *Oncidium* is a large and varied tribe, with flowers in white, cream, pink, and red. In addition, some are short and compact, while others produce a robust fan of leaves and flower stalks over 1m (3ft) long that have to be staked. Most bloom in autumn, but there are plants that will bloom in spring, summer, and winter. Some species need a fair bit of attention, but hybrids, such as Sweet Sugar and the chocolate-scented Sharry Baby, are perfect for beginners. Place in a light position, out of direct sunlight.

TEMPERATURE CONTROL

Depending on the variety, *Oncidium* needs either cool, intermediate, or warm conditions, so check that you can provide the right environment before buying. Cool-loving plants need a temperature of 16°C (61°F) during the day and a minimum of 10°C (50°F) at night, while intermediates thrive in 18-24°C (64-75°F) during the day and 13-16°C (55-61°F) at night. Warm-loving plants need at least 21°C (70°F) during the day and 16°C (61°F) at night.

TOP TIP: ENCOURAGING FLOWERING

Oncidium are generally floriferous, but some people find that plants bought in flower are difficult to coax into bloom again. To ensure they thrive, make sure the temperature regime is correct and that the plants are getting enough light. Water regularly, but less so in winter, and use a liquid orchid feed (following the instructions on the pack) with every other watering to encourage flower production.

Oncidium *Sharry Baby's* *spikes of dark red, pink, and white flowers are long-lasting and beautifully scented.*

Dendrobium 🏠

Plant used
Dendrobium
Momozono 'Princess'

Height and spread
H 60cm (24in)
S 30cm (12in)

Aspect
Bright, but not in
direct sun

Temperature needs
Cool conditions, with
a minimum of
10°C (50°F)

Flowering time
Spring

Suitable pot size
15cm (6in)

**Suitable container
material**
Plastic, placed inside
a decorative
container

Compost type
Orchid compost

Thousands of these show-stopping divas are available, with plants varying in size, from those that grow to ankle height to lofty specimens that soar well above 1m (3ft). These orchids are recognisable by the cluster of slender, cane-like structures (pseudobulbs) that either produce flowers and leaves down their length, or hold clusters of blooms on top. Most *Dendrobium* plants like cool conditions, with a daytime temperature of about 16°C (61°F) and a minimum night-time temperature of 10°C (50°F). However, there are some that need warmer temperatures to thrive.

MAINTAINING PLANTS

Dendrobium plants prefer a light position with shade from direct sunlight; an east-facing windowsill is ideal. Water plants regularly from spring to autumn, but less so in winter. It's important not to overwater or roots can rot. Like most orchids, they are fairly hungry and need a liquid feed with every third watering. To raise the humidity around them, either grow several plants on a pebble tray filled with water, making sure the level is below the top of the pebbles, or mist in the morning with a hand spray, leaving plenty of time for the moisture to dry out before evening.

D. Momozono 'Princess' bears heads of eye-catching pink, yellow, and white flowers.

CHOOSING DENDROBIUMS

D. nobile *produces large, pale pink flowers with darker pink marks and a yellow throat. These sit on top of 45cm (18in), cylindrical stems and appear in spring.*

D. Sonia *is an exotic beauty, the flowers of which are often used to make floral garlands in Hawaii; they are an intense pink with contrasting cream-coloured markings.*

D. Sweet Dawn *fills a room with natural floral fragrance. The star-shaped white flowers with a yellow centre are generally produced from autumn to spring.*

D. fimbriatum *produces pretty fringed flowers the colour of orangeade, with a dark brown centre, and appear in spring. This orchid likes cool conditions.*

Cool cymbidiums

These showy orchids are among the easiest to grow, as they thrive at normal indoor temperatures and will flower for months in winter when little else is in bloom. Flowers come in many striking shades and are held in large sprays on slender spikes, while some are fragrant. They also require very little care and attention.

Plant used
Cymbidium Lisa Rose

Height and spread
H 60cm (24in)
S 90cm (36in)

Aspect
Partial shade in summer; bright light in winter

Temperature needs
Varies and depends on variety – most will die below about 7°C (45°F), and will not thrive above 25°C (77°F).

Suitable pot size
15cm (6in)

Suitable container material
Plastic, placed inside a decorative pot

Compost type
Orchid compost

Valued for their large sprays of colourful flowers, *Cymbidium* bloom for up to ten weeks, usually during winter and spring. New breeding has led to thousands of vibrant varieties, with flowers in shades of white, yellow, red, pink, and green, many of which are attractively speckled. Some have whopping flower stalks 1m (3ft) high, but there are plenty of compact varieties for small spaces that grow to no more than 30cm (12in).

Although they are easy to care for, the compost must be kept moist during the growing season – but never overwater, as this can cause rotting. In winter, reduce watering to keep plants on the dry side. For the best floral display, add a few drops of specialist liquid orchid feed to every other watering. Support flower spikes with a cane to prevent flopping, and cut back stems almost to the base when the blooms have faded.

TEMPERATURE REQUIREMENTS

In summer, a temperature of 16–25°C (61–77°F) is perfect for a *Cymbidium*. You can set them in a bright position in a cool room, out of direct sunlight, or place them outside, as long as they are in a sheltered spot protected from the sun. Remember to bring them back indoors well before frosts threaten in autumn.
In winter, lower the temperature to 10–14°C (50–57°F); a place in a cool greenhouse, conservatory, or on bright windowsill is ideal.

A huge variety of Cymbidium *are available in a vast range of colours, including this pink* Cymbidium Lisa Rose.

TOP TIP: REPOTTING ORCHIDS

Orchid roots will soon fill a container, and plants will need repotting every few years to prevent checked growth. *Cymbidium* flower best if a little pot-bound, so will not need repotting as frequently as other plants. Choose a pot that's just a few centimetres wider than the original. First, prepare the root ball: slide it out of the original container and remove any dead or shrivelled growth, and dead roots. Tap the root ball gently to dislodge loose compost. Put a handful of compost in the bottom of the new pot, place the plant on top, and then fill in around it with orchid compost, up to the original level.

Cymbidium selections

C. hookerianum *is a stunning species with delightfully scented, apple-green flowers that appear in winter.*

C. *Showgirl* *boasts pink-blushed, white flowers that are speckled red; they are produced throughout winter and spring.*

C. *Pontac 'Mont Millais'* *is a tall variety with dramatic, dark maroon-red flowers that appear in winter.*

C. *Portelet Bay* *produces large white flowers with broad petals and bright red centres in winter.*

C. *Golden Elf* *is a summer-flowering variety, with large bright yellow flowers that are sweetly scented. Plant it in a contrasting contemporary black container to create a stylish arrangement.*

Slipper orchids *Paphiopedilum*

At first glance you could be forgiven for thinking that these flowers look too perfect to be real. Intricately patterned, they come in a wide range of colours and shapes, all with an unusual slipper-like pouch. To enjoy these long-lasting blooms at home, just give them the growing conditions they need to thrive.

EASY ORCHIDS

Plant used
Paphiopedilum
hybrid

Height and spread
H & S 15–30cm
(6–12in)

Aspect
Bright, but not
direct sunlight

Temperature needs
Varies, depending
on variety

Suitable pot size
15cm (6in)

**Suitable container
material**
Plastic, placed inside
a decorative pot

Compost type
Orchid compost

Slipper orchids are extremely popular thanks to their showy, colourful flowers and their foliage, which is sometimes attractively spotted. Although not the easiest orchid to grow, it's certainly not the most challenging and will thrive with a little care and attention. There are many different varieties of slipper orchid worth growing, ranging in height from 15–30cm (6–12in) when in flower. The blooms are either borne singly or in clusters and are highly distinctive, comprising an upper sepal, two swept-back petals, and a pouch at the front that gives this orchid its common name.

Water plants regularly, allowing the compost to almost dry out between waterings, but don't overwater. They like humidity, so either group plants together and stand them on a gravel tray filled with water, or wipe down leaves with a soft damp cloth.

LIGHT AND HEAT REQUIREMENTS

Slipper orchids like a light position out of direct sun, such as an east-facing window. They fall into three groups, each relating to temperature requirements, so check that you can give the plant what it needs before you buy. Those that like cool conditions need a temperature of 16°C (61°F) during the day and a minimum temperature of 10°C (50°F) at night; intermediates prefer a daytime temperature of 18–24°C (64–75°F) and 13–16°C (55–61°F) at night; and warm-loving plants require a daytime temperature of at least 21°C (70°F), and 16°C (61°F) at night.

*Centre: **Feed your slipper orchids** fortnightly with half-strength orchid fertilizer, and reduce to monthly in autumn and winter.*

TOP TIP: DIVIDING SLIPPER ORCHIDS

After several years the roots of your *Paphiopedilum* will have filled its container, and it will need to be repotted into a larger pot with fresh orchid compost. Alternatively, you can divide your plant in spring, when it's not in flower, to produce two plants. Remove the orchid carefully from its pot. Loosen the congested root ball and look for a natural break between the leaves of the plant. Then gently ease the root ball apart to produce two plants. Remove any dead roots and repot one section into the original pot with fresh compost and the other into a new container.

Choosing slipper orchids

P. *Clair de Lune* is a highly prized hybrid, with a single lime-green and white flower on each stem.

P. **callosum** is extremely easy to grow and boasts a tall flower spike emerging between heavily mottled leaves.

P. **fairrieanum** bears a single purple-veined flower that rises above a clump of strap-shaped leaves in autumn.

P. **insigne** is a compact orchid with pale green leaves and single flowers that appear from autumn to spring.

P. **venustum** produces very exotic-looking flowers on slender stems from winter to spring.

P. **villosum** is a compact orchid, bearing stems of 15cm (6in) reddish flowers with light-green pouches.

P. **Pinocchio** is a small orchid whose flower spike holds several yellow-green blooms with pinky-yellow pouches.

P. *Maudiae 'Coloratum'* produces 30cm (12in) stems, bearing single dark red flowers that are attractively striped.

EASY ORCHIDS

Frost-proof fuchsias

Blooming continuously from midsummer until well into autumn, hardy fuchsias are among the few flowering container plants that are happy in some shade. Choose from elegant single bells to fat, blowsy, frilly-skirted blooms, and team them with busy Lizzies and foliage plants. Their leaves will be cut down by frost, but plants should revive again in spring.

PLANTS FOR SHADE

Plants used
Fuchsia 'Genii';
Chlorophytum
comosum; purple
Heuchera;
plain-leaved ivy

Height and spread
Fuchsia: H 90cm
(36in) S 75cm (30in);
Chlorophytum
H 15cm (6in) S 30cm
(12in); Heuchera
H & S 50cm (20in);
ivy S 60cm (24in)

Aspect
Partial shade
or full sun

Temperature needs
Ivy and heuchera
are fully hardy.
Fuchsia 'Genii':
min. -5°C (23°F).
Chlorophytum:
min. 7°C (45°F).

Suitable pot size
30cm (12in)

Suitable container material
Stone, terracotta,
metal

Compost type
Soil-based compost,
eg, John Innes No 2

Tall and elegant, or compact and floriferous, there are many hardy fuchsias to choose from. *Fuchsia* 'Genii' has the added bonus of golden-yellow spring foliage that turns bright green as it matures. Use its decorative leaves and flower-laden stems to form a colourful centrepiece in a container arrangement, matched with metallic purple-leaved heucheras, variegated spider plants, and trailing ivy.

Although hardy fuchsias are much tougher than bedding varieties, most lose their top growth after a sharp frost, but they are easily rejuvenated by pruning back to undamaged growth in the spring – you will see green shoots appearing along the lower stems as temperatures rise. Remove any weak, damaged, or diseased stems at the same time. Also place pots of fuchsias close to house walls or in a sheltered site to protect plants from the worst of the winter weather.

HARDY FUCHSIA OPTIONS

Whatever your garden style, there's a fuchsia to match. For a dwarf type, try 'Tom Thumb', with its red and mauve flowers, or its cousin 'Lady Thumb' (*see opposite*), which is about the same size. If you want a slightly larger plant, look out for 'Alice Hoffman', which has semi-double pink and white flowers, or 'Mrs Popple' (*see opposite*). Dark purple and crimson 'Riccartonii' is a taller form, and makes a striking feature in a large mixed container, or keep it compact by pruning the stems back in spring.

TOP TIP: CREATING BUSHIER PLANTS

Hardy fuchsias respond well to pruning when young, which encourages bushy growth and more flowers. Using your fingers, pinch out the leading shoot at the top of the plant when it has developed three sets of leaves. This will result in a number of sideshoots developing. Pinch these back when they too have developed three sets of leaves. As the plant grows, remove wayward shoots to keep a bushy shape.

Forms of Fuchsia **magellanica** *are reliably hardy and produce red, pink, or white single flowers.*

Hardy fuchsia choices

Fuchsia magellanica *var.* molinae *is a large plant with delicate, single, pale pink flowers from midsummer.*

Fuchsia *'Lena'* *is a very hardy selection with double white and magenta flowers held on lax arching stems.*

Fuchsia *'Mrs Popple'* *is almost fully hardy. An upright bushy shrub, it has rich scarlet and purple single flowers.*

Fuchsia *'Lady Thumb'*, *a tiny form ideal for windowboxes or wall pots, has semi-double pink and white blooms.*

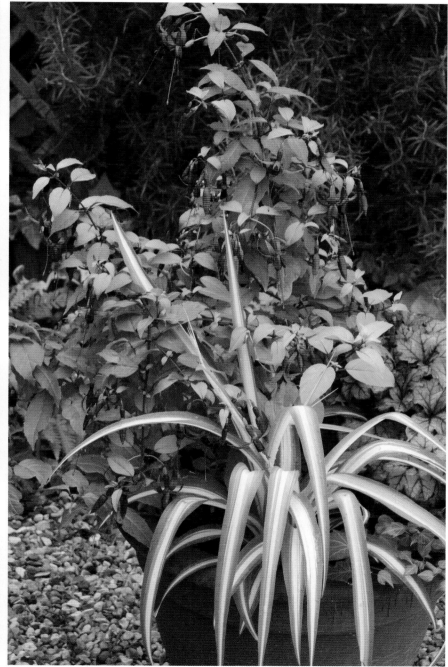

A colourful medley of flowers and foliage, this combination of Fuchsia 'Genii', dark-leaved heuchera, spider plant, and ivy will produce the best display when given a liquid fertilizer every month in summer.

Mini fernery

Don't let a dank spot in shade get you down. Make the most of it with a pot of tactile, leafy ferns guaranteed to transform the gloomiest of corners with year-round colour and texture. Choose a selection with different foliage forms and mix evergreens with deciduous types for a variety of winter shades.

Plants used
Asplenium scolopendrium Cristatum Group; *Athyrium niponicum* var. *pictum*; *Polystichum makinoi*

Height and spread
Asplenium scolopendrium Cristatum Group: H 60cm (24in) S 80cm (32in); *Athyrium niponicum* var. *pictum*: H & S 20cm (8in); *Polystichum makinoi*: H & S 60cm (24in)

Aspect
Sheltered, shady

Temperature needs
Hardy to -15°C (5°F)

Suitable pot size
30–45cm (12–18in)

Suitable container material
Terracotta, stone, glazed terracotta, metal

Compost type
Grow in a mix of 3 parts multi-purpose compost, 1 part soil-based compost, and 1 part sharp sand.

*Centre: **Group ferns together** in a shallow container to create a focal point in a shady corner of the garden.*

Most gardens have a difficult shady area where nothing seems to grow, but a container of mixed ferns will provide lush, verdant hues in these unpromising sites. Good choices include the hart's tongue fern, *Asplenium scolopendrium,* with its leathery, wavy-edged leaves, the feathery evergreen holly fern, *Polystichum makinoi,* and the Japanese painted fern, *Athyrium niponicum* var. *pictum,* whose fronds are blushed pinky red. Although these three ferns work well together in a container, there are many others you can use, but aim to achieve a combination of different leaf shapes, shades, and textures. Robust, vigorous, and tall-growing ferns, such as *Matteuccia struthiopteris,* or the shuttlecock fern, are best given a pot of their own.

When choosing containers for ferns, opt for something clean and simple; these plants are not garden divas and anything too fancy will draw attention away from their subtle good looks. Ferns are also not deep rooted and do well in shallow pots.

CREATING A MICROCLIMATE

Most ferns enjoy damp, shady conditions that mimic those on the forest floor where they grow in the wild. Avoid open, exposed positions, as the sun and wind will scorch their leaves. To ensure plants thrive, keep the compost damp at all times, summer and winter, and feed plants annually in spring with a slow-release granular fertilizer. Choose your ferns carefully to ensure they all prefer the same conditions; those here enjoy damp shade, but the male fern, *Dryopteris filix-mas,* suits dry shade.

TOP TIP: SPRING CARE

Most ferns are tough, fully hardy plants that more or less take care of themselves. However, the outer fronds of some evergreens may look a bit battered or tired after a long winter, so tidy them up by removing old leaves before new fronds unfurl in spring. Leave the dried bronze leaves of deciduous ferns to provide colour and contrast in winter, and then cut these off when you see new growth appearing at the base of the plant in spring. Also remove weeds and any debris lodged between the leaves.

Hardy fern options

Adiantum venustum, *the evergreen Himalayan maidenhair fern, has bronze-pink new growth in spring.*

Asplenium scolopendrium, *or hart's tongue fern, forms dense clumps of evergreen, leathery, upright fronds.*

Dryopteris affinis, *the golden male fern, is a semi-evergreen, waist-high plant with long feathery fronds.*

Dryopteris erythrosora *has knee-high stems of beautiful fine fronds. It is a deciduous plant and new growth is red.*

Matteuccia struthiopteris, *the stately shuttlecock fern, is a robust, tall, upright deciduous fern that suits a large pot.*

Polypodium vulgare 'Cornubiense' *is the common polypody fern. A compact plant, it bears glossy evergreen fronds.*

Polystichum setiferum *Divisilobum Group* *is a bushy evergreen with tall, tapering fronds with brown midribs.*

Polystichum polyblepharum, *known as the Japanese tassel fern, is a compact evergreen with yellow fronds in spring.*

Foliage collections

Hostas and heucheras thrive in containers and look stunning when combined with colourful flowers or grouped together on their own. There are hundreds of different forms of both plants in a wealth of colours, shapes, and sizes. Try a collection of hostas for a cool leafy display, or heucheras in a rainbow of colours for a bolder scheme.

Hostas

Plants used
Hosta 'Francee';
Hosta 'Krossa Regal';
Hosta fortunei var.
albopicta f. *aurea*;
Hosta 'August Moon'

Height and spread
H & S 20–75cm
(8–30in)

Aspect
Shade

Temperature needs
Fully hardy

Suitable pot size
20cm (8in)

Suitable container material
Any

Compost type
Soil-based compost, eg, John Innes No 3

Group together hostas for a rich mix of colours, shapes, and forms. Those here are H. *'Francee',* H. *'Krossa Regal',* H. fortunei var. albopicta f. aurea, *and* H. *'August Moon'.*

Hostas make elegant foliage groups for shady sites. To create the best show, choose varieties with different shapes and leaf colours, and make a tiered display with larger plants at the back and more compact types towards the front. Plants range in height from mound-forming miniatures a few centimetres tall, such as *H. fortunei* var. *albopicta* f. *aurea,* to those whose foliage reaches over 60cm (24in).

Water hostas regularly in spring and summer, and feed in early spring with a slow-release granular fertilizer. Plants spread slowly to form quite large clumps over time; either move them into larger pots or divide them up and replant healthy sections in pots of fresh compost.

TOP TIP: SLUG DETERRENT

Hostas are magnets for slugs and snails, but you can easily protect plants in pots by sticking a band of copper tape around the outside. Widely available from garden centres, the copper emits a tiny electrical charge that deters leaf-munching molluscs trying to cross it.

Heucheras

Plants used
Heuchera 'Can-can';
Juncus effusus f.
spiralis (corkscrew
rush); Teucrium
scorodonia 'Crispum'

Height and spread
Heuchera: H & S
50cm (20in);
Juncus: H 45cm
(18in) S 60cm (24in);
Teucrium: H 35cm
(14in) S 25cm (10in)

Aspect
Partial shade

Temperature needs
Fully hardy

Suitable pot size
30cm (12in)

**Suitable container
material**
Terracotta, plastic,
stone

Compost type
Multi-purpose with
added soil-based
compost, eg, John
Innes No 3

Heucheras, or coral plants, produce lively displays in partially shaded areas with their evergreen leaves and spires of tiny bell-shaped flowers in spring and summer. While they look great on their own or displayed as a collection, they also make good companions for other plants in a container scheme. For example, the metallic purple 'Can-can' contrasts beautifully with a backdrop of crinkle-leaved *Teucrium*, while the spiral leaves of a corkscrew rush echo the tall stems of the heuchera.

To maintain your displays, water heucheras regularly and ensure that the compost does not dry out over summer. Feed plants in early spring with a slow-release granular fertilizer. Pots can be left outside all year, but store them in a sheltered spot over winter to protect them from excessive rainfall. Heucheras will be happy in their pots for several years, but may eventually need to be divided or moved into a larger pot.

EVIL WEEVIL

Heucheras are largely trouble-free, but can be damaged by vine weevils; the adults eat notches around the leaves, while the grubs munch on the roots, causing plants to wilt and die. Protect plants by drenching containers with a biological control containing nematodes that eat vine-weevil larvae (*see also p.245*).

Blend Heuchera *'Can-can'* with the corkscrew rush, Juncus effusus f. spiralis, and Teucrium scorodonia *'Crispum' to produce a mound of colourful foliage and spires of flowers.*

PLANTS FOR SHADE

CHOOSING HEUCHERA VARIETIES

H. *Amber Waves* *makes a compact clump of scalloped-edged leaves that are golden yellow and pink. In spring they are topped with sprays of dainty cream flowers.*

H. *Plum Pudding* *has rich purple leaves that look good all year, but are particularly valuable in winter. The foliage makes a great foil for the pale pink summer blooms.*

H. *Silver Scrolls* *bears masses of pink summer flowers on red stems above a mound of heavily veined, burgundy, evergreen leaves overlaid with shades of metallic silver.*

H. brizoides *may not be as brightly coloured as other heucheras, but it makes a clump of rich green leaves that shows off its sprays of white flowers to perfection.*

Beautiful begonias

If you're looking for plants that provide exotic foliage and colour all year, nothing beats begonias. This decorative tribe of house plants are blessed with striped, streaked, swirled, or splashed foliage in the most amazing hues, and dainty blooms that are generally less flamboyant than their summer-bedding cousins.

PLANTS FOR SHADE

Plants used
Begonia rex hybrids;
Pilea depressa

Height and spread
Begonia rex: H 25cm
(10in) S 30cm (12in);
Pilea depressa:
S 20cm (8in)

Aspect
Bright position out
of direct sun

Temperature needs
Min. 10°C (50°F)

Suitable pot size
30cm (12in)

**Suitable container
material**
Metal, plastic

Compost type
Multi-purpose
compost

Modern breeding has resulted in a raft of striking new begonia cultivars, producing bright, cheery, exciting plants that deserve pride of place in a modern home. Until recently begonias suffered from an image problem and were widely thought of as old-fashioned and rather dreary. Most of the plants under attack were the dark-leaved varieties of *Begonia rex*, and although some of those melancholic varieties still exist, new hybrids look anything but antiquated, and suit contemporary galvanized containers, whose unfussy style helps to show off the foliage to its best advantage. Choose selections with large leaves emblazoned with silver and metallic purple markings that shimmer in the light, or in colours to suit your décor, and team them with trailing plants, such as the tiny-leaved *Pilea depressa*, to soften the edges of the display.

Begonias aren't particularly deep-rooted, so if you are using tall containers, plant them in plastic pots that fit snugly inside your decorative ones. Then fill the base of the tall containers with bits of broken polystyrene or pebbles to help build up the height, and pop the begonias in their plastic pots on top.

WATERING NEEDS

Begonias will soon sulk, wilt, or lose their lustre if you neglect to water them. Water the compost carefully from above with a long-necked watering can. It's important to avoid splashing the leaves as they are quite sensitive and easily damaged. Allow the surface of the compost to dry out before watering again.

Centre: **Pair begonias
with trailing plants**
*in tall contemporary
containers to brighten
a modern décor with
colour and texture.*

TOP TIP: YEAR-ROUND CARE

Begonias are hungry plants that will not perform well if deprived of food. To keep them happy and to ensure they produce lots of colourful leaves, feed them every fortnight from spring to autumn with a general-purpose liquid fertilizer. They also like to be kept warm all year round, ideally between 18–21°C (64–70°F), and they need a bright position out of direct sunlight, which may scorch their leaves. Remove any fallen flowers or damaged leaves to prevent them from rotting on the surface of the compost.

Choosing begonias

Begonia aconitifolia *has cane-like stems, deeply lobed leaves flecked with silver, and pendulous pink flowers.*

Begonia benichoma *is a bushy begonia with serrated pink leaves that take on a silvery sheen as they mature.*

Begonia masoniana *is often called the iron cross begonia due to the distinctive dark markings on the textured leaves.*

Begonia serratipetala *is a shrub-like begonia with long serrated leaves with pink spots and clusters of pink flowers.*

Begonia 'Merry Christmas' *is closely related to Begonia rex, with huge leaves adorned with rich pink markings.*

Begonia 'Silver Queen' *is an upright begonia with pink autumn flowers and leaves embellished with silver marbling.*

Begonia 'Fire Flush' *has deep-green and maroon leaves highlighted with fine red hair, and scented pink flowers.*

Begonia 'Plum Rose' *has large leaves enriched by a glitzy combination of silver, pink, and green markings.*

PLANTS FOR SHADE

Foliage for a shady spot

Every home has its share of low-lit areas, where most flowering house plants fail to prosper. However, there are some tough, resilient types grown for their attractive foliage that will thrive in gloomy sites. These three offer contrasting forms and habits, and would look great as a group.

Mother-in-law's tongue *Sansevieria*

PLANTS FOR SHADE

Plant used
Sansevieria trifasciata 'Laurentii'

Height and spread
H 60cm (24in)
S 30cm (12in)

Aspect
Shade, although will grow equally well in direct light.

Temperature needs
Min. 10°C (50°F)

Suitable pot size
15–20cm (6–8in)

Suitable container material
Plastic pots inside decorative outer containers of any material

Compost type
Well-drained, soil-based compost, eg, John Innes No 2

Grown for its sword-shaped leaves that boast dark horizontal stripes and gold edges, this succulent is a great choice for a shady spot. With a reputation for being virtually indestructible, it will put up with draughts, dry air, and drought. A single plant can look a bit lonely, so turn these architectural plants into a feature by displaying them in groups. Despite growing fairly tall, these plants do well in small containers and do not need frequent repotting. To keep them looking good, water when the compost has dried out, and dust the leaves occasionally.

TOP TIP: MAKING NEW PLANTS

Mother-in-law's tongues spread readily, sending up new leaves from underground stems. In time, dense clumps form that may become too large for their pots. To keep plants in check, tease the rootball apart to make several smaller plants; replant these in fresh compost.

Spiky tongues of variegated foliage create a dramatic focal point on a table, sideboard, or shelves.

Devil's ivy *Epipremnum aureum*

Plant used
Epripremnum aureum

Height and spread
S 1.5m (5ft)

Aspect
Best with some indirect light

Temperature needs
Min. 15°C (59°F)

Suitable pot size
20cm (8in)

Suitable container material
Plastic, ceramic, glazed terracotta

Compost type
Well-drained, multi-purpose compost

The devil's ivy can be grown as a climbing plant up a large support, or allow its long stems to cascade over the sides of a container raised up on a wooden stand, small table, or shelf. Alternatively, try growing it in a hanging basket or wall-mounted container where you can appreciate its glossy, heart-shaped, yellow-splashed leaves.

Not for the darkest corner, this plant needs some light or the variegation will fade. For the best performance, clean the leaves every few weeks to remove any dust, and mist them occasionally with a hand-held spray. If the stems become too long, pinch them back to keep the plant within bounds and to encourage bushy growth. Water whenever the compost dries out during the growing season, but reduce the amount you give over winter. Feed monthly in summer with a foliage feed.

Trail the leaves of a devil's ivy over the sides of a stand, and place it in an area where it gets some indirect light.

Hard fern *Blechnum gibbum*

Plant used
Blechnum gibbum

Height and spread
H & S 60cm (24in)

Aspect
Partial shade

Temperature needs
Min 15°C (59°F)

Suitable pot size
15–20cm (6–8in)

Suitable container material
Plastic, metal, glazed terracotta

Compost type
Soil-based compost, eg, John Innes No 2

Ferns are among the most forgiving plants for a shady room, and the hard fern is one of the most desirable. Boasting long, leathery, deeply divided fronds, it produces a mass of stiff foliage. As the fern ages it forms a distinctive black trunk, giving rise to its other common name, the dwarf tree fern.

WATERING NEEDS
Hailing from the tropics, this fern predictably likes warmth and humidity, making it a good choice for a bathroom, although it won't be very happy next to a draughty window. If you don't have a humid area for your plant, raise moisture levels by misting the leaves every few days with a hand-held spray, which will also remove dust from the foliage. Ensure the compost is always moist, using warm water, and feed with a slow-release granular fertilizer in spring.

Large, deeply divided fronds produce a beautiful display in a simple terracotta container.

Colourful clematis

Many people think of clematis as rampant climbers, only suitable for growing through trees or adorning house walls and pergolas, yet there are many compact varieties that can be grown in large pots. Train these colourful climbers up ornamental supports and use them to decorate patios and to add height to borders.

Plant used
Clematis Ooh La La

Height and spread
H 90–120cm (3–4ft)
S 60cm (24in)

Aspect
Sun or dappled shade

Temperature needs
Hardy to -15°C (5°F)

Suitable pot size
45cm (18in)

Suitable container material
Use plastic pots in outer containers of wood, stone, metal, or terracotta

Compost type
Soil-based compost, eg, John Innes No 3

If you don't have any space in a border close to a wall, fence, or house, you can still enjoy clematis by growing those that are naturally compact or have been bred specifically for containers. Both types need a large pot and a place in the sun or partial shade. Although their vigour may be curtailed in cramped quarters, these Lilliputian climbers are as floriferous as their larger relations, and the new varieties will be covered from top to bottom in blooms during the summer. One such plant is *Clematis* Ooh La La, from the Evipo Boulevard patio range; its large pink flowers, with a darker stripe running down each petal, look stunning in a classic wooden planter.

PRUNING AND TRAINING

You can grow compact clematis up a wigwam of canes, an obelisk, or a fan-shaped trellis panel pushed into the container. Cover supports by regularly tying in new shoots with soft twine. To keep clematis within bounds and flowering prolifically, give them an annual prune. Spring- and early summer-flowering clematis should be pruned when the blooms fade, cutting to just above a leaf joint. Double-flowering varieties and those that flower twice in summer need pruning in winter or early spring; shorten long stems and remove weak or dying shoots. Cut all the stems of late summer- and early autumn-flowering clematis to healthy buds just above the compost in late winter or early spring.

*Centre: **Modern hybrids**, such as the pink-striped C. Ooh La La, have been bred to thrive in large patio containers.*

TOP TIP: MIX AND MATCH VARIETIES

Clematis look great on their own, but you can create an even more eye-catching display by growing two different varieties together. Pink flowers go well with white, dark blue, or purple blooms, or try an elegant white and purple mix, such as Ice Blue, with its blue-flushed white flowers, and Kingfisher, as shown here.

Clematis for containers

Clematis *'Vyvyan Pennell'* *is a very showy clematis for midsummer interest with large, double, lilac flowers.*

Clematis *Fleuri* *is a bushy little climber with a profusion of violet flowers from late spring until mid-autumn.*

Clematis *'Fireworks'* *produces glowing purple and magenta flowers that adorn plants from early to midsummer.*

Clematis florida *var.* florida *'Sieboldiana'* *bears large white flowers from late spring to autumn.*

Clematis *'The President'* *is a summer-flowering variety with large flowers that are a rich shade of bluey-purple.*

Clematis *'Niobe'* *bears single, velvety red flowers with a boss of yellow stamens from late spring to autumn.*

Clematis *Chantilly* *has pale pink flowers with a darker stripe that appear from summer to early autumn.*

Clematis *'Arabella'* *has small, mauve and purple flowers. Its non-climbing stems need tying in to their supports.*

HIGH CLIMBERS

Soaring annuals

Some of the greatest spectacles are short lived, and these annual climbers are a case in point. They last just one season, but in that time produce a blaze of beautiful flowers on twining stems. Use them in combination with other annual flowers and foliage plants, or create a confection of colour by planting two together.

HIGH CLIMBERS

Rhodochiton

Plants used
Rhodochiton atrosanguineus;
Cerinthe major var.
purpurascens;
Plectranthus zatarhendii

Height and spread
Rhodochiton: H 1m
(3ft); *Cerinthe*:
H & S: 30cm (12in);
Plectranthus:
S: 60cm (24in)

Aspect
Sun or partial shade

Temperature needs
Not hardy below 0°C
(32°F).

Suitable pot size
45cm (18in)

Suitable container material
Ceramic, terracotta, stone

Compost type
Soil-based compost, eg, John Innes No 3

Stems of earthy red, pendulous *Rhodochiton* flowers make a striking statement when wrapped around a wigwam of bamboo canes. The bare stems at the base of the plant can be hidden by the silvery-blue bushy foliage of *Cerinthe* plants, and the sides of the pot softened with trailing *Plectranthus*. Perfect as a focal point or to break up a sea of patio slabs, *Rhodochiton* will provide a sophisticated splash of colour from summer to autumn. Add some slow-release granular fertilizer to the compost when planting up, and keep plants well watered during the summer. If your display starts to flag in summer, give it a boost with a tomato feed.

TRAINING PLANTS
Rhodochiton has twining leafstalks and will climb naturally when established, but it needs a helping hand to get started. After erecting your wigwam of canes in a large pot, plant a climber at the foot of each, and secure stems to the canes with soft twine. Plant the other annuals between the bamboo canes.

TOP TIP: SAVING SEED

Although it is a perennial, *Rhodochiton* is often grown as an annual, as it is not frost hardy. It is best started from seed each year, and you can save your own seeds from old plants. Allow the pods to dry out, then break them open to extract the seeds. Store seeds in a labelled jar until spring.

Create an exciting arrangement with colour and height by grouping Rhodochiton *with* Cerinthe *and trailing* Plectranthus.

Morning glory *Ipomoea* and *Convolvulus*

Plant used
Convolvulus tricolor

Height and spread
H 40cm (16in)
S 30cm (12in)

Aspect
Full sun

Temperature needs
Min. 7°C (45°F)

Suitable pot size
30–45cm (12–18in)

Suitable container material
Terracotta, metal, ceramic, wood

Compost type
Soil-based compost, eg, John Innes No 3

Ipomoea is an easy-to-grow annual climber, known as morning glory, that produces masses of delicate flowers from summer until the first frosts. Growing to 2m (6ft) or more, it is perfect for training up supports in large pots. Dwarf morning glory, *Convolvulus tricolor*, is also an annual, but reaches just 40cm (14in) and can be tied in to a low support, or allowed to scramble through other plants. Both *Ipomoea* and *Convolvulus* are best combined with other flowers, as their blooms often close during the hottest part of the day. Water plants freely, and apply a balanced liquid fertilizer every month.

COLOUR OPTIONS

There are many morning glories to choose from, and flowers vary in shape from trumpets to tubes. Colours include white, pink, purple, and blue, while many are bicoloured.

Convolvulus tricolor

Black-eyed Susan *Thunbergia*

Plant used
Thunbergia alata

Height and spread
H 1.8m (6ft)

Aspect
Sun

Temperature needs
Min. 10°C (50°F)

Suitable pot size
30–45cm (12–18in)

Suitable container material
Terracotta, metal, ceramic

Compost type
Soil-based compost, eg, John Innes No 3

Cheery yellow flowers with a distinctive black "eye" cover this vigorous climber from mid-summer to autumn. Superb in a large container, where it can be grown up a wigwam of canes, trellis, or an ornamental obelisk, this plant needs a sunny spot and regular watering to thrive. Also, apply a balanced liquid fertilizer every month. Although it's a perennial, black-eyed Susan is usually grown as an annual from seed each year. Seeds germinate easily, and you can start them off indoors in early spring so that the young plants will be of a good size and ready to start flowering soon after you plant them outside, when the risk of frost has passed.

PLANTING PARTNERS

Black-eyed Susan looks great as a centrepiece among white petunias, yellow nasturtiums, and the yellow foliage of trailing *Ipomoea batatas* 'Margarita'. Alternatively, mix yellow *Thunbergia* with orange- or white-flowered varieties, or plant them with French beans (*see pp.176-7*).

Thunbergia alata **makes an impressive summer show.**

Fragrant climbers

Bring flowers and scent up to nose level with these fragrant climbers. Both produce small blooms that belie their heavy perfume, which is guaranteed to give your garden a lift all summer long. Star jasmine also sports glossy evergreen foliage that turns bronze in the winter, and sweet peas can be grown easily from seed each spring.

Star jasmine *Trachelospermum*

Plant used
Trachelospermum jasminoides

Height and spread
H up to 2.5m (8ft) if pruned

Aspect
Sun or partial shade

Temperature needs
Hardy to -5°C (23°F)

Suitable pot size
30cm (12in)

Suitable container material
Stone, terracotta, ceramic, metal, wood

Compost type
Soil-based compost, eg, John Innes No 3

Star jasmine, *Trachelospermum jasminoides*, is a vigorous evergreen with glossy dark green leaves that make the ideal backdrop for its small, heavenly-scented, white summer flowers. The plant can grow to 9m (28ft) in the ground, but with regular pruning it is easy to keep in check in a large pot. The more compact *Trachelospermum asiaticum* is a good alternative, and has similar foliage and jasmine-scented flowers. Happy in sun or partial shade, both are frost hardy, but will need protecting in harsh winters. Water plants regularly in the growing season, and feed annually in spring with a slow-release granular fertilizer.

SUPPORTING PLANTS
Plants in pots can be pushed up against a wall, fence, shed, or the leg of a pergola, and trained against wires fixed to the support. Alternatively, place trellis, an obelisk, or wigwam of canes in a pot to provide a free-standing support, or train the stems over a sturdy metal arch set between two pots of star jasmine.

> ### TOP TIP: PRUNING STAR JASMINE
> Star jasmine grows quite vigorously and will soon look untidy unless it's given an annual trim. Prune plants in spring. First, cut out any dead, diseased or congested growth. Then prune out any wayward shoots to maintain a tight, compact shape. You may also need to thin out new shoots as they appear later in spring and throughout summer. Although plants are self-supporting, you can tie in shoots with soft twine to fill gaps on your support.

Trachelospermum jasminoides *provides a tower of scented starry flowers in summer.*

Sweet peas *Lathyrus odoratus*

Plant used
Lathyrus odoratus

Height and spread
H 2m (6ft)

Aspect
Full sun

Temperature needs
Hardy to -15°C (5°F)

Suitable pot size
30cm (12in) or larger

Suitable container material
Terracotta, stone, ceramic

Compost type
Soil-based compost, eg, John Innes No 3

Native to southern Italy, sweet peas comprise a large clan of annuals that will fill your garden with colour and scent from early summer to the first frosts in autumn. Perfect for large pots, where their stems can be trained up cane supports or an ornamental obelisk, sweet peas come in shades of pink, red, blue, purple, and white, with two-tone flowers also on offer.

Although seedlings are readily available to buy in spring, you'll have a greater choice if you raise your own from seed. In spring, sow seeds 1cm (½in) deep in tall cell trays, and place them in a coldframe, greenhouse, or cool room to germinate. Keep the compost moist, and when seedlings have four leaves, pinch out the top pair with your fingers, which encourages side-shoots to form. The well-rooted sweet peas can be planted into pots outside from mid-spring.

PROLONGING FLOWERING
Although sweet peas can flower continuously until autumn, they need nurturing to ensure a long-lasting display. Water plants regularly and drench the compost with a weak solution of liquid fertilizer every fortnight. Also remove blooms as soon as they start to fade, or regularly pick bouquets for the home, to prevent the plant diverting its energy into making seeds, which halts flower production.

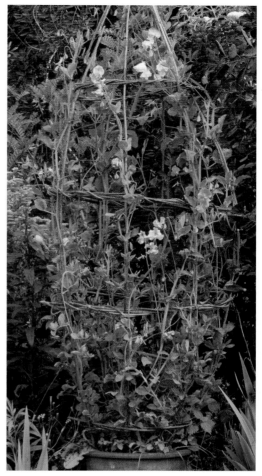

Make a rustic support for sweet peas by twisting flexible willow stems around a pyramid of sturdy poles.

CHOOSING SWEET PEA VARIETIES

'Blue Ripple' is a stunning form, with long slender stems of highly scented, white, frilly-edged flowers with distinctive blue markings on the edge of the petals.

Heirloom Mixed is a showy mixture of heavily scented, old-fashioned varieties, with large flowers in a wide range of eye-catching colours.

'Matucana' is a dark and desirable climber. An old-fashioned sweet pea that has been grown since the 18th century, it produces strongly scented maroon and purple flowers.

'Jayne Amanda' is a Spencer cultivar with large frilly flowers that characterize this group. It has warm pink blooms 3.5cm (1½in) across, which are perfect for cutting.

Jasmines for the home

Covered with masses of small starry flowers that emit a heady perfume, tender climbing jasmines put on a vertical show to delight the senses for much of the year. Plant them in large pots and train their long trailing stems along a wall or twine them around a plant support to fill your home with the natural scent of these sophisticated climbers.

Madagascar jasmine *Stephanotis*

Ideal in a partially shaded site, Stephanotis *thrives when fed monthly while in growth with a balanced liquid feed.*

HIGH CLIMBERS

Plant used
Stephanotis floribunda

Height and spread
H 60cm (24in)
S 2m (6ft) in a large pot

Aspect
Sun or partial shade

Temperature needs
Min. 13°C (55°F)

Suitable pot size
20cm (8in)

Suitable container material
Glazed terracotta, ceramic

Compost type
Soil-based compost, eg, John Innes No 2

This evergreen climber makes an attractive house plant all year round. Its dark green, leathery leaves provide a dramatic foil for the waxy white flowers which appear in large clusters from spring until autumn.

Widely available, Madagascar jasmines are often sold in small pots, ready trained with their long stems twisted around a hoop of wire. Although the hoop will suffice for a while, it will eventually become congested, at which stage the plant will need a larger support structure and a bigger container. Repot by carefully removing the ties and unwinding the stems. Plant the jasmine in the centre of the new pot, secure a piece of trellis or an obelisk in it, and wind the stems around the uprights, tying them in with soft twine. If necessary, cut back long shoots after flowering.

To keep the plant happy, keep the compost moist at all times, decreasing watering in the winter. From time to time, wipe the leaves with a damp cloth to remove dust, and mist the foliage occasionally to increase humidity.

SITING PLANTS
This plant loves a bright position, but should be kept out of direct sunlight in summer. A light, airy sitting room where you can get maximum enjoyment from the scented flowers is an ideal location, but do not place it in the bedroom as the perfume can be a little too strong. Avoid moving it around when in bud or bearing flowers, as the sudden changes of temperature can cause both to drop prematurely.

White jasmine *Jasminum polyanthum*

Plant used
Jasminum polyanthum

Height and spread
H & S 1.5m (5ft)

Aspect
Bright light, away from direct sun

Temperature needs
18°C (64°F)

Suitable pot size
20–30cm (8–12in)

Suitable container material
Plastic, stone, glazed terracotta, ceramic

Compost type
Soil-based compost, eg, John Innes No 2

Its flowers may be small, but what they lack in size they make up for in fragrance. Borne in prolific numbers during winter and spring, the white star-shaped blooms open from pink buds and have a knock-out scent. Although jasmines are often sold trained on a metal hoop, this is rarely adequate for this vigorous evergreen plant. Pot it up into a large container and retrain the stems up a more substantial support, such as an obelisk or wigwam. To keep it healthy, ensure the compost never dries out, and feed every month with a balanced liquid fertilizer while in active growth. This plant grows quickly and can become straggly and choked with stems if left to its own devices. Prune annually after flowering to control its size and maintain a tidy plant.

TEMPERATURE CONTROL

Keep jasmines in a cool room with temperatures of around 18°C (64°F); any warmer and it will produce lots of growth at the expense of flowers. In early autumn, encourage the formation of new buds by placing it outside during the day for about four weeks, bringing it back inside in late afternoon to avoid frost damage. After this, return it to a cool room.

Single, white, highly scented flowers appear in late winter and early spring, brightening up the gloomy months.

HIGH CLIMBERS

TOP TIP: REMOVING SPENT BLOOMS

Faded jasmine flowers tend to stick to the plant, giving it an unsightly appearance. It's a fiddly and time-consuming job, but removing the spent blooms with a pair of sharp scissors will keep the plant tidy and encourage the production of more blooms. Cut the old flower stalks back to the main stem.

Flying colours for the home

Let these flowering exotics paint walls of colour in your home with their exquisite blooms and green foliage. They are tender climbers and produce an abundance of flowers along their twining stems over many months. Purple coral peas bloom from late winter to early summer, while the glory lily and bougainvillea both flower in summer.

Glory lily *Gloriosa*

Plant used
Gloriosa superba 'Rothschildiana'

Height and spread
S 2m (6ft)

Aspect
Sunny, but shaded from direct sun

Temperature needs
Min. 8°C (46°F)

Suitable pot size
30cm (12in)

Suitable container material
Plastic inside a decorative container

Suitable compost
Multi-purpose compost

Few climbing plants make a more arresting sight than the glory lily in summer, when its slender stems are festooned with large red flowers. Measuring 8cm (3in) across, each bloom consists of six wavy, swept-back petals with yellow margins. Native to the tropics of Africa, this self-clinging climber can easily scale 2m (6ft) and will happily scramble through a tall obelisk or other robust support in a large container. Place your plant in a sunny, light, warm conservatory or room.

WINTER CARE

After the glory lily's flowers start to fade, stop feeding and reduce watering (*see Top Tip box below*). The leaves will then turn yellow and the plant will become dormant over winter. Remove the dead growth from the surface of the container, and do not water your glory lily again until new shoots start to appear above the surface of the compost the following spring.

Create a tower of vibrant flowers by weaving stems of Gloriosa superba 'Rothschildiana' through an obelisk.

TOP TIP: ENCOURAGE FLOWERING

To flower well the glory lily needs a position in a warm, light place, with some protection from the sun in summer. Water well during the growing season, and give plants a boost by feeding with a balanced liquid fertilizer every fortnight. Raise humidity levels by misting the leaves occasionally – do this in the morning so that the plant can dry out before evening.

HIGH CLIMBERS

Bougainvillea

Plant used
Bougainvillea glabra

Height and spread
S up to 8m (25ft),
but can be restricted
to size of support

Aspect
Full sun – shade will
cause leaves to drop

Temperature needs
Not reliably hardy
below 0°C (32°C)

Suitable pot size
Min. 15cm (6in)

**Suitable container
material**
Plastic inside a
decorative container

Suitable compost
Multi-purpose
compost

A sun lover for a windowsill or conservatory, there are many fabulous *Bougainvillea* to choose from. As well as *B. glabra*, which comes in pink, purple and white, try *B. x buttiana* with cream flowers, the pale yellow *B. x buttiana* 'Enid Lancaster', or, for the most eye-catching display, select bright pink *B. x buttiana* 'Raspberry Ice', which also sports variegated foliage.

GROWING BOUGAINVILLEA

Trim back plants to suit your space, and grow up frames, around hoops, or along wires as an espalier. Water and feed plants regularly in the growing season. *Bougainvillea* can flower for up to ten months a year in a conservatory, and will be happy outside on a patio in summer, but it needs a frost-free place over winter. Forms of *B. x buttiana* also become dormant in winter and lose their leaves, which then reappear in spring.

Bougainvillea glabra *produces white blooms.*

Purple coral pea *Hardenbergia violacea*

Plant used
*Hardenbergia
violacea*

Height and spread
S up to 2m (6ft)

Aspect
Light, out of
direct sun

Temperature needs
Not reliably hardy
below 0°C (32°C)

Suitable pot size
30cm (12in)

**Suitable container
material**
Plastic inside a
decorative container

Suitable compost
Soil-based compost,
eg, John Innes No 3

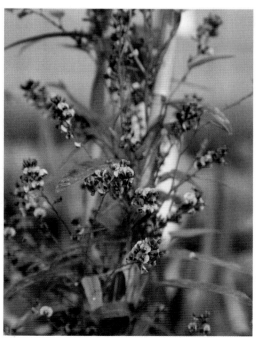

Hardenbergia violacea *has delicate purple flowers.*

Between late winter and early summer, this evergreen climber makes itself a welcome house guest by providing an amazing show of small purple flowers held in long clusters. The wiry branches of this Australian native are self-climbing, but you may need to tie in the shoots with soft twine to train them evenly over a support, such as an obelisk or trellis.

CARE FOR CORAL PEAS

Grow plants in a light area indoors, but make sure they have some protection from direct sun. A conservatory or large sitting room that receives plenty of natural light is perfect.

Although they are quite drought tolerant when grown in the ground in their native environment, plants need watering regularly when in pots, but allow the compost to almost dry out between each watering. Feed monthly in the growing season with a liquid fertilizer, and restrict the height of the plant to keep it within bounds by pruning after flowering.

HIGH CLIMBERS

Early bulbs

Perfect for chasing away those winter blues, daffodils, dwarf irises, and snowdrops are the earliest plants to flower, appearing when there's little else of interest in the garden. Plant your favourite bulbs in autumn to guarantee an early flush of colour, but wait until spring to plant snowdrops when they are in leaf, as this produces better results.

Daffodils *Narcissus*

Plants used
Narcissus 'Salome'
Myosotis scorpioides

Height and spread
Narcissus 'Salome':
H 45cm (18in)
Myosotis
H & S 20cm (8in)

Aspect
Sun or dappled shade

Temperature needs
Hardy to -15°C (5°F)

Suitable pot size
20cm (8in)

Suitable container material
Terracotta, stone, plastic, metal, wicker baskets, recycled containers

Compost type
Bulb fibre

Rustic woven willow baskets and terracotta pots make ideal containers for daffodil displays. Choose a tall variety, such as *Narcissus* 'Salome', as a centrepiece and underplant with white forget-me-nots whose tiny white flowers and foliage complement those of the daffodil.

Plant daffodil bulbs in autumn 10cm (4in) deep and place pots in a sunny or semi-shaded, sheltered spot. If squirrels or cats are a problem, secure a piece of chicken wire over the top until growth appears in late winter. Pots should not need watering over winter, but water during dry spells when they are in bud and flower. Feed with a liquid fertilizer when blooms have faded and allow foliage to die down naturally.

GOOD VARIETIES FOR POTS
There are thousands of daffodil varieties to choose from, with tiny or tall types, and single or double flowers. Among the best low-growing daffodils are 'Jack Snipe', 'Hawera', 'Pipit', and 'Tête-à-Tête', or try taller forms, such as 'Acropolis', 'Ice Follies' and 'Carlton'.

TOP TIP: PLANTING PARTNERS

Create striking combinations by underplanting daffodils with other spring-flowering plants. A carpet of white grape hyacinths (*Muscari*) and white daffodils make pretty partners, or use contrasting purple crocuses, dwarf irises, or violas. Blue *Corydalis* and grape hyacinths work well with yellow daffodils.

Narcissus *'Salome'* *makes a beautiful display of white petals and peachy-yellow trumpets.*

Dwarf iris *Iris reticulata*

Plant used
Iris reticulata

Height and spread
H 10cm (4in)

Aspect
Full sun

Temperature needs
Hardy to -15°C (5°F)

Suitable pot size
10–15cm (4–6in)

Suitable container material
Terracotta, stone, recycled containers

Compost type
Well-drained, soil-based compost, eg, John Innes No 3

Iris reticulata lifts the spring garden with dainty blooms.

Irises are usually associated with borders, but there are a number of ankle-high plants that are perfect for spring pots. Native to mountainous regions of Europe and Asia, *Iris reticulata* grows to just 10cm (4in) and looks smart when planted *en masse* in a terracotta bowl. Plant bulbs in early autumn 5cm (2in) apart and about 5cm (2in) deep, and place containers in a sunny spot to flower. Apply a liquid fertilizer when flowers fade and allow foliage to die down naturally.

DIFFERENT COLOURS

Dwarf irises come in many different colours. *I. reticulata* 'Cantab' has pale blue flowers, and *I.reticulata* 'J.S. Dijt' is deep purple. For pale primrose flowers, choose *I. winogradowii*, or try *I. danfordiae* with its bright yellow, sweetly scented blooms. Another perfumed iris, 'Edward', has orange-marked blue flowers.

Snowdrops *Galanthus*

Plant used
Galanthus nivalis

Height and spread
H 8–30cm (3–12in)
S 5–8cm (2–3in)

Aspect
Dappled shade

Temperature needs
Most are hardy to -15°C (5°F)

Suitable pot size
10–15cm (4–6in)

Suitable container material
Terracotta, stone, recycled containers

Compost type
Soil-based compost, eg, John Innes No 3

Grown for their instantly recognisable nodding white flowers, snowdrops are the first flowers to appear in late winter and early spring. There are hundreds of different types to choose from, varying in height from 8cm (3in) to 30cm (12in), with flowers in many shapes and sizes. Many have exquisite green markings beneath their white petals, and plants are best displayed on tables or ledges so you don't have to stoop to fully appreciate their hidden petticoats.

PLANTING SNOWDROPS

Snowdrops will grow quickly if they are bought and planted in the spring while actively growing, or "in the green", as it is often called. Ensure the snowdrops are planted at the same depth as they were before they were lifted from the ground – the point where the green leaves start to turn yellow should be level with the surface of the compost. Dried bulbs are available in the autumn, but snowdrops may not establish well from them.

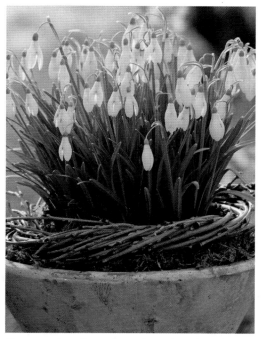

Plant snowdrops in small pots for early spring colour.

Elegant tulips

With a vast array of colours and forms to choose from, you can create dramatic tulip displays from mid- to late spring, brightening up patios and adding punch to borders schemes. These seasonal stars make beautiful focal points in tall pots of mixed plants, or use diminutive types *en masse* in bowls or baskets.

Plants used
Tulipa 'Abu Hassan';
Erysiumum cheiri
(wallflower);
Myosotis scorpioides
'Royal Blue'
(forget-me-nots)

Height and spread
Tulipa 'Abu Hassan':
H 50cm (20in);
Erysium: H & S 20cm
(8in); *Myosotis:*
H 30cm (12in)
S 20cm (8in)

Aspect
Full sun

Temperature needs
Hardy to -15°C (5°F)

Suitable pot size
30–45cm (12–18in)

**Suitable container
material**
Stone, terracotta,
plastic, wood,
baskets

Compost type
Multi-purpose
compost

Icons of the spring garden, tulips are incredibly versatile and provide exceptional value in the spring garden. Choose from elegant double flowers in pastel shades that resemble peonies, simple cups of rich colour, or frilly-petalled "parrots", which mimic the feathers of exotic birds. For a dramatic patio display, plant the eye-catching *Tulipa* 'Abu Hassan', with its mahogany-red goblets, above a sea of burnt orange, red, and yellow wallflowers and clouds of tiny blue forget-me-nots in a range of Victorian chimney pots. Alternatively, create a more subtle scheme with pale pink *Tulipa* 'Angélique', white forget-me-nots, variegated thyme, and purple violas.

To produce dazzling tulip displays, plant the bulbs at a depth of 10cm (4in) in plastic pots in autumn, and then in early spring fill the gaps around the edges with other spring flowers. The utilitarian pots can then be plunged into a chimney pot or other decorative container and set in a sunny position to bloom.

CARING FOR TULIPS
Protect bulbs from foraging squirrels by covering the compost with chicken wire, tucking it down the sides to keep it in place, and remove it in spring when shoots appear. Keep the compost moist during dry spells, and deadhead flowers as they start to fade. Once your displays have gone over, you can simply remove the plastic pots and replace them with summer-flowering plants.

TOP TIP: LAYERING TULIPS WITH OTHER BULBS

Tulips make superb partners for other bulbs, such as daffodils and grape hyacinths. First, add a layer of compost to the bottom of the pot and plant the biggest bulbs, followed by a 5cm (2in) layer of compost and the next-largest bulbs. Add another layer of compost, plant the smallest bulbs, and cover them with compost.

*Centre: **Tall chimney pots** raise tulips up closer to eye level, allowing a better appreciation of their colourful flowers.*

Tulip options

Tulipa *'Artist'* *is a viridiflora type, with shapely flowers decorated with green, pink, and orange markings.*

Tulipa *'Estella Rijnveld'* *is a parrot tulip that produces a globe of intricately fringed petals in red and white.*

Tulipa *'China Pink'* *produces lily-like candy pink flowers on tall, graceful stems from mid- to late spring.*

Tulipa *'Ballerina'* *is a scented lily-shaped tulip bearing marmalade-coloured flowers with pointed petals.*

Tulipa *'Queen of Night'* *has deep purple-black single flowers that contrast well with light blue forget-me-nots.*

Tulipa *'Spring Green'*, *a viridiflora tulip, produces slightly feathered ivory white flowers with green stripes.*

Tulipa clusiana *is a desirable species whose small white flowers marked with a dark pink stripe appear in late spring.*

Tulipa *'West Point'* *is a clear, lemon yellow, lily-flowered tulip with graceful, swept-back, pointed petals.*

Blossom in pots

There's nothing shy and retiring about a shrub or tree laden with spring blossom. The flowers, some of which are sweetly scented, are borne in great profusion, and provide head-height displays on a patio or terrace. Choose dwarf forms of trees, as these will be the happiest in containers, and keep plants well fed and watered.

Lilac *Syringa*

Plants used
Syringa vulgaris 'Andenken an Ludwig Späth'; *Viola cornuta*; *Hedera helix* (ivy)

Height and spread
Syringa: H 2m (6ft) S 1m (3ft);
Viola: H 15cm (6in) S: 40cm (16in);
Hedera: S 45cm (18in)

Aspect
Full sun

Temperature needs
Hardy to -15°C (5°F)

Suitable pot size
45cm (18in)

Suitable container material
Stone, glazed terracotta

Compost type
Soil-based compost, eg, John Innes No 3

Much admired for their long sprays of heavily scented late-spring flowers, lilacs are most often thought of as border plants. However, those that have the potential to reach 7m (22ft) in open ground, such as the reddish-purple-flowered 'Andenken an Ludwig Späth', will grow to just a fraction of that size when confined to a pot. Add interest to your displays with a skirt of ivy and perennial horned violet (*Viola cornuta*), which produces a carpet of tiny lilac flowers. Keep plants well watered throughout the growing season, and feed annually in spring with a slow-release granular fertilizer.

DWARF OPTIONS FOR CONTAINERS
Large lilacs can be grown in containers, but those that are naturally dwarf or slow growing will generally perform better and be happiest for longer in a pot. Among the best are the pale pink, dwarf Korean lilac, *S. meyeri* 'Palibin', and purple *S. pubescens* subsp. *patula* 'Miss Kim'. The cut-leaf lilac, *S.* x *laciniata*, is another option; it grows to just 2m (6ft) and bears purple flowers.

TOP TIP: PRUNING LILACS

Avoid deadheading lilacs until you can see two shoots beneath the fading flowerheads – removing them before this could jeopardize next year's display. To maintain an open, bushy shape, remove one or two old stems in winter, cutting them to the base. This will result in a flush of new growth in spring.

Glorious, sweetly scented purple blossoms adorn Syringa *'Andenken an Ludwig Späth' in late spring.*

Crab apple *Malus*

Plant used
Malus 'Adirondack'

Height and spread
H 1.5m (5ft)
S 1m (3ft)

Aspect
Full sun

Temperature needs
Hardy to -15°C (5°F)

Suitable pot size
45cm (18in)

Suitable container material
Stone, glazed ceramic

Compost type
Soil-based compost, eg, John Innes No 3

If you've only got space for one tree on your patio, a crab apple is hard to beat. Naturally compact, it forms a rounded or narrow, upright tree that is easy to maintain with minimal pruning. To keep plants in good condition, water pots regularly and remove some of the old soil in early spring, replacing it with slow-release granular fertilizer added to fresh compost.

TWO SEASONS OF INTEREST
Crab apples are great value, providing two seasons of interest. In spring their branches are covered with blossom, followed in autumn by round or oval fruits that last for a few months. The crabs come in many sizes and colours: 'Red Sentinel' has glossy red fruit, while 'Butterball' bears golden-yellow apples. Some plants, such as *M. transitoria,* have three seasons of interest, with autumn leaf colour to add to its charms.

Malus *'Adirondack' is a good choice* for a deep container, and bears star-shaped white flowers and orange-red fruit.

Cherry *Prunus*

Plant used
Prunus 'Kiku-shidare-zakura' (syn.'Cheals Weeping')

Height and spread
H & S up to 3m (10ft)

Aspect
Full sun

Temperature needs
Hardy to -15°C (5°F)

Suitable pot size
45cm (18in)

Suitable container material
Stone, glazed terracotta, plastic

Compost type
Soil-based compost, eg, John Innes No 3

Flowering cherries sparkle with spring blooms, lighting up patios and gardens with their seasonal bouquets. The Cheal's Weeping cherry or *Prunus* 'Kiku-shidare-zakura' is one of the best, its pink buds opening to reveal double flowers held in dense clusters among the bronze-flushed, glossy new foliage. Easy to care for, this small tree needs pruning just occasionally to remove dead or diseased stems, and to tidy any wayward branches. Other flowering cherries suitable for growing in pots include 'Pink Perfection', 'Fukubana' and 'Beni-yutaka'.

WATERING NEEDS
Cherry trees grown in containers must be watered regularly to ensure the compost never dries out completely, especially over summer and in late winter when flower buds are forming. If you lead a busy life, consider installing an automatic irrigation system to ensure trees are kept moist. In spring, remove the top layer of soil and apply a slow-release granular fertilizer mixed with fresh compost.

Prunus 'Kiku-shidare-zakura'

Early season flower displays

Cheer up your spring garden with a basket filled with dainty flowers and lush grasses, and display it on a table or windowsill. Alternatively, keep things simple and plant colourful low-growing alpines in troughs or small pots grouped together to create a miniature spectacle. All of these flowering beauties are easy to grow and require very little aftercare.

Colourful basket of blooms

Plants used
Erysimum 'Poem Lavender'; Viola 'Etain'; Aubrieta 'Silberrand'; Alopecurus pratensis 'Aureus'

Height and spread
Erysimum: H 30cm (12in) S 40cm (16in); Viola: H & S 15cm (6in); Aubrieta: H 8cm (3in) S 30cm (12in); Alopecurus: H & S 30cm (12in)

Aspect
Sun or partial shade

Temperature needs
Hardy to -15°C (5°F)

Suitable pot size
45cm- (18in-) long windowbox or basket

Suitable container material
Terracotta, stone, ceramic, wood, basket

Compost type
Multi-purpose compost with added soil-based compost, eg, John Innes No 3

Water your spring basket during dry spells, and when the plants become too congested, repot into a larger container.

When creating a flower display, start with the tallest plant for your centrepiece, such as the scented wallflower, Erysimum 'Poem Lavender'. Small, nodding violas and the tumbling tiny mauve blooms of Aubrieta add to the picture, while grasses, such as the foxtail grass, Alopecurus, complete the display.

Ensure your basket or pot has drainage holes at the bottom and fill with a mix of soil-based and multi-purpose compost. Plant densely, but ensure the top of the compost is 5cm (2in) below the basket rim to allow space for watering.

TOP TIP: DEADHEADING VIOLAS

For a long-lasting display, spend a few minutes every day or two removing fading flowers. This not only ensures that the basket looks its best, but deadheading also encourages the plants to put all of their energy into making showy flowers rather than seeds.

Spring alpines

Plant used
Saxifraga stribrnyi

Height and spread
H 10cm (4in)
S 20cm (8in)

Aspect
Full sun

Temperature needs
Hardy to -15°C (5°F)

Suitable pot size
20cm (8in) shallow
or pan-shaped pots

Suitable container material
Terracotta, stone

Compost type
Soil-based compost,
eg, John Innes No 2,
with added grit

They may be small, but alpines are charming plants blessed with attractive foliage and pretty flowers. Among the most popular alpines are saxifrages, a diverse group of evergreen plants that includes *Saxifraga stribrnyi*, whose small silvery rosettes will spread readily across the surface of a pot filled with well-drained compost. Many saxifrages flower in summer or autumn, so check labels before you buy. Other good choices for spring colour include *S.* Southside Seedling Group, with its tight leaf rosettes and white flowers spotted with red, and *S. sancta* which has bright green spiky leaves paired with cup-shaped yellow flowers.

Although alpines come from mountainous terrains and are incredibly tough, most need protection from excessive winter rain to prevent rotting, and a site in full sun. Plant them in gritty compost to improve drainage, and top with a gravel mulch to keep the foliage dry. Feed annually in spring with a granular fertilizer.

GROUPING PLANTS

To make a more dramatic statement with these diminutive plants, group several pots filled with different alpines. Alternatively, combine a few plants in a trough or antique ceramic sink. You can also group them with bulbs, such as species tulips, and late-flowering daffodils.

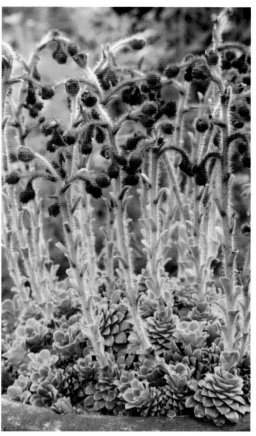

Spring-flowering saxifrages make a low mound of textured foliage, which erupts with stems of dainty flowers.

CHOOSING SPRING ALPINES

Aubrieta species form a carpet of soft grey-green leaves, and generally produce pink or purple, single or double flowers, although other shades are available.

Gentiana acaulis is an evergreen perennial that forms a carpet of dark green leaves masked in spring by trumpet-shaped blue flowers. A good choice for dappled shade.

Leontopodium alpinum, commonly known as edelweiss, produces grey leaves topped by dainty white flowers in spring. It needs well-drained soil and full sun.

Androsace villosa var. jacquemontii produces a low cushion of silky, hairy leaf rosettes, and deep pinky-purple flowers, with yellow or green eyes.

Dramatic spring finale
Rhododendron and *azalea*

See out spring in style by growing rhododendron and azaleas in containers. Available in a wide range of colours and sizes, most need a large pot and space to show off their stems of glossy leaves and blowsy flowers, although some dwarf forms are more compact and suit small patios, balconies, and terraces.

SPRING SPECTACLES

Plants used
Rhododendron 'Gunborg';
Tiarella 'Snow Blanket';
Viola 'Etain';
Lysimachia nummularia 'Goldilocks'

Height and spread
Rhododendron:
H 1m (3ft) S 60cm (24in); *Tiarella:*
H 15cm (6in)
S 30cm (12in);
Viola: H & S 15cm (6in); *Lysimachia:*
H 10cm (4in)
S 90cm (36in)

Aspect
Sun or partial shade

Temperature needs
Most are hardy to -15°C (5°F)

Suitable pot size
45cm (18in)

Suitable container material
Stone, glazed terracotta, ceramic

Compost type
Soil-based ericaceous compost, eg, John Innes Ericaceous Compost

Centre **A tall standard rhododendron** *creates a sparkling flower display above a carpet of bedding and trailing plants.*

Many admire the vibrant flowers of rhododendrons and azaleas, but not everyone has the acid soil they need to thrive. The solution is to grow these attractive shrubs in containers filled with ericaceous compost, a formulation devised to suit the specific needs of acid-loving plants.

Growing standards with a clear stem allows space for underplanting to extend the interest. For example, the rose-pink flowers of *Rhododendron* 'Gunborg' look stunning above a frill of *Tiarella*, with its pretty lobed foliage and delicate flower spires. Trailing *Lysimachia* is a good choice for softening the edges of the containers, while duotone violas provide an additional splash of spring colour. 'Gunborg' is a yakushimanum rhododendron, a group known for their slow growth and compact habit. A form that has been grafted on to a straight stem makes a tall plant, but in a smaller area, use an ungrafted specimen. Other yakushimanum to choose from include 'Dreamland', 'Dopey', and 'Lemon Dream'.

PRUNING AND TRAINING
To keep shrubs in shape, remove faded flowers to prevent seeds from forming; use your thumb and forefinger, and avoid damage to the new buds beneath. Most plants need just a light tidy-up after flowering by cutting back or removing wayward stems, and rub off any buds that appear along the clear stems of standards.

TOP TIP: PLANTS WITH SIMILAR NEEDS

Rhododendrons and azaleas are not the only acid-loving plants that you can grow in pots. *Pieris*, camellias (*right*), magnolias, and *Skimmia* all require similar soil conditions. Feed all these plants in spring with granular fertilizer formulated for acid-lover worked into the top layer of compost.

Choosing acid-loving shrubs

Rhododendron *'Palestrina'* *is a dwarf evergreen azalea with white flowers. Protect with fleece over winter.*

Rhododendron *'Temple Belle'* *has evergreen rounded leaves accompanied by bell-shaped, pink spring flowers.*

Rhododendron augustinii *is a bushy evergreen and produces large violet-blue flowers in mid-spring.*

Rhododendron *'Fragrantissimum'* *has highly scented, large white flowers. It is tender and needs frost protection.*

Rhododendron *'Louise Dowdle'* *is a compact, spreading, evergreen azalea with large, brilliant pink flowers.*

Rhododendron luteum *is a very highly scented deciduous azalea with glorious canary yellow, late-spring flowers.*

Rhododendron *'Yellow Hammer'* *is an upright evergreen with tubular flowers that often bloom again in autumn.*

Rhododendron yakushimanum *is a compact, domed species with rose-pink flowers that fade to white or pale pink.*

Spring bouquets

When spring bulbs start to bloom outside in the garden, match their vibrant displays with colour indoors by growing flowering house plants. Azaleas, cyclamen, and cinerarias are traditional favourites, but you can give them a modern makeover by teaming them with funky or elegant containers to match your home.

Indian azalea *Rhododendron simsii*

Plant used
Rhododendron simsii
white hybrid

Height and spread
H & S 35cm (14in)

Aspect
Bright, but not
in direct sunlight

Temperature needs
12–15°C (54–59°F)

Suitable pot size
15cm (6in)

**Suitable container
material**
Plastic, inside a
decorative pot

Compost type
Ericaceous compost

Indian azaleas are compact, evergreen house plants that produce masses of flowers in a wide range of colours, including white, pink, purple, and red, together with bicolours. Although they are related to hardy rhododendrons, these tender types need winter protection, requiring a minimum temperature of 12°C (54°F) to thrive. However, they also suffer in a hot environment, so try to keep temperatures below 24°C (75°F). In winter, buy plants with a profusion of tight buds; avoid those with lots of open flowers, as the display will be short lived.

GROWING AZALEAS
Place Indian azaleas in a cool, brightly lit area, but not in direct sunlight. Keep the compost moist while plants are in bud and flowering, ideally using rainwater as they are not fond of hard tap water. Dry compost at this key time can cause both buds and blooms to fall prematurely. Feed azaleas every fortnight with fertilizer formulated for acid-loving plants, and remove faded blooms to extend the flower display.

TOP TIP: SUMMER CARE
After plants have finished flowering, do not feed, and water less frequently, allowing the compost to almost dry out before giving more.

In summer, repot plants in ericaceous compost, and after all danger of frost has passed, place your azaleas in a sheltered, shaded area outside. Increase watering and start feeding again as the plant comes back into growth. Bring plants back indoors in early autumn before frosts threaten.

Plant Indian azaleas in plastic pots and set these inside more decorative containers in a cool room indoors.

Cyclamen *Cyclamen persicum*

Plant used
Cyclamen persicum

Height and spread
H 20cm (8in)
S 15cm (6in)

Aspect
Bright, but not
in direct sunlight

Temperature needs
Min. 13–16°C
(55–61°F) in winter

Suitable pot size
15cm (6in)

Suitable container material
Plastic, inside a
decorative pot

Compost type
Soil-based compost,
eg, John Innes No 2

The swept-back petals and nest of marbled leaves can look old-fashioned when a cyclamen is grown in a dowdy container, but give it a sleek glazed pot and this traditional house plant won't look out of place in a modern home. Slow to raise from seed, it's best to buy ready-grown plants. When flowering, keep the compost moist, and feed every fortnight with a high potash liquid feed. After the blooms have faded, stop watering and place the pot on its side until midsummer. Then repot into a slightly bigger pot, ensuring the tuber is just above the compost surface.

SITING PLANTS
Cyclamen wilt, foliage turns yellow, and plants perform poorly if they are in the wrong spot. They dislike warm dry air and too much light, and thrive on a cool, north-facing windowsill away from radiators. They also enjoy being misted occasionally to raise humidity levels.

Cyclamen persicum

Cineraria *Pericallis x hybrida*

Plant used
Pericallis x *hybrida*
Senetti Series

Height and spread
H 45cm (18in)
S 25cm (10in)

Aspect
Bright, but not
in direct sunlight

Temperature needs
Min. 7°C (45°F)

Suitable pot size
15cm (6in)

Suitable container material
Plastic, inside a
decorative pot

Compost type
Multi-purpose
compost

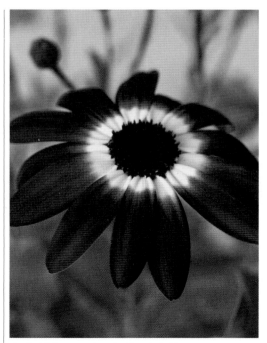

The bold flowers of *Pericallis* x *hybrida* Senetti Series

Popular winter and spring house plants that will brighten up your indoor space, cinerarias come in a wide range of colours. The large, daisy-like flowers that rise above clumps of triangular-shaped leaves are available in pink, white, blue, purple, coppery orange, and red, often sporting a contrasting white centre. Technically perennials, cinerarias are best added to the compost heap after flowering as they are difficult to maintain and rarely perform well the following year. Keep plants healthy by never allowing the compost to dry out, and feed every fortnight with a balanced liquid fertilizer.

GROWING PLANTS FROM SEED
Although plants are readily available, it's easy to grow cinerarias from seed. At any time from spring to midsummer, fill a small pot with seed compost, and sow on the surface. Cover pots with a plastic bag sealed with a rubber band, and put in a light place to germinate. Remove the bag when seedlings appear.

Roses for containers

The classic choice for a country garden scheme, roses tend to need plenty of elbow room to produce their romantic, often scented, flowers. However, breeders have developed many equally beautiful compact forms, perfect for containers. Most rose nurseries offer a good selection and they are all easy to care for.

Plants used
Rosa Regensberg; *Bacopa* 'Snowflake' (syn. *Sutera cordata* 'Snowflake')

Height and spread
Rosa: H & S 75cm (30in); *Bacopa:* H 10cm (4in) S 30cm (12in)

Aspect
Full sun

Temperature needs
Rosa is hardy to -23°C (-10°F); *Bacopa* is not hardy below 0°C (32°F)

Suitable pot size
45cm (18in)

Suitable container material
Stone, terracotta, glazed ceramic, plastic

Compost type
Soil-based compost, eg, John Innes No 3

When selecting a rose for a container, look for patio roses or miniatures, which are ideal for small pots. Many compact ground cover shrubs, standards, and patio climbers are also suitable, but need larger containers. *Rosa* Regensberg (syn. 'Macyoumis') is a floriferous patio rose, with large sweetly scented blooms that look as if they have been hand painted. Roses like plenty of air and light, and don't take kindly to large plant partners that will steal many of the nutrients in the compost. However, a low growing carpet of *Bacopa* is perfect, softening the sides of a container with its dainty foliage and small white flowers.

When planting a rose in a container make sure that the graft union (knobbly join between the roots and stem) is just beneath the surface of the compost. If you're planting a rose from late autumn to late winter, trim back stems to 10cm (4in) in length to encourage lots of new growth in spring. Place the pots in a sunny position and water plants freely in spring and summer.

PRUNING ROSES

Remove faded blooms regularly, as this promotes the production of more flowers and will extend the display. Prune plants annually in early spring to retain an attractive shape and to remove dead, diseased, or spindly growth. To rejuvenate roses, in late winter or early spring cut back all the stems by half to healthy buds, or to within 8cm (3in) of the previous year's growth.

TOP TIP: FEEDING ROSES

Roses are thirsty and hungry plants. As well as watering regularly, feed them every couple of weeks with a fertilizer high in potash to encourage flowering – you can buy products formulated specifically for roses. Also, get plants off to a flying start in spring by mixing slow-release fertilizer granules into the compost surface.

Centre: **Choose pots in contrasting colours** *to bring out the hues of your patio roses, such as these blue containers and pale pink* Rosa *Regensberg.*

Rose choices

Rosa *Sweet Dream* *is a bushy patio rose with sweetly scented, fully double, apricot-coloured blooms.*

Rosa *Stacey Sue* *is a continuous-flowering miniature rose, with fully double, soft pink blooms.*

Rosa *Queen Mother*, *a floriferous patio rose, produces clusters of beautiful pink flowers and glossy mid-green foliage.*

Rosa *Drummer Boy* *is a dwarf bush that bears clusters of double, lipstick-red flowers throughout summer.*

Rosa *Anna Ford* *has lightly fragrant, semi-double flowers that start off bright orange and turn red as they age.*

Rosa *Baby Masquerade* *is a miniature rose ideal for a small pot, with yellowish flowers edged with pink.*

Rosa *Chatsworth* *bears a succession of deep pink flowers from summer until early winter that fade as they mature.*

Rosa *Baby Love* *is a patio rose that produces canary-yellow summer flowers followed by orange hips.*

SUMMER BLOOMS

Shrubby staples

Shrubs provide great background colour and structure for more showy perennial flowers, but some also perform a star turn of their own with summer blooms and other decorative features. Hebes offer pretty evergreen foliage, hydrangeas produce beautiful flowers and attractive seedheads, and hibiscus have large blooms and a graceful shape and form.

Hydrangeas

Plants used
Hydrangea
macrophylla
Endless Summer
Twist-n-Shout

Height and spread
H & S 1m (3ft)

Aspect
Dappled shade

Temperature needs
Hardy to -15°C (5°F)

Suitable pot size
45cm (18in)

Suitable container material
Stone, terracotta, glazed ceramic, plastic

Compost type
Soil-based compost, eg, John Innes No 3 (some need ericaceous compost)

Offering large heads of summer flowers in a wide range of colours, hydrangeas also sport decorative seedheads in autumn and winter. Forms of *H. macrophylla*, known as mopheads, have rounded domes of flowers, while *H. paniuculata* produces cone-like flowerheads. New mophead cultivars provide even greater value with extended flowering seasons. The Endless Summer range is a good example, with long-lasting flowers that look like scattered confetti, and red-tinted autumn foliage.

Hydrangeas like moist soil conditions, and plants should be covered with fleece in spring to protect them from late frosts. Most also benefit from annual pruning, but the method you use depends on the species (*see Top Tip box below*).

COLOUR OPTIONS
Hydrangeas come in shades of pink, red, purple, blue, white, and near-green. The colour of the flowers is determined by the compost. Pink types need alkaline soil, while ericaceous compost is required for blue and purple forms.

> ### TOP TIP: PRUNING HYDRANGEAS
>
> Allow the spent flowers of *H. macrophylla* to remain on the plant over winter to protect the new growth below. In mid-spring, use secateurs to cut stems down to the first strong pair of buds. To prune forms of *H. paniculata*, which flower on stems made in the current year, prune back all the stems in early spring to a pair of healthy buds about 25cm (10in) from the base. If either hydrangea becomes congested, remove a quarter of the older branches in spring.

Hydrangea *Endless Summer* *blooms all summer on old and new stems, and should be pruned like a mophead.*

Hebes

Plant used
Hebe 'Johnny Day'

Height and spread
H & S 60cm (24in)

Aspect
Sun, sheltered

Temperature needs
Hardy to -5°C (23°F)

Suitable pot size
20cm (8in)

Suitable container material
Terracotta, stone, glazed ceramic

Compost type
Soil-based compost, eg, John Innes No 3

Grown for their handsome evergreen leaves and spikes of blue, purple, white, or pink flowers, hebes make excellent container specimens. Some are large, so check labels before you buy and select those that are naturally compact, such as 'Johnny Day', 'Silver Queen', 'Watson's Pink', 'Rosie', and Hebe topiaria. All are magnets for butterflies and bees, and require little maintenance apart from regular watering in the growing season, and some slow-release general fertilizer in spring.

OVERWINTERING TENDER TYPES
Few hebes enjoy being whipped by cold winds and some are quite tender, so unless your garden is very sheltered, protect their foliage during windy, wintry weather with horticultural fleece. If you have a tender type, move it to a cool, light, frost-free place indoors over winter.

The young foliage of *Hebe* 'Johnny Day' is deep purple.

Hibiscus *Hibiscus syriacus*

Plant used
Hibiscus syriacus Blue Bird (syn 'Oiseau Bleu')

Height and spread
H 2m (6ft)
S 1.2m (4ft)

Aspect
Full sun

Temperature needs
Hardy to -15°C (5°F)

Suitable pot size
30–45cm (12–18in)

Suitable container material
Stone, terracotta, metal, glazed ceramic

Compost type
Well-drained, soil-based compost, eg, John Innes No 2

If you want to add a Mediterranean touch to your patio, terrace, or garden, you can't beat a shrubby hibiscus for pure flower power. The blooms come in many different colours and sizes, but Blue Bird is one of the best, with large purple-blue flowers with cream centres set against a foil of dark green, lobed leaves. Perfect for a sunny, sheltered area, this deciduous shrub will put on a head-turning spectacle from midsummer to early autumn. Plant in a large container of soil-based compost, such as John Innes No 2, and water plants regularly in summer. Add some slow-release granular fertilizer to the compost in spring.

WHEN TO PRUNE
For the best show of flowers, prune plants in spring. Start by shortening last year's shoots to maintain an attractive shape and bushy habit. Then remove any dead, diseased, or crossing branches that may rub each other and cause a wound. Finally, take out some older stems, to prevent congested growth.

Hibiscus *Blue Bird* is covered with purple-blue flowers in late summer.

SUMMER BLOOMS

Versatile dahlias

Flamboyant, glamorous, and alluring, dahlias are the divas of the horticultural world. Emerging on slender stems above decorative foliage, their head-turning blooms draw the crowds from mid- to late summer until the first frosts in autumn. Provide simple containers that do not distract from your star performers.

Plants used
Dahlia 'Gallery Art Deco'; *Thymus* 'Silver Posie'

Height and spread
Dahlia: H & S 45cm (18in); *Thymus:* H 30cm (12in) S 45cm (18in)

Aspect
Full sun

Temperature needs
Not reliably hardy below 0°C (32°F)

Suitable pot size
30cm (12in)

Suitable container material
Glazed ceramic, stone, terracotta

Compost type
Soil-based compost, eg, John Innes No 3

Perfect for illuminating a sun-baked patio or border, dahlias comprise a large group of tuberous perennials ranging in height from 30cm (12in) to 3.5m (11ft) whoppers. Natives of Mexico, dahlia blooms are incredibly diverse, and include plain, striped, and speckled types. You can also choose from flowers resembling little pompoms, waterlilies, or spiky balls of narrow, pointed petals, known as cactus dahlias, and leaves range from bright green to smouldering dark purple. While many are too large to squeeze into a container, plenty more have been bred for patio pots, including the Gallery Series, which are compact and floriferous, and available in a range of colours. Dahlias make striking centrepieces in large summer arrangements, alongside petunias and foliage plants, such as variegated thyme.

GROWING DAHLIAS FROM TUBERS
Dormant tubers can be planted indoors in mid-spring. Half-fill a 10cm (4in) pot with multi-purpose compost, place the tuber on top and cover with compost. Set pots on a light windowsill or in a greenhouse, but do not water. When shoots appear, water lightly – you can increase the amount of water you give them as they grow. The dahlias will be ready for planting into larger containers outdoors when all danger of frost has passed in late spring. Water plants regularly in the growing season, and apply a liquid tomato fertilizer every couple of weeks in summer.

TOP TIP: OVERWINTERING TUBERS

When frost blackens the foliage, prise the tubers from the compost and remove as much of the soil as you can. Cut back the stems to about 15cm (6in) and allow the tubers to dry for a few weeks. Place in seed trays filled with dry compost and store in a frost-free place until spring. Then pot them up as described above.

*Centre: **The dazzling orange and red flowers** of Dahlia 'Gallery Art Deco' explode from a cool frill of scented thyme.*

Choosing dahlias

Dahlia *'Tally Ho'* *produces post-box red flowers that are shown to perfection against dark greeny-black foliage.*

Dahlia *'Pink Giraffe'* *is a knee-high variety with pink and white variegated flowers with swept-back petals.*

Dahlia *Gallery Series* *comprises a range of compact dahlias named after painters and art movements.*

Dahlia *'Small World'* *has long stems of pure white pompom flowers held above neat clumps of green foliage.*

Dahlia *'Yellow Hammer'* *is a dwarf dahlia, with clear yellow flowers and contrasting near-black foliage.*

Dahlia *'Purple Gem'* *is ideal for a large container, and produces hand-sized, deep purple, cactus-style flowers.*

Dahlia *'Roxy'* *is a popular form, with a striking combination of dark purple foliage and magenta-pink flowers.*

Dahlia *'David Howard'* *produces smoky-orange flowers held in sharp relief against a foil of dark leaves.*

Dazzling highlights

Dull corners of a patio, bare walls, or an empty windowledge can be quickly transformed into an exuberant area with a few prized summer flowers. Gerberas, pelargoniums, and blanket flowers are among the best for injecting intense colour with their long-lasting blooms. All are drought-resistant and make excellent container plants.

Gerbera

SUMMER BLOOMS

Plant used
Gerbera (Landscape Series) 'Mount Rushmore'

Height and spread
H & S 35cm (14in)

Aspect
Sun or partial shade

Temperature needs
Min. 5°C (41°F)

Suitable pot size
20cm (8in)

Suitable container material
Terracotta, plastic, stone, glazed ceramic

Compost type
Multi-purpose compost

A striking group of perennials, gerberas have daisy-like flowers that sit like saucers on top of stout stems and bloom all summer long. There are many suitable for containers, including the Landscape Series, a group of herbaceous perennials that have been bred for their compact growth and long season of large flowers. Among the showy varieties in this series is the pinky-red 'Mount Rushmore', pink bicoloured 'Everglades', and 'Klondike', which has orange flowers. Apart from adding a splash of colour to gardens, the flowers can also be cut for indoor displays.

PLANT CARE
Ready-grown plants are available from garden centres and nurseries, and can be placed outside in pots of multi-purpose compost after the last frosts in late spring. Keep the compost damp and feed plants every four weeks with a balanced liquid fertilizer. Remove faded flowers to prolong the floral display, and bring plants back indoors before frosts threaten in autumn.

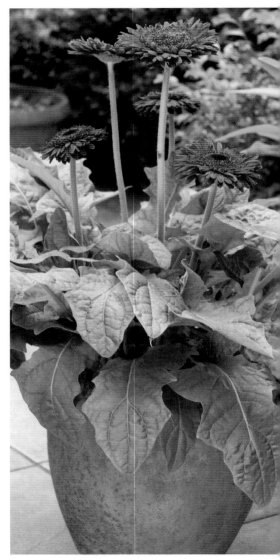

Gerbera *'Mount Rushmore'* needs no competition from planting partners to make an impact on a patio or terrace.

TOP TIP: PLANT HARDY GERBERAS

Most gerberas are frost tender and cannot be left outside all year, but a new breed of hardy gerberas is now available, such as the Everlast and Garvinea Series. Perfect for growing in pots in summer, they can then be overwintered in a sunny area in a border, or given a sheltered site by the house.

Pelargonium

Plant used
Pelargonium 'Trend
Scarlet Red'; *Lobelia*

Height and spread
H 25cm (10in)
S 15cm (6in)

Aspect
Full sun

Temperature needs
Not reliably hardy
below 0°C (32°F)

Suitable pot size
15cm (6in) or larger

**Suitable container
material**
Terracotta, glazed
ceramic, stone

Compost type
Soil-based compost,
eg, John Innes No 2

Scarlet pelargoniums make a good partner for lobelia.

Evocative of French and Spanish courtyard gardens, pelargoniums lend a Mediterranean tone to designs, and are prized for their long-lasting flowers. Countless different varieties are available, in shades of red, white, pink, purple, and orange. Blooms are held on stout stems above rounded foliage, which is often scented, variegated, marked, or veined.

ANNUAL CARE

Feed plants every month while in flower with a high-potash fertilizer, and water regularly – once a week should suffice for most containers. Remove fading flowerheads to encourage more to form. Pelargoniums can survive year after year if you cut the stems back by about two-thirds before frost threatens in autumn. Stow pots in a frost-free place in winter, keeping the compost slightly damp, but not too wet.

Blanket flower *Gaillardia*

Plant used
Gaillardia x
grandiflora

Height and spread
H 90cm (3ft)
S 45cm (18in)

Aspect
Full sun

Temperature needs
Fully hardy

Suitable pot size
30cm (12in)

**Suitable container
material**
Terracotta, glazed
ceramic, stone

Compost type
Soil-based compost,
eg, John Innes No 3

With daisy-like blooms that can measure up to 14cm (5½in) in diameter, blanket flowers are eye-catching, bushy perennials that perform continuously from early summer to autumn. The compact cultivars of *Gaillardia* x *grandiflora* are most suitable for pots. Try 'Kobold', with yellow-tipped red petals; 'Goldkobold', which has golden blooms; or 'Dazzler', with its yellow-edged orange blooms.

Plant in pots of soil-based compost and set plants in a sunny spot. Keep the pots well watered, feed with a balanced liquid fertilizer every month after flower buds appear, and deadhead regularly to prolong blooming.

GROWING PLANTS FROM SEED

Although many varieties of blanket flower are readily available as plugs or young plants, there are some that will flower in their first year if grown from seed. In late winter, fill small pots with compost, sow seeds and cover with a thin layer of vermiculite. Keep at 13–18°C (55–64°F), and when seedlings are large enough to handle, separate the roots carefully and grow plants on in individual pots.

Gaillardia x *grandiflora* has long-lasting blooms.

SUMMER BLOOMS

Alpine collection

As the saying goes, the best gifts come in small packages, and this is certainly true of alpines. Tiny but tough, many provide a year-round show of textured evergreen foliage, together with a dazzling array of colourful blooms from spring until autumn. Collect together a few with different attributes in a pot for a dynamic display.

Plants used
Mixed alpines

Height and spread
H up to 15cm (6in)
S up to 30cm (12in)

Aspect
Full sun

Temperature needs
Fully hardy

Suitable pot size
15–20cm (6–8in)

Suitable container material
Terracotta, stone

Compost type
Soil-based compost, eg, John Innes No 3, with extra grit

Alpines are a diverse group of miniature beauties that include bulbs, perennials, and conifers, as well as diminutive trees and shrubs. Some form ground-hugging mats, just 1cm (½in) tall, while the largest will slowly grow to reach a modest 60cm (24in). Many of the varieties within this Lilliputian tribe are evergreen, with beautiful foliage for 12 months of the year, but it's the flowers that provide the razzle dazzle. Blooms come in a wide variety of colours, shapes, and sizes, and by choosing plants carefully you can have a succession of flowers from spring until early autumn. One of the most attractive ways to show them off is to plant a collection in a stone trough or old ceramic sink to create a miniature alpine landscape. Smaller groups also look good in pots, together with succulents, but check plant labels and bring containers under cover in winter if you choose tender succulent varieties, such as *Pachyphytum* and *Oscularia*.

PLANTING AND CARING FOR ALPINES
Alpines hate wet roots and require well-drained compost to thrive. Use soil-based John Innes No 3, mixed with some extra horticultural grit, which should be washed first to remove any residues. Ensure plants are not set too deeply in the soil, as this may rot their foliage, and cover the surface of the compost with decorative gravel to keep the lower leaves dry. Also, set your containers on pot feet or pebbles to maintain good drainage.

To keep plants healthy and vigorous, place them in a sunny hot spot, and water once or twice a week in the growing season. Remove any dead or tatty foliage when you see it.

Sempervivum arachnoideum *is known as the cobweb houseleek, due to the fine white hairs that cover the foliage.*

TOP TIP: UNUSUAL CONTAINERS

Alpines grow in thin, dry soils in their natural habitats, and their drought tolerance makes them easy to grow in tiny pots and unusual containers. Be really creative and try growing them in recycled food tins, large shells, hollowed-out gourds, colanders, or even old boots. There's no limit to what you can use; the only requirement is that your receptacle has a big-enough gap for you to push in some gritty compost, and that it has drainage holes in the bottom.

Alpine plant options

Helianthemum *'Rhodanthe Carneum'*, *is a low-growing, spreading shrub with masses of pink flowers in summer.*

Sedum rupestre *is an evergreen with succulent leaves and short spikes of bright yellow summer flowers.*

Phlox subulata *'Lilacina', known as moss phlox due to its hairy leaves, has lavender-blue flowers in late spring.*

Sempervivum tectorum *is a dramatic houseleek that produces dense mats of robust, burgundy-red leaf rosettes.*

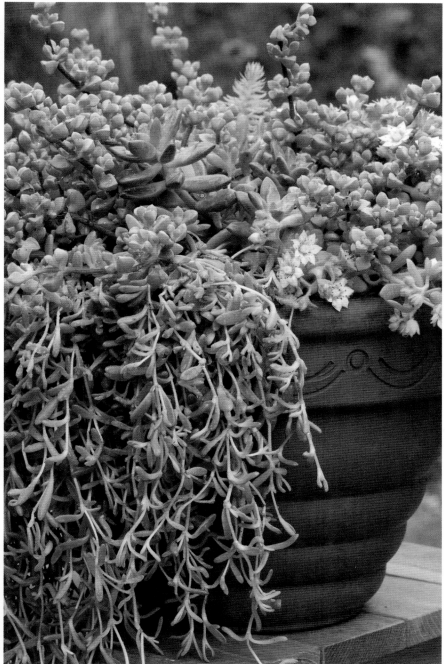

Mix together alpines and succulents *with different habits, shapes, and foliage to create an eye-catching summer display. Those here include* Delosperma, Sedum sedoides, Sedum rupestre, *and the tender* Oscularia deltoides *and* Pachyphytum.

Outdoor aquatics

If you would like a pond but think your garden is too small, make a container water feature. Many aquatic plants grown for their attractive foliage or beautiful flowers will thrive in the shallow water, allowing even the most space-strapped gardeners to enjoy dwarf water lilies and a wealth of other colourful aquatics.

Water lilies *Nymphaea*

SUMMER BLOOMS

Plant used
Nymphaea odorata var. *minor*

Height and spread
S 45cm (18in); planting depth 25–30cm (10–12in)

Aspect
Partial shade, with sun for some of the day

Temperature needs
Hardy to -5°C (23°F)

Suitable pot size
Min. 45cm (18in) wide and 30cm (12in) deep

Suitable container material
Aquatic baskets inside watertight glazed terracotta, half-barrel, or plastic containers

Compost type
Aquatic compost

The undisputed stars of the garden aquatics, water lilies are elegant plants grown for their cup-shaped or star-like flowers, which appear from late spring until the first frosts. Although most need a large pool, many diminutive types are happy in a 30–45cm (12–18in) deep container.

Plant water lilies in aquatic baskets filled with aquatic compost, and place them in a watertight container, such as a glazed ceramic pot or half-barrel. Site containers in a partially shaded spot. Top up the water level in hot weather and remove dying leaves and flowers as you see them. Place lilies in a sheltered area close to the house, or a frost-free place over winter.

TOP TIP: CHOOSING TINY LILIES

There are many dwarf water lilies to choose from, but the following are among the best. *N. tetragona* has small pure white flowers; *N.* 'Pygmaea Rubra' bears rosy-red blooms; *N.* 'René Gérard' has delicate pink flowers (*right*); and *N.* 'Pygmaea Helvola' has tiny star-shaped yellow blooms.

Nymphaea odorata **var.** *minor produces small, fragrant, star-shaped blooms that look stunning in a glazed blue container.*

Beautiful buckets

Plants used
Equisetum hyemale;
Zantedeschia hybrid;
Lobelia siphilitica

Height and spread
Equisetum hyemale:
H 75cm (30in) S 30cm
(12in); *Zantedeschia*
hybrid: H & S 30cm
(12in); *Lobelia*
siphilitica: H 60cm
(24in) S 30cm (12in)

Aspect
Partial shade

Temperature needs
Fully hardy, except
Zantedeschia, which
is not hardy below
0°C (32°F)

Suitable pot size
Min. 30cm (12in)

Suitable container
material
Aquatic baskets
inside any
watertight container

Compost type
Aquatic compost

A colourful plastic or metal bucket makes an effective container for a group of compact aquatics. Not only will it accommodate several of these fascinating plants, but it is small enough to squeeze on to the tiniest patio, terrace or balcony. Good choices include the cardinal flower, *Lobelia siphilitica*; *Equisetum hyemale,* with its striped, bamboo-like stems; and *Zantedeschia,* the tender forms of which come in many colours and are ideal for containers, as they can be easily brought under cover over winter.

Plant in one or two aquatic baskets filled with aquatic compost, adding a layer of gravel on top to help stabilize the soil surface, and set these in the bucket. If possible, fill with rainwater from a butt, leaving a 5cm (2in) gap between the water surface and lip of the container, and place in a partially shaded spot. Ensure that the plants are at the correct depth of water, raising them up on large pebbles if necessary.

CARING FOR AQUATIC PLANTS
Regularly remove dead and dying leaves, and any flowers as they start to fade. When the baskets become congested with growth, remove the plants, divide and replant them in new baskets. Any tender plants must be moved to a light, frost-free place over winter.

Equisetum hyemale and Zantedeschia are best planted with their root balls 10cm (4in) below the water; the blue Lobelia siphilitica is happier with its root ball at water level.

CHOOSING AQUATICS FOR CONTAINERS

Lobelia cardinalis *produces lofty spires clad with red flowers, which make the cardinal flower stand out. Set the top of the root ball at water level and protect plants over winter.*

Juncus ensifolius *is a shallow water lover best planted with its root ball at the surface. It makes a clump of grassy leaves topped by tiny brown pompom flowerheads.*

Iris laevigata, *commonly known as the Japanese water iris, likes its roots 10cm (4in) below the surface. Its blue flowers are held on tall stems, and it's best in a large pot.*

Caltha palustris *has beautiful buttercup-like spring flowers, held on 60cm (24in) stems that contrast well with the round leaves. Set the top of the root ball at water level.*

Star performers

There are many tender plants that put on great flower displays in the garden in summer, but perhaps none are as spectacular as these three. Rose of China, lantana, and flowering maples perform their star turns at this time of year, bearing exotic blooms over a long period. Before frosts threaten in autumn, bring them back inside to see out the winter in the warmth of your home.

SUMMER BLOOMS

Rose of China *Hibiscus rosa-sinensis*

Plant used
Hibiscus rosa-sinensis 'Athene'

Height and spread
H 1.2m (4ft)
S 60cm (24in)

Aspect
Bright, but out of midday sun in summer

Temperature
Min. 10°C (50°F)

Suitable pot size
30cm (12in)

Suitable container material
Stone, glazed ceramic, terracotta, plastic

Compost type
Soil-based compost, eg, John Innes No 3

The large flowers of the rose of China possess exotic good looks and its many cultivars come in vibrant shades, ranging from dark red to yellow and white. The bold flowers often measure 10cm (4in) in diameter, and feature a cluster of elegant stamens in the centre. Most have glossy, dark, evergreen leaves, but 'Cooperi' has showy pink, white, and green variegated foliage. Available as standards or as bushy shrubs, rose of China needs protection from frosts, but thrives in a sunny site outdoors during the summer.

WATERING AND FEEDING

Pot up plants in soil-based compost in a large container. Water regularly in summer, and feed monthly with a balanced liquid fertilizer to encourage a great show of colour. In early spring, apply a slow-release granular fertilizer. Before frosts threaten, move plants to a bright room indoors and reduce watering, allowing the compost to almost dry out between applications.

TOP TIP: DEADHEADING AND PRUNING

For a long-lasting floral spectacle, remove faded flowers regularly to ensure plants do not waste energy on producing seeds. Plants do not require much pruning; just reduce the length of stems in late winter to keep plants within bounds and maintain an attractive shape. This will also encourage bushy growth.

Hibiscus rosa-sinensis **'Athene'** *produces breathtaking golden blooms with red eyes.*

Lantana *Lantana camara*

Plant used
Lantana camara
'Sunkiss'

Height and spread
H & S 1.2m (4ft)

Aspect
Full sun

Temperature
Min. 10°C (50°F)

Suitable pot size
30cm (12in)

Suitable container material
Terracotta, stone, glazed ceramic, plastic

Compost type
Soil-based compost, eg, John Innes No 3

Butterflies love the nectar-rich flowers of this evergreen shrub from South Africa and South and Central America. The flowerheads comprise tiny flowers that open in succession from the outer edges to the centre. Plants are often sold as standards with a bushy, lollipop-shaped head.

Grow *Lantana* in a bright place indoors and in summer place pots outside in a sheltered, sunny area. Water plants regularly and feed monthly with a balanced liquid fertilizer after flower buds appear. Also apply a slow-release granular fertilizer in spring.

COLOUR CHOICES

Available in white, yellow, orange, pink, and red, the flowers often appear two-tone as they open from buds of different hues. 'Sunkiss' has orange and red flowers, 'Feston Rose' is pink and yellow, and 'Mine d'Or' has golden yellow blooms.

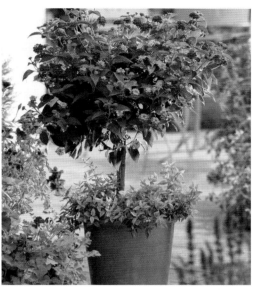

Lantana with *Abelia* x *grandiflora* 'Kaleidoscope'.

Flowering maple *Abutilon* x *hybridum*

Plant used
Abutilon x *hybridum*

Height and spread
H 1.2m (4ft)
S 60cm (24in)

Aspect
Light, bright position

Temperature
Not hardy below 0°C (32°F)

Suitable pot size
30cm (12in)

Suitable container material
Terracotta, stone, glazed ceramic, plastic

Compost type
Soil-based compost, eg, John Innes No 3

Part of a large plant group, flowering maples are named after the shape of their leaves, not because they are related to maple trees. Plants are available in many colours, including white, yellow, orange, and pink, as well as red. Choose a large container for your *Abutilon*, as plants can grow up to 1.2m (4ft) in height, and create a striking scheme by teaming a scarlet-flowered plant with a simple white, glazed pot with a cracked antique finish.

YEAR-ROUND CARE

Flowering maples are tender, and best grown in a conservatory or a light room indoors; move them to a sunny position in the garden when the threat of frost has passed. Ensure the compost does not dry out in summer and feed monthly with a balanced liquid fertilizer to prolong the flower display. In winter, when the plant is under cover, reduce watering, and apply a slow-release granular fertilizer in early spring. Prune plants in autumn to maintain a good shape.

Flowering maples produce vibrant blooms.

Small jewels

They may be small, but these house plants make up for their size with a long floral display of delicate blooms. Available in a rainbow of colours, Cape primroses will flower on and off all year, while African violets brighten the home from late spring and throughout summer. Both plants are quite easy to care for, and thrive on east- or west-facing windowsills.

Cape primroses *Streptocarpus*

SUMMER BLOOMS

Plants used
Streptocarpus 'Gwen';
Streptocarpus 'Katie'

Height and spread
H & S 30cm (12in)

Aspect
Bright, but avoid
direct sunlight

Temperature
Min. 13°C (55°F)
in winter

Suitable pot size
20cm (8in)

**Suitable container
material**
Any

Compost type
Multi-purpose
compost

Cape primroses form a compact, bushy rosette of heavily textured, strappy leaves beneath a bouquet of dainty flowers held on slender stalks. They come in many vibrant single colours, or produce two-toned, striped, or veined blooms in striking hues. The plants are most floriferous in the summer months, but the Crystal Series of *Streptocarpus* flower on and off all year round.

Place Cape primroses in a bright position, but ensure they are not in direct sunlight or the flower colours will start to fade and leaves may scorch. An east- or west-facing windowsill is ideal. Plants can be moved outside in the summer, but ensure they are in dappled shade.

Streptocarpus **'Gwen' and 'Katie'**
*make a beautiful pair, with their
medley of white and purple shades.
The glass-bead mulch lends a hint
of glamour to the display.*

WATERING AND FEEDING

Water plants regularly, allowing the compost to dry out completely between applications, and feed monthly while they are in flower with a half-strength liquid fertilizer that is high in potash. Most plants need a rest over winter, but some, including the Crystal Series or winter-flowering forms, require feeding and watering as usual.

TOP TIP: WINTER CARE

For most *Streptocarpus*, reduce watering in winter and do not feed plants. Cape primroses can remain on an east- or west-facing windowsill, but they will need to be protected from very cold conditions, so bring them into the room at night if your windows are single-glazed. Remove dead flowers and leaves, and keep a close eye out for mealy bugs, taking action to control the pest if necessary (*see p.243*). Increase watering again in the spring.

African violets *Saintpaulia*

Plant used
Saintpaulia
Spectra-Color Series

Height and spread
H & S 25cm (10in)

Aspect
Bright position, not
in direct sunlight

Temperature
18–25°C (64–77°F)

Suitable pot size
15cm (6in)

Suitable container material
Plastic pots placed
inside a decorative
container

Compost type
Multi-purpose
compost

Considered unfashionable by many, today's African violets are a world apart from the single colours and sparsely flowering varieties of old. Modern breeding has led to a floriferous tribe of plants that put on a great display for much of the year, if you give them the care they need. The single, semi-double, or double flowers are available in a wide range of shades, with petals that often have margins or centres of a different colour. Plants also range in size, from micro-miniatures, with leafy rosettes only 8cm (3in) in width and height, to large varieties measuring more than 40cm (16in).

Looking after African violets is easy. Water from below by standing pots in a tray of water until the top of the compost is moist. Allow the compost to dry out between waterings and feed every six weeks with a half-strength dose of liquid fertilizer that is high in potash. Place in a bright area in summer, out of direct sunlight.

Like all African violets, the Spectra-Color hybrids, grown here with mind-your-own-business, need a site by a south-facing window in winter.

CHOOSING AFRICAN VIOLET VARIETIES

S. 'Fancy Pants' *is a beautiful form, with a rosette of dark leaves beneath a mass of sophisticated, single, white flowers with frilly petals edged in pinkish-red.*

S. 'Delft' *is a real head-turner, with its wavy-edged blooms above dark leaves. The large, semi-double cornflower-blue flowers have contrasting yellow centres.*

S. 'Kristi Marie' *is a relatively large plant, spreading up to 40cm (16in). It has dark green leaves that provide the perfect foil for its white-edged, bright red flowers.*

S. 'Rococo Anna' *is grown for its large, double, deep-pink flowers, which are borne in profusion above a rosette of mid-green leaves with lighter undersides.*

Topiary designs

The sharp outline of closely clipped topiary makes a compelling statement, adding structure and colour to a winter garden. So, whether you want a cone, spiral, dome, or a menagerie of animals, grab your shears and start clipping; or if you are wary of making your own, buy a ready-formed plant from a nursery.

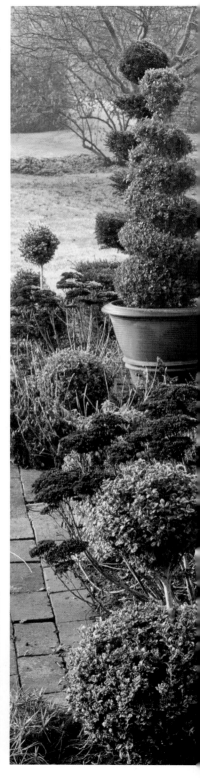

COLD-SEASON DISPLAYS

Plant used
Buxus sempervirens, (box) spiral

Height and spread
H 1.2m (4ft)
S 45cm (18in)

Aspect
Sun or partial shade

Temperature needs
Hardy to -15°C (5°F)

Suitable pot size
45cm (18in)

Suitable container material
Terracotta, stone, wood, metal

Compost type
Soil-based compost, eg, John Innes No 3

Whether they are grown in a pair of sleek galvanized steel containers outside your front door or in terracotta pots on a patio, topiary shapes are guaranteed to catch the eye. Balls, cones, cubes, lollipops, spirals, or cloud-pruned trees add a dash of formal elegance whatever the weather, but they are most treasured in winter when there's little of interest in the garden, providing much-needed structure, texture, and verdant colour.

Holly, privet, shrubby honeysuckle (*Lonicera nitida*), viburnum, laurel, phillyrea, yew, bay, and many other evergreen plants respond well to close clipping, but the most popular topiary plant is box. If you're adventurous, you could start a piece of topiary off from scratch, but it's far easier to buy a ready-trained shape that you can maintain with a pair of sharp secateurs, clippers, or topiary shears. Ensure that pots of topiary are kept well watered and work some slow-release fertilizer granules into the compost in spring. Also feed with a liquid fertilizer after clipping.

WHEN TO PRUNE

Most topiary should be pruned in early summer and again in late summer to give it a crisp outline over winter. However, yew only needs pruning once in midsummer, while fast-growing shrubs, such as box, may need cutting up to four times a year. It's possible to trim simple shapes, like cones and balls, by eye, but for more accurate straight edges use a cane as a guide.

*Centre: **Box spirals provide a vertical accent** in a winter border, flanked by contrasting topiaries and the rich bronze seedheads of sedums.*

TOP TIP: TRIMMING SPIRALS

Topiary spirals may look like they would be tricky to keep in shape, but they are easy to maintain. Working from top to bottom, shape the upper surface of the spiral, removing the foliage as far back as the main stem. Work your way down the spiral, maintaining its curved edges and standing back now and then to check the shape.

Plants for topiary

Ilex crenata *'Mariesii'* is a very slow-growing form of Japanese holly with tiny leaves ideal for shaping.

Lonicera nitida *'Baggesen's Gold'*, or shrubby honeysuckle, has golden foliage that grows densely if clipped.

Hedera helix *is common ivy. Its fast-growing, leafy stems can be easily manipulated over topiary frames.*

Viburnum tinus *'Variegatum'* is a bushy shrub with gold-edged green leaves, perfect for simple shapes.

Taxus baccata*, or yew, responds well to close clipping and is ideal for geometric or intricate topiary shapes.*

Laurus nobilis *is the herb, bay. Its bushy form is often used for lollipop shapes and pyramids in a herb garden.*

Autumnal effects

If your displays start to flag as autumn approaches, give them a boost with dainty blooms, dramatic foliage, and bright, cheerful berries. Michaelmas daisies come in many colours and are ideal for late floral displays, while many shrubs grown for their fiery leaves or bead-like fruits grow well in containers, boosting drab patios and borders.

Bedding asters *Callistephus* species

COLD-SEASON DISPLAYS

Plant used
Bedding asters;
Bacopa (syn. *Sutera cordata*)

Height and spread
Asters: H & S 25cm (10in); bacopa:
S 30cm (12in)

Aspect
Full sun

Temperature needs
Not hardy below
0°C (32°F)

Suitable pot size
30cm (12in)

Suitable container material
Basket, terracotta, stone

Compost type
Multi-purpose compost

Use a wicker basket for a cottage garden-style scheme of bedding asters and late-flowering trailing plants. Set your basket on a bench or pebbles to aid drainage.

Don't despair if your garden looks a bit jaded following a spectacular show of summer colour. Plant some bedding asters and you'll be rewarded with a stunning display of flowers that will last well into autumn. These compact annual bedding plants are *Callistephus*, and are not to be confused with the genus *Aster*.

To make a rustic container, line a basket with a plastic sheet punctured with drainage holes. Add multi-purpose compost and plant a mix of large- and small-flowered bedding asters, together with trailing *Bacopa*. Place in the sun and keep plants well watered for a long display.

TOP TIP: CHOOSING ASTERS FOR POTS

Annual bedding asters provide a season of colour, but for a show year after year, grow perennial species. The New York Michaelmas daisy, or *Aster novi-belgii*, has the brightest colours, while *Aster amellus* (right) is compact and floriferous. Both are great for pots.

Autumn leaves

Plant used
Hydrangea
quercifolia

Height and spread
H & S 1.2m (4ft)

Aspect
Sun or partial shade

Temperature needs
Fully hardy

Suitable pot size
45cm (18in)

Suitable container material
Terracotta, glazed
ceramic, stone

Compost type
Soil-based compost,
eg, John Innes No 3

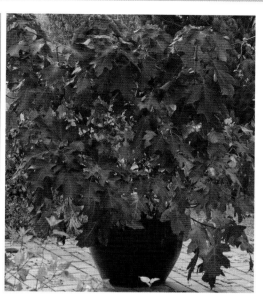

Hydrangea quercifolia **makes a mound of fiery foliage.**

Many shrubs earn their keep in containers by providing gardens with breathtaking autumn colour. Commonly known as oak leaf hydrangea, *Hydrangea quercifolia* is among the best, and produces an attractive mound of deeply lobed green leaves that in autumn take a dramatic turn as they fire up in shades of red and purple before falling. Other gems with superb autumn colour include the Japanese maples (*see pp.68–69*); a slow-growing form of smoke bush, *Cotinus coggygria* 'Young Lady'; the winged spindle bush *Euonymus alatus* 'Compactus'; the Eastern redbud *Cercis canadensis* 'Forest Pansy'; and *Liquidambar styraciflua* 'Gumball', a compact sweet gum with burnt orange foliage.

All are sizable shrubs and require large pots or half barrels and soil-based compost. Keep plants well watered, and feed annually in early spring with an all-purpose granular ferilizer.

Berry choices

Plant used
Dwarf *Hypericum*
hybrid

Height and spread
H 1m (3ft)
S 1.5m (5ft)

Aspect
Full sun or partial
shade

Temperature needs
Fully hardy

Suitable pot size
30cm (12in)

Suitable container material
Terracotta, glazed
ceramic, stone

Compost type
Soil-based compost,
eg, John Innes No 3

Berried plants add colour and form to an autumn patio display. Good choices include dwarf hybrids of *Hypericum*, such as *H*. 'Magical Red', which bear colourful red or pink fruits following sunshine-yellow summer flowers, and *Cotoneaster salicifolius* 'Gnom', which is a low-growing form that does well in a pot if clipped to keep it neat. Although its evergreen leaves make it welcome all year, the main season of interest is autumn when the branches drip with masses of bright red berries.

COLOUR CHOICE
For a blaze of berries, match a *Hypericum* or *Cotoneaster* with other fruit-bearing plants in showy colours. Make a statement with a *Callicarpa bodinieri* var. *giraldii* 'Profusion', whose amazing metallic violet berries cling to the bare branches in autumn and winter, and *Viburnum opulus* 'Xanthocarpum' with its plump yellow berries. Plant all in large pots of soil-based compost, and feed in spring with an all-purpose granular fertilizer.

Many *Hypericum* species bear striking berries.

Evergreen grasses

If you're looking for an exciting way to create a fantastic spectacle during the cold months of the year, plant pots of evergreen grasses and sedges. Tough, graceful, and easy to care for, they provide a shot of colour to brighten the bleakest day, and are often topped with long-lasting seedheads that catch the light and rustle in the breeze.

COLD-SEASON DISPLAYS

Plants used
Stipa tenuissima;
Carex comans
'Bronze Perfection';
Eragrostis elliottii

Height and spread
Stipa: H & S 60cm
(24in); *Carex:* H 30cm
(12in) S 40cm (16in);
Eragrostis H 80cm
(32in) S 60cm (24in)

Aspect
Sun or partial shade

Temperature needs
Hardy to -15°C (5°F)
Eragrostis hardy to
-5°C (23°F)

Suitable pot size
20–30cm (8–12in)

Suitable container material
Stone, terracotta,
glazed ceramic,
metal

Suitable compost
Soil-based compost,
eg, John Innes
No 3

Evergreen grasses really earn their keep. They look good all year, but are prized in winter for their colours, shapes, and textures. They also boast several other attributes, such as the gentle rustle of the leaves as they sway in the wind, and their dancing seedheads. There is a wide selection of grasses, sedges, and grass-like plants to choose from, including *Carex*, *Festuca*, *Acorus*, *Stipa*, and *Ophiopogon*. Some have upright habits, while others produce a fountain of arching leaves. Perfect alongside other plants in a container, you can also group several grasses together, combining a selection of different colours and shapes.

Site pots in sun or partial shade and water regularly, especially in summer. However, do not overwater, and place containers on "feet" or large pebbles to allow excess moisture to drain away. Feed monthly with a liquid fertilizer during the growing season.

GROOMING PLANTS

Evergreen grasses can become choked with dead leaves and debris over time, which inhibits their growth. To remove these from soft-leaved forms, put on gardening gloves and then comb your hands through the foliage from top to bottom. Use secateurs to remove dead or damaged foliage from wide-leaved grasses.

TOP TIP: DIVIDING

When happy, evergreen grasses will grow vigorously, eventually filling their original containers. In spring, either move them into larger pots or divide them in two. To do this, remove the plant from its pot and pull apart the root ball carefully by hand or, if the roots are very congested, use a sharp knife to cut it down the middle. Before repotting the sections in fresh compost, use a pair of secateurs to remove any dead or damaged growth.

Steel-blue Festuca glauca *forms a compact head of spiky foliage, ideal for windowboxes and small pots.*

Choosing grasses for winter

Carex *'Ice Dance'* is a clump-forming sedge with variegated strap-like leaves and brown flowers.

Acorus gramineus *'Ōgon'* makes a cascading clump of yellow, green, and cream variegated leaves; it prefers sun.

Carex flagellifera produces a large, low waterfall of bronze leaves. It is happy in sun or partial shade.

Ophiopogon planiscapus *'Nigrescens'* is not a true grass, but its dramatic black, grass-like leaves are invaluable.

Combine grass and container colours and forms to make an exciting garden display. Stipa tenuissima and Carex comans are evergreen, while the deciduous Eragrostis retains its leaves until late autumn.

Winter at home

If cold gloomy days get you down, bring some cheer into your home with a range of colourful house plants. Amaryllis provide big, bold blooms in the depths of winter, while bush lilies, with their beefy, strap-like leaves and vibrant orange flowers, make a dramatic statement. The bright fruits of Christmas cherries complete the picture.

Amaryllis *Hippeastrum*

Plants used
Hippeastrum varieties; *Syngonium podophyllum;* ferns

Height and spread
Hippeastrum:
H 75cm (30in)
S 30cm (12in);
Syngonium:
H & S 40cm (16in)

Aspect
Light with some direct sun

Temperature
18–24°C (64–75°F); cooler when in bloom

Suitable pot size
15cm (6in) or larger

Suitable container material
Metal, glazed terracotta, plastic

Compost type
Soil-based compost, eg, John Innes No 2

With bold, flamboyant flowers on top of sturdy stems that don't need staking, amaryllis cannot fail to impress. This bulbous plant often receives undivided attention, since it has very little competition when it bursts into flower in the depths of winter. Choose from deep red, pink, pale green, white, and striped forms. Packing a few bulbs together in a wide, shallow, container and underplanting with foliage helps to disguise the stems and plain leaves, producing a dazzling indoor scheme with the blooms performing the starring role.

SURVIVAL STRATEGY
Provide plants with plenty of light, including some direct sun. Keep the compost moist when in active growth, and feed fortnightly with a liquid fertilizer. After flowering, stop watering, and allow the bulbs to dry off and the leaves to wither. Start watering again in the autumn to bring plants back into growth. In the second year, repot in fresh compost after the summer dormancy, and then feed and water regularly.

Create an exotic winter display with amaryllis grouped together with leafy goosefoot plants (Syngonium) and ferns.

TOP TIP: PLANTING DRY BULBS

In early autumn, buy dry bulbs and soak them in a basin of lukewarm water for a few hours to soften them. Choose a pot just larger than the bulb and fill the base with compost. Place the bulb on top and fill in with more compost, leaving the top third of the bulb protruding. Water and leave in a warm spot.

Bush lily *Clivia*

Plant used
Clivia miniata

Height and spread
H 70cm (28in)
S 60cm (24in)

Aspect
Bright, light position
out of midday sun

Temperature
18°C (64°F);
min: 7°C (45°F)

Suitable pot size
15–20cm (6–8in)

Suitable container material
Glazed terracotta,
metal, plastic

Compost type
House plant compost

A combination of long, strap-like, glossy leaves and dense heads of large dramatic flowers make *Clivia* a much-prized house plant. The flowers are produced on top of sturdy stems in late winter or early spring, and colour options include red, orange, yellow, or apricot flowers. Plant these lily-like plants in a small pot in house plant compost; they enjoy cramped conditions, so do not worry if you see the roots pushing out of the top of the pot.

WATERING AND FEEDING

It is difficult to water root-bound plants from above, so place containers in a bucket of water, leave until the top of the compost is moist, then remove and allow to drain. Water plants regularly during the growing season, keeping the compost moist but not too wet. Feed plants regularly during this time with a liquid fertilizer.

Clivia miniata produces bright vase-shaped flowers.

Christmas cherry *Solanum*

Plant used
Solanum pseudocapsicum

Height and spread
H & S 30cm (12in)

Aspect
Full light but away
from midday sun

Temperature
18–24°C (64–75°F);
min: 10°C (50°F)

Suitable pot size
15–20cm (6–8in)

Suitable container material
Glazed terracotta,
metal, plastic

Compost type
House plant compost

Christmas cherries are usually grown as annuals, and the bright red berries of this pretty little plant bring a ray of sunshine to gloomy winter days. Unripe berries are green, and then turn yellow, orange, and finally red, but they are often all displayed at the same time, giving the plant a multi-coloured effect. Dwarf varieties are ideal for small, decorative pots. A word of warning: the berries may look edible, but they are poisonous, and plants must be kept out of the reach of children and pets.

PLANTING NEEDS

Plant in pots of house plant compost, keep them well watered, and feed regularly with a liquid fertilizer. Reduce watering and stop feeding when the berries wither at the end of winter; resume regular care after a few weeks.

Solanum pseudocapsicum

Forced bulbs

Narcissus and *Hyacinthus*

When it's too cold to step out of your back door, cheer yourself up by bringing the garden inside. Pots of colourful bulbs will instantly brighten up a dreary winter's day and fill your home with a combination of beautiful blooms and heady scent.

Plants used
Narcissus and *Hyacinthus* species

Height and spread
Narcissus: H 20cm (8in); *Hyacinthus:* H 20cm (8in)

Aspect
Bright and sunny, away from direct heat

Temperature needs
Fully hardy outside; happy indoors at 20°C (68°F)

Suitable pot size
15–20cm (6–8in)

Suitable container material
Terracotta, ceramic, glazed terracotta, glass

Compost type
Bulb fibre

Daffodils and hyacinths naturally flower in spring, but it's possible to produce a display in winter if you carry out a technique called "forcing". To do this, buy bulbs in early autumn that are labelled "Prepared", "For Forcing", or "Heat-treated". These have been grown especially for indoor displays.

Either plant single bulbs in small pots, or try groups of three or five in shallow bowls filled with bulb fibre. Hyacinths should be planted with the top half of the bulb showing above the compost, while the pointed tips of narcissus bulbs should be just below the surface. Water the pots lightly after planting, then place them in a box and store in an unheated shed or garage. Check them after about ten weeks, and when bulbs have shoots 2.5cm (1in) long, move the pots to a cool windowsill indoors. When flower buds appear, bring them into a warmer room to bloom, and keep the compost damp at all times.

SITING BULBS IN THE HOME

For long-lasting blooms, display plants in a cool, sunny place, such as a tabletop near a south-facing window. Avoid siting pots near a direct source of heat, such as a radiator, as this will cause them to quickly fade. Don't overdo the hyacinths; a single pot will have ample flowers to fill a room with scent. After flowering, discard bulbs or allow the foliage to fade and plant in the garden.

TOP TIP: CHOOSING HEALTHY BULBS

Healthy bulbs should be plump, firm, and unblemished, so before buying, inspect them carefully. Reject any that are mouldy, bruised, shrivelled, or show premature signs of growth, and also leave those that have lost their outer skins. Give the remaining bulbs a squeeze; if they are soft, they are probably rotten.

Forced daffodils and hyacinths will flower in the depths of winter, and are very easy to grow from prepared bulbs.

Bulb choices

Hyacinthus orientalis *'Blue Jacket'* produces dense spikes of sweetly scented blue flowers and dark leaves.

Hyacinthus orientalis *'City of Haarlem'* is an old favourite, with spikes of highly perfumed yellow flowers.

Hyacinthus orientalis *'Ostara'* has heavily scented, violet-blue, bell-shaped flowers, marked white at the edges.

Hyacinthus *'Pink Pearl'* produces fat spikes packed with bright pink flowers that emit a wonderful fragrance.

Narcissus *'Avalanche'* produces short stems, each carrying over a dozen scented white flowers with yellow cups.

Narcissus *'Cheerfulness'* has double, creamy-white flowers with egg-yolk yellow centres and a knock-out scent.

Narcissus *'Ice Follies'* has large, pale yellow cups that stand proud of white petals on knee-high flower stalks.

Narcissus *'Salome'* bears creamy-white petals and yellow cups that age gracefully to a peachy colour.

FRUIT AND VEGETABLES

Many delicious edibles thrive in containers on a patio, balcony, or terrace, bringing allotment gardening closer to home. Use the advice in this chapter to select a range of crops that suit cramped conditions and discover which plants will best suit your garden aspect. Also try new varieties of fruit and vegetables that are not available in the shops, to widen your culinary experience.

Plant strawberries in large baskets to produce bumper summer crops, and use wooden crates to grow your own onions. Thornless blackberries have been bred for large pots, while chard grows easily from seed.

Planning your crops in pots

With so many grow-your-own fruit and vegetables to choose from, it's worth taking a little time to explore your options. Some varieties of fruit, for example, have been bred especially for containers, while many unusual vegetables are only available as seed, and well worth growing. Use the seasonal sowing and planting guide opposite to help plan your gardening year.

Choosing crops for containers

When planning your container collection of fruit and vegetables, choose those that are easy to grow and produce abundant crops, or select unusual varieties that are not available to buy in the shops. All the edibles in this chapter will grow well in a container or growing bag, and produce a good harvest. You can also obtain more advice about specific cultivars and how well they will cope with cramped growing conditions from specialist seed companies and nurseries.

In addition, choose your containers and compost carefully, ensuring that they will suit your chosen crops. Details of both are in the boxes adjacent to the plant entries in this chapter.

Choose compact plants, such as herbs, chillies, and tomatoes for small pots on a sunny patio, roof terrace, or balcony. Set pots on crates to improve drainage.

Siting your pots

Most vegetables and fruits require sun to thrive, so if your plot is shady your choices will be limited to leafy crops, rhubarb, mint, parsley, and chives, among others, but few crops tolerate deep shade.

Also find a sheltered area out of strong winds, which can blow over pots and reduce insect numbers and pollination rates. Protect crops in exposed sites with a semi-permeable windbreak that allows some air to pass through.

Tomatoes demand a warm, sunny spot, which ensures their fruits ripen well before the frosts in autumn. Grow plants under cover in early spring to lengthen the growing season.

Rhubarb is happy in a slightly shaded site but will suffer if grown in deep shade. To thrive, plants must be watered well.

VEGETABLE AND HERB SOWING AND PLANTING GUIDE

LATE WINTER/EARLY SPRING
Sow seeds of these crops under cover from late winter to early spring and transplant outside after the frosts.

MID- TO LATE SPRING
Sow seeds directly into pots outside, and transplant crops sown inside into larger pots outdoors after the frosts.

EARLY TO MIDSUMMER
Sow directly into pots outside. Sow small quantities of fast-maturing crops over a few weeks for a long harvest.

LATE SUMMER TO AUTUMN
Sow spring-maturing crops directly into pots outside from late summer to early autumn. Some may need cloches.

Column 1 (Late winter/early spring):
- Aubergines *p.166*
- Basil *p.198*
- Bay *p.196*
- Carrots *pp.186–7*
- Chamomile *p.195*
- Chicory *p.160*
- Chives *p.163*
- Courgettes *p.167*
- French beans *pp.176–7*
- Ginger *p.203*
- Horseradish *p.184*
- Kohlrabi *p.173*
- Leeks *p.190*
- Lemon grass *p.202*
- Lettuces *pp.156–7*
- Onions and shallots *p.170*
- Orach *p.161*
- Oregano *p.201*
- Oriental leaves *pp.158–9*
- Pak choi *p.173*
- Parsley *p.200*
- Peas *pp.180–1*
- Peppers *pp.168–9*
- Potatoes *pp.182–3*
- Radishes *p.162*
- Sage *p.197*
- Spinach *p.175*
- Spring onions *p.163*
- Swiss chard *p.172*
- Tomatoes *pp.164–5*

Column 2 (Mid- to late spring):
- Basil *p.198*
- Beetroot *p.185*
- Carrots *pp.186–7*
- Chicory *p.160*
- Chives *p.163*
- Coriander *p.203*
- Endives *p.191*
- Fennel *p.194*
- French beans *pp.176–7*
- Horseradish *p.184*
- Kale *p.174*
- Kohlrabi *p.173*
- Lemon balm *p.195*
- Lettuces *pp.156–7*
- Mint *pp.192–3*
- Orach *p.161*
- Oriental leaves *pp.158–9*
- Pak choi *p.173*
- Peas *pp.180–1*
- Potatoes *pp.182–3*
- Pumpkins and winter squashes *pp.188–9*
- Radishes *p.162*
- Rosemary *p.201*
- Runner beans *pp.178–9*
- Sorrel *p.161*
- Spinach *p.175*
- Spring onions *p.163*
- Swiss chard *p.172*
- Thyme *p.198*
- Winter cabbage *p.191*

Column 3 (Early to midsummer):
- Beetroot *p.185*
- Carrots *pp.186–7*
- Chicory *p.160*
- Coriander *p.203*
- Courgettes *p.167*
- Endives *p.191*
- Fennel *p.194*
- Kale *p.174*
- Kohlrabi *p.173*
- Leeks *p.190*
- Lettuces *pp.156–7*
- Oriental leaves *pp.158–9*
- Pak choi *p.173*
- Parsley *p.200*
- Peas *pp.180–1*
- Peppers *pp.168–9*
- Pumpkins and winter squashes *pp.188–9*
- Spinach *p.175*
- Thyme *p.198*
- Winter cabbage *p.191*

Column 4 (Late summer to autumn):
- Chicory *p.160*
- Chives *p.163*
- Garlic *p.171*
- Lettuces *pp.156–7*
- Mint *pp.192–3*
- Oriental leaves *pp.158–9*
- Peas *pp.180–1*
- Radishes *p.162*

WEATHER WATCH

Although this seasonal advice is accurate for most areas, if you live in a warmer climate by the coast, for example, you may be able to plant your crops outside a little earlier. Conversely, in colder sites, delay planting vulnerable seeds and plants outside until the last frosts have passed, which may be in early summer. Cover pots with fleece if unexpected late frosts are forecast.

For autumn-sown plants, protect from severe frosts by placing a cloche or a few sheets of horticultural fleece over your containers. Alternatively, bring them close to the house or into an unheated greenhouse.

Fresh lettuce

Among the easiest vegetables to grow, lettuces are ideal for pots, where they can be more easily protected from marauding slugs and snails. The widest selection is available in seed form, and the cut-and-come-again types are ready to pick just a few weeks after sowing. Try a mix of lettuces for different textures and tastes.

Plants used
Dazzle and Green Frills lettuces

Height and spread
H up to 20cm (8in)
S up to 30cm (12in)

Aspect
Sun or partial shade

Temperature
Fully hardy

Harvesting period
Summer to winter

Suitable pot size
15cm (6in) or larger

Container material
Metal, terracotta, plastic, baskets

Compost type
Multi-purpose compost

Lettuces are not only delicious when picked fresh from the garden, but they also make decorative features in pots. Fill a container, large or small, with some multi-purpose compost and sow your seed thinly on the surface. In small containers, try to sow about three or four seeds of butterheads, cos, and crispheads, which form a heart, or just sprinkle cut-and-come-again varieties more densely, as you will not need to thin these out. Sow a few pots each week for a continuous supply of leaves throughout the summer, but remember that seeds will not germinate if the temperature is above 25°C (77°F). When heart-forming varieties reach a few centimetres in height, thin them out to appropriate spacings, which will be given on the packet of seeds, or a little closer.

CARING FOR LETTUCES

Keep your lettuces well watered at all times, especially in hot weather when you will have to water daily, and move pots to a slightly shaded spot in the height of summer. Lack of water or too much heat will cause the plants to "bolt" and produce long flowering stems — the leaves then become bitter. However, do not allow the compost to become waterlogged or the lettuces will rot. Most multi-purpose composts contain enough nutrients to sustain lettuces for a few weeks, but after that, give them a boost with a nitrogen-rich fertilizer formulated for leafy crops. The main pests to look out for are slugs and snails. Inspect plants every few days and pick off any culprits.

TOP TIP: HARVESTING LEAVES

Allow the butterhead, cos, and crisphead varieties to mature into solid heads of leaves, and then slice the main stem off at the base with a sharp knife. Cut-and-come-again types can be harvested in one go by cutting all the leaves off a few centimetres above the base. New leaves should then regrow, giving you a second crop. Alternatively, just pick off a few leaves as and when you need them; more will then grow to replace them. Growing some of each type gives you the best of both worlds.

An old tin bath makes a good home for a collection of Green Frills and dark red Dazzle cut-and-come-again lettuces.

SALADS

Choosing lettuce varieties

'Nymans' *is a two-tone lettuce with burgundy leaves and bright green bases. Slow to bolt and mildew-resistant.*

'Winter Density' *is a compact variety with dark green hearts that offer fresh greens in winter from autumn sowings.*

'Bubbles' *has distinctive crumpled leaves with a very sweet flavour. Its compact habit makes it perfect for pots.*

'Lollo Rosso' *has crisp frilly leaves that add colour and texture to salads and are a feature in pots in the garden.*

'Pandero' *is a delicious mini red cos lettuce with crisp leaves that develop a good colour and are mildew-resistant.*

'Tintin' *is slightly larger than a 'Little Gem'; it has a great flavour and bubbly leaves with a crisp heart.*

'Salad Bowl' *has wavy-edged leaves that can be left to produce a loose head, or treat it as a cut-and-come-again.*

'Little Gem' *is a popular variety that produces upright, dark green, crunchy hearts with an excellent sweet flavour.*

SALADS

Oriental leaves

They may be small but these salad leaves are big on flavour, and when combined with flowers, they make a pretty ornamental display. Easy to grow, the tasty crops are ready to harvest within weeks of sowing – micro greens are even quicker – and all require little care, apart from watering and picking the leaves regularly to keep the plants productive.

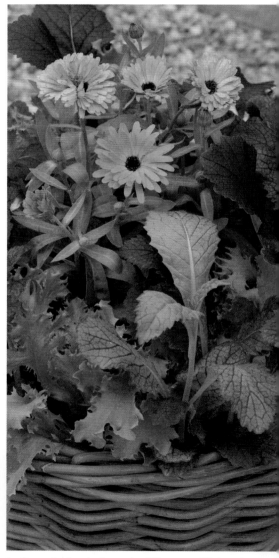

Leafy mustard and mizuna should be cropped little and often to keep plants productive and prevent them bolting.

Mustard and mizuna

Plants used
Mustard 'Red Giant'; mizuna; *Calendula* (pot marigold)

Aspect
Sun or partial shade

Temperature
Not hardy below 0°C (32°F)

Harvesting period
Spring to autumn

Suitable pot size
Min. 20cm (8in)

Suitable container material
Any

Compost type
Multi-purpose compost

A wicker basket makes a decorative container for a vibrant mix of tasty oriental leaves and orange pot marigolds. The mizuna's serrated leaves contrast well with the rounded, purple foliage of mustard 'Red Giant', and both will add a peppery kick to salads. The pot marigold doesn't just help to brighten up the basket, its edible petals can also be tossed into salads.

To grow the leaves, mix together a pinch of mustard and mizuna seed, then sow across the surface of a container filled with multi-purpose compost. Raise your marigolds separately, sowing seed in pots and transferring a few seedlings into the container when they reach 15cm (6in). Alternatively, buy young plants.

CARING FOR CROPS
Water regularly, especially during hot weather, to ensure the compost is always moist; dry soil will cause the salad leaves to turn bitter and the plants to bolt. To ensure a regular supply of fresh leaves, cut them as you need them from the outside edge of the plants.

TOP TIP: SOWING SALAD LEAF SEEDS

Sow seeds of mustard, mizuna, rocket, or salad leaf mixes in pots filled with multi-purpose compost. Sow seeds thinly across the surface of your container and cover with 1cm (½in) compost. Firm gently, then water. Thin out overcrowded seedlings when they are large enough to handle; eat the thinnings.

Rocket

Plant used
Rocket

Aspect
Sun or partial shade

Temperature
Frost tender

Harvesting period
Late spring to early autumn

Suitable pot size
20cm (8in)

Suitable container material
Any

Compost type
Multi-purpose compost

The peppery leaves of rocket are ideal for adding heat to salads or blitzing together with olive oil to make a fiery version of pesto sauce. Seeds will germinate readily at any time between early spring and early autumn, and a single container will provide tasty pickings for several weeks if you harvest leaves regularly, which also prevents plants flowering and going to seed. Although a large pot will provide you with armfuls of leaves, this is a great crop for sowing in small containers, such as windowboxes. Water plants regularly to ensure the compost doesn't dry out.

PEST PROTECTION
Cover up your leaves with fine mesh to prevent cabbage white butterflies laying their eggs. These will later hatch into ravenous caterpillars that will munch their way through your crops.

Hot, peppery rocket leaves.

Micro greens

Plants used
Micro greens

Aspect
Full sun

Temperature
Grow indoors

Harvesting period
Spring to late autumn

Suitable pot size
A seed tray or recycled shallow container

Suitable container material
Plastic

Compost type
Vermiculite

Micro greens are ready to harvest in just a few days.

Prized by top chefs, micro greens are diminutive vegetable seedlings that are harvested between six and 21 days after germination. They may be small but their flavour is intense. Micro crops grow well in seed trays, plastic punnets, or other shallow containers with good drainage. Add a 2cm (1in) layer of vermiculite to your container, then scatter seeds liberally over the surface, and do not cover them. Stand the container in a tray filled with water, and leave until the surface of the vermiculite is wet, then drain. Place the container on a sunny windowsill in a warm room, and don't let the vermiculite dry out. Harvest crops with scissors when they have formed their first leaves.

WHAT TO GROW
Lots of vegetables make tasty micro leaves. Try Chinese and Oregon sugar pod peas, sunflowers, broccoli, rocket, radish, beetroot, celery, Swiss chard, and red mustard. Herbs, such as basil, fennel, coriander, and chervil, are also options.

Spicy salad mix

If you can't face another boring green salad, these three fantastic leaves will perk up your palate and your plate with their distinctive flavours and colourful leaves. Chicory is famously bitter; orach tastes a little like salty spinach; and sorrel has a mild citrus flavour. You'd be hard pressed to find the last two in a supermarket, but luckily they are easy to grow.

Chicory

Plant used
Chicory 'Treviso
Precoce Mesola'

Aspect
Full sun

Temperature needs
Fully hardy

Harvesting period
Summer to winter

Suitable pot size
45cm (18in)

Suitable container material
Terracotta, plastic,
glazed ceramic

Compost type
Multi-purpose
compost

Chicory is famed for its bitter leaves, and there are three types on offer. Sugarloaf and red chicory, which is better known as radicchio, are grown for their leaves, while Belgian or Witloof forcing chicory produces tender white hearts, known as "chicons", when deprived of light.

All seeds are started the same way. Sow them thinly across the surface of a pot filled with seed compost and cover with 1cm (½in) of sieved compost. Water and place in a sunny site. When seedlings have a few leaves, transplant three into a 45cm (18in) pot. Spring sowings provide summer leaves, while seeds sown in summer will be ready from autumn through to winter.

TOP TIP: BLANCHING CHICORY

Once forcing chicory has developed a good head of leaves in late autumn, cut the tops off, leaving a 5cm (2in) stump. Water plants well, then cover the stumps with an upturned bucket to exclude any light, and stand in a frost-free place. Your blanched chicons will be ready to harvest after a month.

'Treviso Precoce Mesola' is a really colourful radicchio, with white-ribbed, red-flushed leaves.

Sorrel

Plant used
Red-veined sorrel

Aspect
Sun or partial shade

Temperature needs
Fully hardy

Harvesting period
Spring to early
autumn

Suitable pot size
30cm (12in)

**Suitable container
material**
Plastic, terracotta,
glazed ceramic

Compost type
Soil-based compost,
eg, John Innes No 2

Difficult to find in shops, sorrel is a perennial herb grown for its tangy, slightly citrussy leaves. It's perfect for adding flavour to green salads or perking up soups. Most sorrels are let down by their looks, but the red-veined variety (*Rumex sanguineus*) has attractive bright green leaves with distinctive red markings. Buckler-leaved or French sorrel (*Rumex scutatus*) is also worth growing for its green, shield-shaped leaves, which have a slight green-apple flavour.

GROWING SORREL
Sow seeds in spring 1.5cm (½in) deep, thinning out seedlings to a final spacing of 30cm (12in). Young plants are also available. Plant into the middle of a container filled with John Innes No 2 compost and keep well watered. Pick leaves when needed, and nip out flowers as soon as they develop, to prevent plants running to seed.

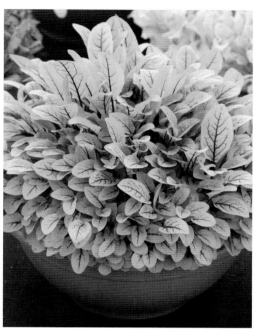

Red-veined sorrel is grown for its mild citrus flavour.

SALADS

Orach

Plant used
Red orach

Height
H 1m (3ft)

Aspect
Partial shade

Temperature needs
Fully hardy

Harvesting period
Early spring to
summer

Suitable pot size
30cm (12in)

**Suitable container
material**
Plastic, terracotta,
glazed ceramic

Compost type
Soil-based compost,
eg, John Innes No 2

Orach is an extremely attractive annual herb that is grown for its spinach-like leaves. It's fast growing and will quickly shoot up to an imposing 1m (3ft).

Sow seeds in small pots of moist compost in late winter or early spring, cover them with a layer of vermiculite and keep moist. Stand pots on a warm windowsill to germinate but avoid direct sun. When seedlings are large enough to handle, transplant them into individual pots to grow on. In mid-spring, plant out into large containers filled with John Innes No 2 compost. Water regularly; if plants become lanky, pinch out the growing tips to encourage bushy growth. To prevent leaf scorch, stand containers in partial shade.

WHAT TO GROW
Red orach (*Atriplex hortensis* var. *rubra*) is a showy plant with reddish-purple triangular leaves. Gold orach has golden foliage, and 'Scarlet Emperor' produces dusky purple and pink, two-tone leaves.

Red orach makes a beautiful plant.

Tangy salad boosters

If your salads are a little on the bland side, spice them up by sowing some fast-growing crops with bags of flavour. Perfect in pots on their own or dotted in gaps around the base of larger plants, radishes, chives, and spring onions are incredibly easy to grow and will shoot up quickly from seeds sown in succession from spring to late summer.

Radishes

Plant used
Radish 'French Breakfast'

Aspect
Sun or partial shade

Temperature needs
Not hardy below 0°C (32°F)

Harvesting period
From spring to autumn

Suitable pot size
20cm (8in)

Suitable container material
Terracotta, metal, plastic, baskets

Compost type
Multi-purpose compost

Perfect for adding a peppery crunch to salads, radishes are a doddle to grow, and often produce mature crops within four weeks of sowing. There are many different types to choose from, in different colours, shapes, and sizes. Short-rooted radishes can be grown in shallow containers, such as windowboxes, while those with longer roots need deeper pots to develop properly.

SOWING SEEDS
Seeds can be sown at any time from late winter to early autumn, but early and late sowings need protecting from frost and heavy rain. Either place pots in a greenhouse or cool light room, or cover them with a bell cloche. Sow seeds thinly across the surface of a pot and cover with a 1.5cm (½in) layer of compost. If seedlings are too crowded, thin out to appropriate spacings. Keep plants well watered, especially during hot, dry spells.

Easy to grow, radishes are a good choice for children to try as they are ready to eat within weeks of sowing.

CHOOSING RADISH VARIETIES

'Scarlet Globe' is a fast-growing variety with round, scarlet roots and crisp white flesh. It is a great choice for a windowbox or shallow pot, or for dotting around other plants.

'French Breakfast' is a popular radish, with slender roots that have a sweet, mild taste. It requires a fairly deep pot to accommodate the long, pinkish-red roots.

'China Rose', known as the Chinese or winter radish, has long, peppery roots that need a very deep pot. It is favoured because it stores well and can be used over winter.

'Cherry Belle' radishes have bright red skins and white flesh, and a sweet, mild flavour. This variety is exceptionally fast-maturing and perfect for small pots on a patio.

Chives

Plant used
Chives

Height and spread
H 30cm (12in)
S indefinite

Aspect
Sun or partial shade

Temperature needs
Fully hardy

Harvesting period
From spring
to autumn

Suitable pot size
20cm (8in)

Suitable container material
Terracotta, metal, plastic

Compost type
Soil-based compost, eg, John Innes No 3

The pungent, mild onion taste of chives gives a boost to salads and other dishes. You can either buy a young plant or grow your own from seeds sown in spring. Sow seeds about 0.5cm (¼in) deep in a small 7.5cm (3in) pot of seed compost, and place in a heated propagator to germinate. You can then pot the seedlings up outside into larger containers of soil-based compost, such as John Innes No 3, in late spring when the weather has warmed up. To harvest, simply cut the leaves as required just above the compost.

REJUVENATING CLUMPS

Chives spread fairly quickly and will eventually fill their containers. At this stage, either move plants into larger pots, or lift them out and divide them in two with a sharp knife. Replant healthy sections in new pots of fresh compost.

Chives are ideal for small pots.

SALADS

Spring onions

Plant used
Red spring onions

Aspect
Sun or partial shade

Temperature needs
Fully hardy

Harvesting period
Summer to
mid-autumn

Suitable pot size
45cm (18in)

Suitable container material
Terracotta, metal, plastic, deep baskets

Compost type
Multi-purpose compost

Grown for their tangy bulbs and stems, spring onions are easy to raise from seed and should be ready for harvesting within 12 weeks of sowing. Seeds can be sown in spring and summer into pots filled with multi-purpose compost; either make shallow rows across the surface and sprinkle the seeds into the grooves, or scatter them thinly on top of the compost and cover with a 1cm (½in) layer of compost. Thin seedlings if necessary. The disease downy mildew can present a problem. If you spot a white fungal growth, remove affected plants immediately.

CHOOSING VARIETIES

There are many varieties of spring onion on offer. 'White Lisbon' is popular for its mild white bulbs and stems with green tops, while 'Vigour King' has a hotter onion taste. 'North Holland Blood Red' has striking dark red bulbs and lower stems with green tops, and adds colour as well as flavour to mixed salads and stir fries.

Red spring onions add colour to a mixed salad.

Sweet tomato treats

Home-grown tomatoes are a world apart from those you can buy in the shops. Whether you grow young plants bought from a garden centre, or sow your own from seed, you will be picking fresh fruits from midsummer until the beginning of autumn. Most tomatoes require large pots or deep baskets to thrive.

Plant used
Tomato 'Tumbling Tom Red'

Aspect
Full sun

Temperature needs
Not hardy below 0°C (32°F)

Harvesting periods
Summer to early autumn

Suitable pot size
30cm (12in) or larger

Suitable container material
Terracotta, baskets, plastic

Compost type
Multi-purpose compost

The taste of tomatoes that have ripened naturally over a long season in the sun is unrivalled and makes growing them yourself well worth the effort. Most are happy in pots, as long as the containers can hold sufficient compost and water. Trailing varieties are perfect in deep hanging baskets or large tubs, while cordon types, which are grown as a single stem against a cane, can be planted in big pots or growing bags (*see p.241*).

A good range of young plants is available from garden centres in spring, but for a wider choice, sow seeds indoors in late winter. Fill a 7.5cm (3in) pot with seed compost, scatter seeds thinly over the surface, and cover them with a layer of vermiculite. Then water the pots and place in a heated propagator until the seeds have germinated. When seedlings are almost 2.5cm (1in) tall, carefully lift them out of the pot, separate the root balls, and plant each one in a 7.5cm (3in) pot. Keep plants in a light, frost-free place, and when roots show at the bottom of the pots, move them into 12.5cm (5in) pots filled with multi-purpose compost. At the end of spring, most tomatoes can be planted outside.

FEEDING REGIME

Tomatoes are greedy crops and need to be fed every week with a tomato fertilizer once the flowers appear. This regime should be increased to two doses a week when the fruit has set, and continued until the last tomato has been picked.

*Centre **Red 'Tumbling Toms'** produce bumper crops in large hanging baskets, given a sunny site, and lots of water and fertilizer.*

TOP TIP: WATERING NEEDS

It's important that tomatoes are never allowed to dry out or all of your hard work raising the plants will be wasted. Irregular watering can cause the tomatoes to split or hard black patches to form on the bottom of the fruits. This is known as blossom end rot, and is caused by a lack of calcium, which is found in water.

Choosing tomato varieties

'Tumbling Tom Yellow' *is perfect for a large hanging basket that will hold plenty of compost and water. The large trusses of sweet, cherry-sized fruit look great cascading over the sides and can be picked all summer long.*

'Totem' *is a short and compact variety, making it ideal for a large hanging basket or even a deep windowbox. Its stocky branches carry a heavy crop of bright red fruits. The sideshoots must be removed to ensure a good crop.*

'Sungold' *produces an abundance of small, sweet, and juicy, bright orange to yellow fruits with very thin skins. Plants are best grown as cordons, with a cane to support the stems, in large pots or growing bags.*

'Moneymaker' *is a long-time favourite, popular for its ease of growth and dependable crops of medium-sized, red fruits that are borne in large trusses. It should be grown as a cordon in a large container or growing bag.*

'Sweet Olive' *produces trusses of olive-shaped fruits that hang down from the stems of this cordon variety. It is easy to grow, and will produce a heavy crop in a pot or growing bag, even if you don't remove all of the sideshoots.*

'Tigerella' *is a decorative variety with orange fruit emblazoned with bright green stripes that looks good in the garden and on the plate. It is a cordon type and produces heavy crops when grown in a large pot in a greenhouse.*

MEDITERRANEAN MIXES

Fruits of the Med

Their plump, juicy fruit and showy blooms make aubergines and courgettes a great choice for a decorative patio display, set among pots of summer flowers and other fruiting crops. Plant them in large containers in a warm sheltered spot, water them well, and let these Mediterranean delights swell to perfection in the heat of the sun.

MEDITERANNEAN MIXES

Aubergines

Plant used
Aubergine 'Pinstripe'

Height and spread
H 60cm (24in)
S 30cm (12in)

Aspect
Full sun

Temperature needs
Not hardy below
0°C (32°F)

Harvesting period
From summer
to early autumn

Suitable pot size
20cm (8in)

Suitable container material
Plastic, terracotta

Compost type
Multi-purpose
compost

Even before the plump fruits start to form, aubergines make beautiful patio plants, with pretty pink flowers and scallop-edged foliage. Although you can buy young plants, the choice of seed is much greater, and the best option if you want more unusual varieties. To grow plants from seed, fill a small pot with seed compost and scatter a few seeds over the surface. Then cover with a layer of vermiculite and put the pot in a heated propagator. When shoots appear, move the pot from the propagator to a light windowsill. Transfer each seedling into a separate pot when they are about 5cm (2in) tall.

TEMPERATURE REQUIREMENTS

Aubergines will not fruit well during wet summers, as they need a long growing season and plenty of warmth. To help overcome this problem, sow seed in late winter. This gives plants more time to establish, resulting in robust growth and a better crop. You can also extend the growing season further by raising them in a warm greenhouse or a conservatory.

TOP TIP: INCREASING YIELDS

Plants grown outside produce about five fruits. For a good harvest, feed aubergines every couple of weeks with a tomato fertilizer as the fruits start to swell. After five fruits have formed, cut off any sideshoots and remove the remaining flowers. Fruits are ready when they are full size and the skin is shiny.

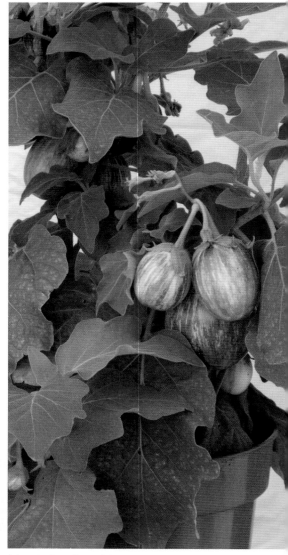

'Pinstripe' is a beautiful aubergine variety, with white-striped mauve fruits and a compact habit ideal for pots.

Courgettes

Plant used
Courgette 'Golden Delight'

Height and spread
H & S 60cm (24in)

Aspect
Full sun

Temperature needs
Not hardy below 0°C (32°F)

Harvesting period
From summer to early autumn

Suitable pot size
30–45cm (12–18in)

Suitable container material
Plastic, growing bags, vegetable bags

Compost type
Multi-purpose compost

Easy to grow from seed, courgettes are among the most productive vegetables you can grow on a patio; a single plant will keep you in fruit all summer. Bearing this in mind, don't get too carried away and pot up lots of plants or you will be sick of the sight of the fruits before long.

Start seeds off in early spring by filling a 7.5cm (3in) pot with seed compost. Plant two seeds on their sides, 2.5cm (1in) deep, and cover with more compost. Water, and put the pot in a propagator or on a sunny windowsill. Keep moist and when the roots of your seedlings show through the drainage holes at the bottom, move individual plants into 12.5cm (5in) pots. When there is no risk from frost, place a single plant in a large pot or colourful growing bag. Water regularly and harvest fruits with a sharp knife when they are about 10cm (3in) long.

'Golden Delight' makes a great patio feature when grown in a pretty vegetable bag. Pick three courgettes a week to keep plants productive.

CHOOSING COURGETTE VARIETIES

'Parador' produces large clusters of head-turning golden yellow fruit, which lend a decorative touch to the garden or patio. They have a great taste and mature early.

'De Nice A Fruit Rond' is perfect if you're looking for something a little different. These spherical green fruits are best picked when they are the size of a golf ball.

'Defender' is a tried and trusted favourite, due to its resistance to cucumber mosaic virus. It produces a bumper crop of large, tasty fruits over a long season.

'Venus' is a compact courgette, ideal for container growing, with uniform, dark green cylindrical fruits that are produced from midsummer through until early autumn.

Fiery peppers

If you like spicy food with a bite, turn up the heat in your garden by growing some chilli peppers. An essential ingredient of many fiery dishes, chillies come in a range of shapes, colours, and sizes, and will grow happily in containers. Not all peppers are hot, so if you prefer a mild flavour, try the sweet ones.

Plant used
'Cheyenne' chilli pepper; *Petunia* Million Bells; *Viola*; *Lotus berthelotii*; Greek basil

Height and spread
Pepper: H 45cm (18in) S 30cm (12in); *Petunia*: H & S 30cm (12in); *Viola*: H & S 20cm (8in); *Lotus*: H 50cm (20in) S 1m (3ft); Basil: H & S 15cm (6in)

Aspect
Full sun

Temperature needs
Not hardy below 0°C (32°F)

Harvesting period
From late summer to early autumn

Suitable pot size
30cm (12in)

Suitable container material
Terracotta, metal, baskets

Compost type
Multi-purpose compost

Centre: **Match orange chillies** *with small violas and contrasting purple petunias. A cascading* Lotus berthelotii *and tangy Greek basil complete this delicious display.*

Peppers are grown for their jewel-like, glistening fruits, which come in a range of colours, including red, green, yellow, orange, brown, and purple. Although they can be grown in a pot on their own, peppers don't attract attention until the fruit develops, so create early interest by planting them in a basket or pot with flowers and herbs. Good companions include purple trailing petunias, violas, silver-leaved *Lotus berthelotii,* and basil.

Buy young pepper plants in spring, or grow them from seed sown indoors in late winter. Seeds germinate easily and will need moving into increasingly larger pots several times before they are ready to go outside in late spring, when all danger of frost has passed. When plants are about 20cm (8in) tall, or before if they start to lean, stake them with a small cane. Pinch out the tops of the shoots when they are about 30cm (12in) tall to encourage lots of fruiting stems to form. The peppers will be ready to harvest from midsummer and can be removed with a sharp knife or secateurs. Picking the fruit regularly helps to ensure the plant puts its energy into producing more crops.

WATERING AND FEEDING

For a good harvest water plants regularly, especially in hot weather, and feed every two weeks with a liquid tomato fertilizer. Start feeding your peppers when the flowers first appear, often while plants are still indoors before the frosts have passed, and continue until all the fruits have been picked.

TOP TIP: SOWING SEEDS

Fill a 7.5cm (3in) pot with good-quality seed compost and sow a few seeds on top. Cover with a fine layer of vermiculite and place the pot in a heated propagator. After the seeds have germinated, move the pot to a windowsill. When plants are about 2.5cm (1in) tall, move to a 10cm (4in) pot.

Chilli and pepper options

'California Wonder' *is a very sweet, mild pepper with brick-red fruit, produced on compact plants.*

'Gourmet' *is a sweet pepper with eye-catching, bright orange fruits that appear on small plants, ideal for pots.*

'Pepper Gypsy' *produces tasty, wide, tapering sweet peppers that start green, and then turn orange and red.*

'Alma Paprika' *is a chilli pepper with fruits that start yellow and turn red. They have a sweet, mildly hot flavour.*

'Cherry Bomb' *is a chilli with round red fruits. They are quite hot, and the plant makes an ornamental patio display.*

'Prairie Fire' *produces hundreds of tiny fruits that make up for their size with an explosive fiery taste.*

'Numex Twilight' *is a compact chilli that produces a large crop of small purple, yellow, orange, and red fruits.*

'Aji Amarillo' *makes a compact plant, laden with long, hot chillies that turn from green to yellow, then orange.*

MEDITERRANEAN MIXES

Potted onions and garlic

Onions, shallots, and garlic are staple ingredients in many kitchens. Growing your own in containers allows you to sample a wide variety of shapes, sizes, and colours, and to enjoy the freshest flavours. All members of the onion family take up very little space and require the minimum of care.

MEDITERRANEAN MIXES

Plants used
Garlic, onions, shallots

Aspect
Full sun

Temperature requirement
Hardy to -10°C (14°F)

Harvesting period
Summer

Suitable pot size
Shallots and onions: 60cm (24in)
Garlic: 30cm (12in) or larger

Suitable container material
Any

Suitable compost
Soil-based compost, eg, John Innes No 3

GROWING ONIONS AND SHALLOTS

Onions and shallots are best grown from sets (small, immature bulbs) planted in spring. Choose a large container, such as a wooden storage crate, that's at least 24cm (10in) deep and 60cm (24in) wide. Fill with soil-based compost and make holes 10cm (4in) apart for onions and 15cm (6in) apart for shallots. Drop a bulb in, ensuring the pointy end is facing upwards, then cover with compost, firm with your fingers and water well. The nose of the bulb should be just visible. Sprinkle over a handful of blood, fish and bone fertilizer and keep well watered. In summer, when the leaves turn brown, crops are ready to harvest. Leave them to dry on a wire rack for three weeks before storing.

GROWING GARLIC

Best planted in autumn or early winter, garlic is divided into two groups: soft-neck garlic, which forms a mass of strappy leaves and stores well; and the hard-neck, stiff-stalked types, which are best used fresh. Split open the bulb and separate the cloves – plant only the largest, healthy ones. Fill a 30cm (12in) container with soil-based compost, then make shallow holes, 10cm (4in) apart, around the outside. Place a clove in each, making sure the flat base is facing downwards. Cover with compost, sprinkle over a handful of blood, fish and bone, water well, and place in a sunny spot. Garlic is ready to harvest in summer when the leaves start to turn yellow.

Plait the stems of your garlic bulbs and store them in a cool, dark place.

TOP TIP: DRYING AND PLAITING GARLIC BULBS

Dried, soft-neck garlic will keep for a long time if stored correctly. The easiest way is to arrange a single layer of bulbs on a slatted wooden tray, keeping them in a cool, dry, dark place, such as a shed. Those with more patience could take a tip from the traditional French garlic seller and try plaiting the leaves together to create a decorative garlic rope. Simply twist off a bulb when you want to use it.

Choosing varieties

Elephant garlic produces huge bulbs of up to 10cm (4in). Enjoy the mild flavour when bulbs are roasted whole.

Shallot 'Mikor' is perfect for storing. This French shallot has reddish skin and white flesh with a pink tinge.

Shallot 'Red Sun' is a neat, spherical bulb with red skin and white flesh. It is delicious chopped into salads.

Onion 'Red Baron' is a red variety that keeps well after harvesting and has a strong, intense flavour.

Plant onions in a wooden box to lend a rustic note to a patio or balcony. Keep bulbs well watered and you will be enjoying fresh crops all summer.

Leaves and stems

Leafy chard, pak choi, and kohl rabi, which also produces delicious swollen stems, form a trio of ornamental edibles that are easy to grow and ready to harvest within a few weeks of sowing. Highly nutritious, use them in the kitchen and to dress up dreary patios or balconies with their vibrant stems and designer good looks.

Chard

TASTY GREENS

Plant used
Mixed chard

Aspect
Sun or partial shade

Temperature
Needs protection over winter

Harvesting period
Spring to autumn

Suitable pot size
Min. 30cm (12in)

Suitable container material
Any

Compost type
Multi-purpose compost

Many vegetables look rather utilitarian in pots, but leafy chard's brightly coloured stems sit comfortably among more decorative displays. Ruby chard has green leaves with red stems and veins, while 'Lucullus' has green leaves with white stems, but for striking looks, nothing beats the zingy red, white, orange, yellow, pink, and purple stems of 'Bright Lights'.

Young plants are available in spring, but chard is easy to raise from seed sown from early to late spring. Sow seeds 2.5cm (1in) deep in a small pot of compost. When seedlings have a few leaves, transplant them into their own pots; repot them again when you see roots growing through the drainage holes. Water regularly and protect plants with fleece or cloches over winter.

HARVESTING STEMS AND LEAVES
Spring sowings of chard are ready to pick after 12 weeks. Harvest what you need by cutting leaves from the outside of the plant. Picking the leaves frequently prompts the plants to produce more, and extends the harvest period.

Feed chard in containers once a month with a nitrogen-rich fertilizer to keep foliage and stems healthy.

TOP TIP: PLANT A COLOURFUL MIX

Rather than growing a single plant in a small pot, create an eye-catching display by planting up a large container with several different-coloured chards. Check that the container you choose has adequate drainage. Fill with multi-purpose compost and space plants 10cm (4in) apart.

Kohl rabi

Plant used
Kohl rabi

Aspect
Full sun

Temperature
Fully hardy

Harvesting period
Summer to winter, depending on sowing time

Suitable pot size
20cm (8in)

Suitable container material
Terracotta, plastic inside decorative pot

Compost type
Multi-purpose compost

You either love or hate the mild turnip taste of kohl rabi, but there's no denying that it makes a fascinating plant for a pot. Pick the young leaves for a salad, or steam as a spinach substitute. Grate the crunchy round stems raw into salads (like celeriac), or steam or boil. 'Olivia' is a pretty, pale green-skinned variety, while 'Violetta' has white flesh and a violet-blue skin.

STARTING FROM SEED
Sow seeds indoors in spring by planting three seeds 2cm (¾in) deep in a small pot of compost. After germination, remove the two weakest seedlings. When they have a few leaves, pot seedlings on into a larger container, and move plants to their final pot outside in summer. Water plants frequently, and harvest six weeks after sowing, when no bigger than a tennis ball; much larger and they start getting woody.

'Purple Vienna' is a stunning crop for a container.

Pak choi

Plant used
Pak choi

Aspect
Full sun

Temperature
Fully hardy

Harvesting period
Summer to autumn

Suitable pot size
20cm (8in)

Suitable container material
Plastic

Compost type
Multi-purpose compost

An oriental vegetable related to the cabbage, pak choi (or bok choy) is steadily increasing in popularity. The leaves can be chopped into salads, or toss both leaves and stems into a stir-fry or lightly steam. Plants can be started from seed, but there's a tendency for them to bolt, so you may find it easier to buy young plants. After a month or so, you can start picking the young leaves from around the outside of the plant. Alternatively, allow the plant to mature fully and harvest the entire head by cutting it off at the base.

WATERING NEEDS
Pak choi has short roots that run close to the surface of the compost, and plants bolt if the compost is allowed to dry out. Apply a mulch of shredded bark, slate chippings, or gravel to retain moisture, and water daily in hot weather and in summer.

Leafy pak choi needs plenty of water.

Pots of dark greens

If you're looking for a nutritious vegetable that's tough, attractive and can be picked over winter, then look no further than leafy kale. After a heavy frost the flavour will even sweeten up. Spinach, too, can be grown to provide rich pickings when there's little else to harvest, but for a real show-stopper, try Mexican tree spinach.

Kale

TASTY GREENS

Plant used
Kale 'Black Tuscany' and 'Dwarf Green Curled'

Aspect
Sun or partial shade

Temperature
Fully hardy

Harvesting period
Winter

Suitable pot size
45cm (18in)

Suitable container material
Plastic

Compost type
Multi-purpose compost

Some members of the brassica or cabbage family look rather utilitarian, but kale is queen of the crops. Many cultivars are blessed with great looks and provide colour, interest, and food over winter. Perhaps the most attractive one of all is 'Black Tuscany' (often called cavolo nero or black cabbage), with its upright "fronds" of near-black, textured leaves.

In spring, sow seeds indoors into small pots of multi-purpose compost, then cover with 2cm (¾in) of compost, and water. When seedlings are big enough to handle, move into individual small pots. In late spring, plant into larger containers outside. If the leaves start to yellow or growth slows, apply a balanced fertilizer.

LOOKING AFTER PLANTS
Keep plants well watered and cover with netting to deter pigeons and cabbage white butterflies. Harvest leaves as required from around the plants, or cut off entire heads. In winter, check plants regularly for windrock, firming the soil around the base of the stems to secure the roots.

TOP TIP: CHOOSING KALE VARIETIES

'Black Tuscany' has crimped, near-black leaves with a peppery flavour. The green leaves of 'Redbor' turn a deep red, while 'Red Curled' has tightly curled red leaves. 'Red Russian' boasts frilly red and green leaves (left), and the compact 'Dwarf Green Curled' will grow happily in open, exposed sites.

Kale 'Black Tuscany' and 'Dwarf Green Curled' provide tasty and colourful leaves over the winter months.

Spinach

Plant used
Mexican tree spinach (*Chenopodium giganteum*)

Aspect
Full sun

Temperature
Fully hardy

Harvesting period
Summer, autumn and winter

Suitable pot size
30cm (12in)

Suitable container material
Plastic

Compost type
Multi-purpose compost

There's no point pretending that spinach will stop you in your tracks when you lay eyes on it. It may be highly nutritious, but it's green and pretty dull. Not so Mexican tree spinach (not related to true spinach), which is a stunning plant, with triangular leaves and magenta shoots, that will add height and colour to a patio display. When young, the leaves are delicious in salads, and mature leaves can be steamed like conventional spinach. The more you pick the foliage, the longer it will continue to crop.

GROWING SPINACH

Sow conventional spinach seeds 2.5cm (1in) deep in pots of multi-purpose compost; Mexican tree spinach is sown on the surface. Thin the seedlings when they are large enough to handle, allowing about 7cm (3in) between plants. Keep pots well watered, especially during dry spells, as plants will bolt if stressed. If growth slows, feed with a nitrogen-rich fertilizer.

Spinach can be sown throughout the year to provide leaves at different times. For a summer crop, sow from early spring to early summer; for winter pickings, sow seed from late summer to early autumn. Plants grown over winter will need protecting from the worst of the weather with cloches or fleece. Harvest by snipping leaves from around the outside of the plants.

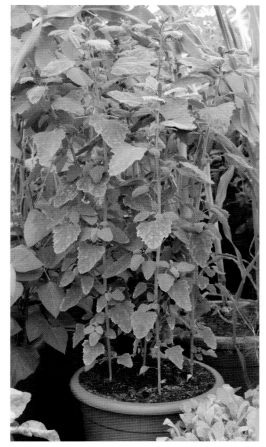

Lofty Mexican tree spinach may need staking.

CHOOSING SPINACH FOR CUT-AND-COME-AGAIN LEAVES

Perpetual spinach is also known as beet spinach. It's a good autumn/winter crop with tender, tasty leaves. Plants can last up to two years if picked regularly.

New Zealand spinach is unrelated to spinach, but it can be harvested and used in the same way. It makes a bushy plant and can be picked until cut down by the first frost.

'Galaxy' has dark green, glossy leaves with a better flavour than the ones that come in those costly supermarket bags. For baby leaves, don't thin out your seedlings.

'Medania' has a mild, sweet flavour. It will keep producing succulent leaves as long as you keep it well watered. It also has good mildew resistance.

Towers of beans

Choose from the old-fashioned varieties of French beans with bags of flavour or modern hybrids that promise succulent stringless pods, and you will never want to eat shop-bought again. Not only do those grown in the garden taste better, but they can be picked and enjoyed when they are young and tender.

PERFECT PODS

Plants used
French bean;
Thunbergia alata
(black-eyed Susan)

Height and spread
French bean:
H 1.5m (5ft);
Thunbergia:
H 1.5m (5ft)

Aspect
Full sun

Temperature needs
Not hardy below 0°C
(32°F)

Harvesting period
From late spring
to early autumn

Suitable pot size
45cm (18in)

**Suitable container
material**
Terracotta, plastic,
stone

Compost type
Multi-purpose
compost

Many people with small plots understandably give beans a wide berth, but climbing French beans are perfect for tiny gardens, as they can be grown in a large pot up an ornamental obelisk or cane wigwam. While some beans are naturally decorative with brightly coloured pods, others are less ornamental and can be teamed with flowering climbers to create a striking combination. For example, you can jazz up a plain green French bean by planting it with a yellow-flowered black-eyed Susan or some sweet peas.

Sow bean seeds indoors in early spring or plant them directly into a large pot of multi-purpose compost outdoors, after all danger of frost has passed. Alternatively, buy young plants from the garden centre. These climbing beans naturally grip their supports, but it's best to give them a helping hand until they're established by tying them to their supports with soft twine. Dwarf varieties of French bean do not need any supports.

CARING FOR FRENCH BEANS

Water plants frugally until they are established, increasing the amount you give them after the first flowers appear and until the last pods have been picked. Also feed plants with a tomato fertilizer fortnightly after the flowers form. Beans will be ready to harvest 8-12 weeks after sowing. Picking pods regularly when they're small and tender encourages the plant to produce more.

TOP TIP: SOWING BEAN SEEDS

Place one seed in a 7.5cm (3in) pot of seed compost and put it in a light, bright, frost-free place until it has germinated. Seedlings will be ready to plant outdoors in late spring. Or sow two seeds, 5cm (2in) deep, in the compost at the base of each leg of your support. When the seedlings have germinated, remove the weakest.

*Centre: **Grow French beans with a black-eyed Susan** in a large pot for a blaze of colour and fresh summer vegetables.*

Choosing bean varieties

'Blue Lake' is an old favourite that produces good-sized pods that are tender and stringless.

'The Prince' is a dwarf French bean that doesn't need staking. It's renowned for its heavy crops of long, flat pods.

'Delinel' produces tasty, slender, stingless beans with a good texture on dwarf plants that don't need staking.

'Purple Tepee' is a dwarf bean that looks and tastes great. Pods are deep purple, turning green when cooked.

'French Rocquencourt' is a very showy dwarf bean that will draw attention with its long golden pods.

'Cobra' is a vigorous variety and requires a large pot. It is valued for its heavy yields of long, tasty pods.

PERFECT PODS

Runner bean feast

A traditional favourite, runner beans are incredibly rewarding to grow. Not only will you enjoy a bumper harvest with the minimum of effort, their flowers are beautiful, too, and there are many tasty seed varieties to choose from, with pods in an assortment of sizes and flavours. Beans will do well in a large pot if given a sturdy support of bamboo sticks or hazel twigs to climb.

Plant used
Runner bean 'Red Rum'

Aspect
Full sun

Temperature needs
Not hardy below 0°C (32°F)

Harvesting period
Summer to autumn

Suitable pot size
45cm (18in)

Suitable container material
Plastic, stone, terracotta

Compost type
Multi-purpose compost

Runner beans are a top-heavy crop, so choose a weighty pot for stability. Depending on the variety, they can grow to 2m (6ft) and will need a support for their long, twining stems, mass of leaves and crop of pods. A bamboo wigwam is simple to make: space four to eight canes 15–22cm (6–9in) apart in a circle and bind the tops together with twine. Dwarf runner beans, which won't grow higher than 60cm (24in), will grow happily in a deep windowbox or patio pot with only a few pea sticks for support.

SOWING, FEEDING, AND WATERING

Start seeds off in small pots indoors in mid-spring for planting outdoors about six weeks later, after the last frost. Alternatively, sow directly into a pot outdoors in late spring or early summer. Sow two seeds 5cm (2in) deep at the base of each cane. Water in well. After germination, leave the most vigorous seedling to climb up the cane and nip out the other. Runner beans are self-supporting climbers and won't need tying in.

Water plants regularly after the first flower buds appear. If the compost is allowed to dry out, the flowers will fall. During dry weather, mist occasionally with a hand-held sprayer to raise humidity levels. When the beans reach the top of their supports, pinch out the growing tips to encourage more stems with pods to form. Runner beans are hungry crops: use a seaweed-based feed weekly, switching to a high-potash fertilizer when flowers form.

TOP TIP: HARVESTING

You can expect to be picking beans about three months after sowing. To ensure a constant supply, harvest them every few days while they are young and tender. The time you leave them to grow before picking depends on the variety. In general, if you leave runner beans too long on the plant they will become tough and stringy, and if you can feel the beans inside the pods, they will be too old and not worth eating.

Picked when young and tender
runner beans need little more than lightly steaming and a drizzle of butter for a delicious dish.

Choosing runner bean varieties

'White Lady' produces pretty white flowers followed by thick, tender pods. The flowers are a favourite with bees.

'Painted Lady' bears such pretty red and white flowers that the long, tasty beans are almost an added bonus.

'Polestar' produces masses of tender, stringless beans with smooth pods and bright scarlet flowers.

'Lady Di' has vibrant red flowers with heavy crops of long, slender, tasty beans with no hint of stringiness.

The runner bean 'Red Rum' needs a large pot and bamboo cane supports for its mass of scrambling stems. Its beautiful red flowers ensure it doesn't look out of place on the patio.

Peas and pods

You don't need loads of space to grow peas, mangetouts, or sugar snaps. These crops climb vertically up supports in large containers, squeezing onto tiny patios and terraces. Plants will reward you with baskets of tender pods to add to traditional fare and Oriental dishes, while young crops are delicious when eaten fresh off the plant.

Peas

Plant used
Peas

Aspect
Full sun

Temperature
Not hardy below 0°C (32°F)

Harvesting period
Summer

Suitable pot size
30cm (12in) or larger

Suitable container material
Plastic, terracotta, fabric or planting bags

Compost type
Multi-purpose compost

Freshly podded peas eaten within seconds of being picked are a melt-in-the-mouth sensation. As well as tasting delicious, some peas also make decorative patio plants, and really earn their keep in the garden. 'Purple Podded' is a heritage variety with dusky purple pods, while 'Blauwschokker' has red and violet flowers, followed by purple pods.

SOWING FROM SEED
Sow pea seeds 5cm (2in) deep in large pots of multi-purpose compost between spring and midsummer. Water well, and when seedlings appear, add supports for the plants to climb up. For an earlier crop, start a few seeds off in small pots indoors in early spring, and plant out the seedlings when the frosts have passed.

Water plants frequently, ensuring the compost does not dry out, but ensure pots have good drainage by standing them on "feet"; place bags on pebbles. Feed with a tomato fertilizer when flowers appear, and harvest pods regularly to encourage more to form.

TOP TIP: STAKING PLANTS

When seedlings are about 5cm (2in) in height, add some supports to prevent plants from collapsing as they grow. Either make a rustic wigwam with twigs, use bamboo canes tied together at the top, or, for an ornamental display, use a decorative tripod. Once they get going, peas will grip the supports with their tendrils, but give young plants a helping hand by securing the stems with soft twine.

White flowers and ripening peas make an ornamental display in a planting bag. Set bags on pebbles to aid drainage.

Mangetouts

Plant used
Mangetouts

Aspect
Full sun

Temperature
Not hardy below 0°C
(32°F)

Harvesting period
Summer

Suitable pot size
30cm (12in) or larger

Suitable container material
Plastic, terracotta, fabric or planting bags

Compost type
Multi-purpose compost

Mangetout ripen throughout summer.

Grown for their flattened tender pods which are eaten whole, mangetout can be steamed or boiled, or added to stir fries. There are many tasty varieties: 'Carouby de Maussanne' has long wide pods that follow attractive purple flowers, or try 'Oregon Sugar Pod', which has broad pods with a intensely sweet flavour.

Sow seeds, water, and feed mangetout as you would peas (*see opposite*). Also provide sturdy supports for the stems, which can grow up to 1–1.5m (3–5ft) in height.

PICKING PODS
Mangetout are best picked and eaten young before they become tough and stringy. As a rule of thumb, pick crops when the pods are about 5cm (2in) long. Harvest frequently to encourage a long-lasting supply of pods to form.

Sugar snaps

Plant used
Sugar snaps

Aspect
Full sun

Temperature
Not hardy below 0°C
(32°F)

Harvesting period
Summer

Suitable pot size
30cm (12in) or larger

Suitable container material
Plastic, terracotta, fabric or planting bags

Compost type
Multi-purpose compost

The fat pods of sugar snaps are eaten whole when the peas inside are fully developed. Sweet, crisp, and tasty, they are the perfect ingredient for stir-fries, or you can steam them for a few minutes so that they still retain their crunch. Sow seeds directly into large pots of multi-purpose compost outside from late spring to mid-summer, and add supports before plants flop.

Sugar snaps require the same growing conditions and watering and feeding regime as peas (*see opposite*). The main pests for all three pod plants are slugs, snails, and birds. Protect containers from slugs and snails with copper bands (*see p.243*) and net plants to keep birds at bay.

WHAT TO GROW
There is a limited selection of sugar snaps to choose from, but it is worth selecting varieties carefully, as some are extremely vigorous and can scale heights of 1.8m (6ft). Among the best for large containers are 'Sugar Ann', which grows to a compact 75cm (30in), and 'Cascadia', which reaches 90cm (3ft).

Sugar snaps are easy to grow.

Perfect potatoes

Chipped, roasted, mashed, sautéed, boiled, or baked, potatoes are an essential ingredient in many favourite dishes. Despite being a root vegetable with a sizable root system, potatoes are relatively easy to grow in pots. Plant in early or mid-spring and they'll be ready to harvest in just a few months.

DELICIOUS ROOTS

Plant used
Potatoes

Aspect
Full sun

Temperature needs
Hardy to -15°C (5°F)

Harvesting period
From late spring to early autumn, depending on type of potato

Suitable pot size
At least 30cm wide (12in) and 30cm (12in) deep

Suitable container material
Plastic; fabric bags

Compost type
Multi-purpose compost

Although there are a great array of different potato varieties available to grow in as many different colours, shapes, and sizes, relatively few of them make it on to the supermarket shelves. If you want to sample some of these more unusual, and often delicious, types you will have to grow your own.

PLANTING POTATOES IN CONTAINERS
Before planting, potato tubers need "chitting" to encourage them to produce shoots. In late winter, place the tubers in a shallow tray, an egg carton, or on sheets of newspaper and leave in a cool, light place. When shoots are about 2.5cm (1in) long, which can take up to six weeks, the potatoes are ready to plant.

Potatoes need a deep and wide container – a plastic dustbin, bucket or fabric potato bag are ideal. Just make sure it has plenty of drainage holes in the base or the tubers will rot. Put a 15cm (6in) layer of compost in the bottom of your container, then place two tubers on top, making sure the sprouts are facing upwards. Cover with another 15cm (6in) layer of compost and water well. When the shoots are about 20cm (8in) tall, add a second layer of compost, leaving just the growing tips poking above the surface. As the stems continue to grow, keep adding more compost until the container is almost full. Keep your potatoes well watered, especially during hot, dry spells, and feed weekly with a seaweed-based fertilizer.

*Centre: **The stems of potato plants** are easily snapped. When growing in containers, push in a few pea sticks for support.*

TOP TIP: HARVESTING CROPS

Potatoes are ready to harvest from early summer to early autumn. Salad and early potatoes should be lifted while the plants are flowering; maincrop types are ready when the foliage dies back. To harvest, tip the container on its side and loosen the compost with your fingers, "combing" through it to scoop up all the tubers.

Choosing potato varieties

'Foremost' *produces neat, round tubers with yellow skins and firm, white flesh. Use as a new and salad potato.*

'Red Duke of York' *has oval-shaped tubers with eye-catching red skins and creamy-white flesh. Good for baking.*

'Accent' *is great for boiling. This early potato has oval tubers with pale yellow skins and flesh. Good slug resistance.*

'Belle de Fontenay' *produces small, yellow, kidney-shaped tubers with waxy flesh. A salad potato that stores well.*

'Yukon Gold' *is a large, yellow-skinned potato that is perfect for baking or frying. It has a rich buttery flavour.*

'Pink Fir Apple' *has knobbly tubers that are impossible to peel, so just scrub them. Delicious served cold in salads.*

'Ratte' *is an old French variety with nutty-tasting, smooth-textured, waxy tubers that can be eaten hot or cold.*

'Charlotte' *is a great tasting, high-yielding salad potato with slender tubers and firm, creamy-yellow flesh.*

Health-promoting roots

You may not have considered growing root vegetables in containers, but as long as you give them a good depth of compost and keep them well watered they should do well. Beetroot is a virtually maintenance-free crop, while perennial horseradish requires a little more hands-on attention, but if you're a fan of the fiery sauce it's well worth the effort.

Horseradish

Plant used
Horseradish

Height and spread
H 75cm (30in)
S indefinite

Aspect
Sun or partial shade

Temperature needs
Fully hardy

Harvesting period
Autumn

Suitable pot size
Min. 30cm (12in)

Suitable container material
Plastic

Compost type
Multi-purpose compost

When planted in the ground, perennial horseradish is an invasive thug, but it can be tamed by growing in a large container. Bare-root plants, known as "thongs", are sold in spring; young plants are available later in the season. To plant thongs, fill a pot with multi-purpose compost, make deep vertical holes with a dibber, then drop in a thong so that the top sits 5cm (2in) beneath the surface of the compost. You'll fit three thongs in a 30cm (12in) pot. Cover over with compost and keep well watered. With its white-splashed foliage, *Amoracia rusticana* 'Variegata' is much showier than the commonly grown green species.

REJUVENATING PLANTS
Horseradish is a vigorous plant that will quickly fill a pot. When you harvest it in autumn rejuvenate your plants at the same time. Upturn the pot and remove about half the slender white roots, then replant the remaining portion in fresh compost. These will stir into life in spring, producing a flush of new leaves.

TOP TIP: STORING ROOTS

Horseradish is best used fresh, but if you have a glut, bundle roots together and place them in a wooden box or tray covered with damp sand. Put the box in a cool, dark, frost-free place. Alternatively, peel and grate roots and dry them in a low oven for a few hours. Store in an airtight container for 2–3 months.

Variegated horseradish makes an attractive foliage plant, and produces the same hot roots as the plain green species.

DELICIOUS ROOTS

Beetroot

Plant used
Beetroot

Height and spread
H 1.8m (6ft)
S 1m (3ft)

Aspect
Full sun

Temperature needs
Fully hardy

Harvesting period
Summer into early autumn

Suitable pot size
30cm (12in)

Suitable container material
Plastic, terracotta

Compost type
Multi-purpose compost

If you have never eaten fresh beetroot before, you're in for a real treat. The roots have a warm, earthy taste that is so much sweeter than anything you will find pickled in vinegar. Tender baby beets are delicious grated raw in salads, while mature roots are best boiled or roasted. Harvest them before they have a chance to develop a woody core – ideally when they are no bigger than 6cm (2½in) in diameter. You can also eat the colourful leaves; harvest them when they are young to add to salads, or steam them like spinach.

If you fancy something different, there is a huge range of variously shaped and coloured roots to try, and all have one thing in common – they are easy to grow.

SOWING SEEDS

Sow seed from mid-spring to early summer. Fill a container with compost, leaving a 5cm (2in) gap between the surface and the rim to allow space for watering. Sow seeds thinly across the surface and cover over with a 2cm (1in) layer of compost that has been sieved to remove any lumps. Keep well watered. When seedlings are large enough to handle, thin them out so that plants are about 12cm (5in) apart, to give the roots plenty of space to develop. Use the thinnings in a salad.

Colourful beetroot are easy to grow from seed; just keep them well watered and you're guaranteed a good crop.

CHOOSING BEETROOT VARIETIES

'Red Ace' grows strongly and is tolerant of dry conditions. It produces dark red roots that are round and uniform in size with a fine, sweet flavour.

'Chioggia Pink' beets are rosy pink on the outside, but when cut open they reveal pretty pink and white concentric circles. Keep well watered to prevent bolting.

'Boltardy' is a very popular variety due to its resistance to bolting. It also matures quickly from an early sowing. Tender spherical roots have a smooth skin.

'Forono' is perfect for slicing due to its long cylindrical roots. Young crops taste particularly good. Delay sowing the seed until mid-spring to prevent bolting.

Crunchy carrots

While we're used to seeing carrots growing in neat rows in the veg patch, they do well in large pots too. You just need to match the type of carrot you grow to the depth of compost: long and tapering varieties will need a deep container, while short, stumpy types are fine in shallow pots and growing bags.

Plant used
Carrot 'Mini Finger'

Aspect
Full sun

Temperature needs
Hardy, although young plants may be damaged by frost

Harvesting period
Late summer to autumn

Suitable pot size
20cm (8in)

Suitable container material
Plastic, terracotta, windowbox

Compost type
Soil-based compost, eg, John Innes No 3

Rounded, stump-rooted carrots are the obvious choice for growing in pots, but if you have a deep enough container you can grow the traditional long-rooted varieties. Ideally, harvest these carrots when young, before there's any hint of woodiness. Wait for them to colour up – in most cases, they will turn orange – and pick them when they are about the width of a finger. Alternatively, grow a Lilliputian patio carrot, such as 'Mini Finger', which has quick-maturing, slender roots.

Early varieties can be sown in early spring, but will need covering with cloches or fleece to protect them from the worst of the weather. From mid-spring to midsummer, carrots can be sown outdoors without any protection.

To make growing carrots worth your while, have several pots on the go; sow seeds in each at fortnightly intervals. Alternatively, divide up a large container or growing bag and stagger the sowing times in different sections. To sow, scatter seeds thinly across the surface of damp compost – space them about 2–3cm (¾–1¼in) apart – and cover with a 1cm (½in) layer of compost.

WATERING AND FEEDING

The compost should remain damp at all times, but take care to avoid overwatering as this will result in lots of leafy top growth at the expense of root development. Watering after the compost has remained dry for several days will cause the roots to split. Fresh soil-based compost contains sufficient nutrients to ensure a good crop without supplementary feeding.

Centre: **Carrot 'Mini Finger'** *produces cylindrical-shaped carrots that will be at their most tender when finger width.*

TOP TIP: PROTECTION FROM CARROT FLY

When seedlings are thinned out, carrot fly are attracted by the smell and lay their eggs. After hatching the larvae burrow into the carrot. As a precaution, avoid thinning by sowing seed thinly, and cover pots with a fine mesh to prevent flies landing.

Choosing carrot varieties

'Bangor' *is best grown in a deep container. This maincrop variety boasts tasty, smooth, cylindrical roots.*

'Carson' *is a tapering carrot with a sweet taste and a crunchy texture. The crops also store well.*

'Chantenay Red Cored 2' *is a delicious, sweet-tasting carrot. The stump-shaped roots are a deep orange colour.*

'Infinity' *has long, slender, roots that are very sweet and crunchy. Can be picked three months after sowing.*

'Amsterdam Forcing 3' *is an old and popular variety with bright orange, sweet-flavoured roots. Delicious raw.*

'Autumn King 2' *produces tasty, red-cored roots that have good resistance to splitting. Needs a deep container.*

'Volcano' *is a very tasty carrot that is frost resistant (good for early sowing) with long, slender, orange roots.*

'Parmex' *is a quick-to-mature, round-rooted carrot with a great taste; roots can be eaten whole.*

Colourful squash

Whether tumbling down the sides of a container or climbing up supports, squashes and pumpkins produce colourful fruits to brighten up the garden in early autumn. They can be stored for up to six months, providing you with tasty flesh that can be roasted, steamed, or boiled in winter dishes. Small fruits also make ornamental table decorations for the home.

Plant used
'Harlequin' and pattypan squashes; small pumpkin

Aspect
Full sun

Temperature
Not hardy below 0°C (32°F)

Harvesting period
Autumn

Suitable pot size
Min. 30cm (12in)

Suitable container material
Plastic, raised beds, growing bags

Compost type
Multi-purpose compost

With their wildly colourful fruits in all manner of shapes and sizes, the choice of winter squashes and pumpkins is vast. As well as tasting delicious, the fruits also look great in containers, raised beds, or growing bags on a sunny, sheltered patio.

Either buy young plants in late spring or start your own off from seeds sown indoors. Sow two seeds on their sides, 2.5cm (1in) deep in small pots from early to late spring, and place in a heated propagator. After germination, remove the weaker of the two seedlings. When roots appear at the base of the pots move seedlings into larger containers, and plant outside after the last frosts. If you don't have room to allow the plants to trail across the ground, train them up supports. Not all are self-supporting, so you will need to tie stems in, and make sure the supports are sturdy enough to take the weight of your plants when they are laden with fruit. Water pots regularly, especially in hot weather.

RIPENING PUMPKINS

To encourage fruits to develop and ripen, they need lots of light and air, so snip off any leaves that are shading them. Harvesting time depends on the variety you grow, but all need picking before the first autumn frosts.

TOP TIP: STORING WINTER SQUASH

After harvesting your pumpkins and squashes, spread them out on a clean surface in a light, sunny spot, such as a shelf in a cool room or a greenhouse bench, for about a week until the skins harden. This process prevents the flesh from drying out during the long winter storage. Your fruits will keep until spring if stored in a cool, frost-free place on a dry layer of cardboard or clean straw.

'Harlequin' and pattypan squashes, and small pumpkins require feeding weekly with a high potash formula, such as tomato fertilizer. Your rewards will be these highly decorative fruits.

Choosing squash varieties

'Turk's Turban' is one of the most colourful squashes available. The pale-lemon flesh tastes a little like turnip.

'Jack Be Little' produces up to eight tiny fruits per plant – just the right size for an individual portion.

'Sweet Dumpling' has up to 10 stripey fruits per plant. Either roast them whole or use for soups and stews.

'Crown Prince' has ribbed, blue-grey skin and orange flesh, which is delicious roasted. Flowers are a magnet for bees.

Small pumpkins may not need extra support, but place heavier fruits in net bags (use those sold with citrus fruit) and tie these to sturdy canes to prevent the stems from snapping.

Winter staples

If you enjoy growing your own food there's no reason for pickings to come to an end in the autumn. Extend the growing season with these hardy crops to add fresh flavours to your dishes throughout the winter months. All can be grown in large pots and are easy to raise from seed or young plants bought from the garden centre.

Leeks

Plant used
Leeks

Aspect
Full sun

Temperature
Fully hardy

Harvesting period
Late autumn to winter

Suitable pot size
30cm (12in) or larger

Suitable container material
Stone, growing bags, plastic, wooden crates

Compost type
Soil-based compost, eg, John Innes No 3

This staple of the vegetable garden is a handsome plant for a pot, thanks to its upright stems and cascading, glaucous leaves. For a good show and decent harvest, plant enough leeks to supply several meals. Grow them in a few inexpensive plastic pots or large containers, such as wooden packing crates, that are at least 35cm (14in) deep.

Plants prefer a sunny, sheltered site and well-drained, soil-based compost. Sow seeds in pots indoors in mid-spring, and plant seedlings in their final containers in late spring or early summer. Keep crops well watered and harvest from late autumn and throughout winter.

TOP TIP: PLANTING OUT SEEDLINGS

Plant leek seedlings in large pots outside in late spring or early summer. First, make holes with a dibber, 20cm (8in) deep and 15cm (6in) apart, and drop a seedling into each. Pour water into the holes and leave to soak away. This draws enough soil over the plants to cover the roots and produce blanched stems.

Feed leeks in pots with a high-nitrogen fertilizer in midsummer to sustain growth until plants are ready to harvest.

Winter cabbage and endive

Plant used
Endive

Aspect
Full sun

Temperature
Fully hardy

Harvesting period
Late autumn to winter

Suitable pot size
Large rectangular trough or 45cm (18in) pot

Suitable container material
Stone, growing bags, plastic

Compost type
Soil-based compost, eg, John Innes No 3

There aren't many vegetables you can pick over winter, but growing cabbages in pots is an ideal way to ensure you have some fresh crops at this time of year. They also make attractive plants that will happily put up with the worst of the weather. There's a good choice of varieties on offer, from smooth-skinned types to the Savoy cabbages, famed for their highly textured, corrugated leaves.

Sow seeds in late spring and plant out the seedlings in midsummer. Use a trough or rectangle container that will fit several cabbage plants and produce a decent-sized crop. Cover pots with netting to keep out cabbage white butterflies, as their caterpillars will gobble up your crops in no time. Water the plants well and feed with a balanced granular fertilizer when planting out.

GROWING ENDIVE

The frilly leaves of endive are highly decorative, but the bitter flavour is an acquired taste. Sow seeds into large troughs in midsummer, then thin out to space plants 20cm (8in) apart. Pick the outer leaves as required, or allow the whole head to mature and cut it off, leaving a short stump. This may resprout with new growth. Cover with a cloche or fleece in winter to extend the harvest.

Endive looks decorative in pots and has a bitter taste that adds a kick to winter dishes.

COOL-SEASON CROPS

SELECTING CABBAGE VARIETIES

'January King 3' is a Savoy-style cabbage and a traditional winter favourite, with large, tasty heads concealed between glaucous, frilled outer leaves.

'Jewel' is resistant to bolting and will happily endure tough winter weather to form a loose head of very tasty, smooth, dark green leaves ideal for winter stews.

'Siberia' lives up to its name and will shrug off frost, snow, and any other winter weather conditions without discolouring. It is a Savoy cabbage with a sweet flavour.

'Tarvoy' has been bred to survive the toughest of winter weather. A Savoy cabbage, it produces an attractive, dense, wrinkly head of dark green, nutritious leaves.

Fresh mint

A favourite garnish for boiled potatoes, tangy spearmint is also used to make classic mint sauce, while peppermint makes a wonderfully soothing tea. But why limit yourself to just "minty" mints when you could also be growing spicy ginger, apple, and even chocolate-flavoured types? With leaf shapes as excitingly varied as their flavours, plant a selection in individual pots.

Plants used
Mentha suaveolens 'Variegata'; *Viola; Bacopa* (syn. *Sutera cordata*)

Height and spread
Mentha: H & S 30cm (12in); *Viola*: H 15cm (6in); *Bacopa* S 30cm (12in)

Aspect
Sun or partial shade

Temperature needs
Fully hardy

Harvesting period
Spring to autumn

Suitable pot size
30cm (12in)

Suitable container material
Terracotta, stone

Compost type
Mix of multi-purpose and soil-based composts

If mint is planted straight into the ground you run the risk of it spreading everywhere. To avoid this problem, keep it safely confined in a container, which you can either stand by the back door within easy reach of the kitchen, or plunge into a gap in the border – just make sure the lip of the container remains above the surface to prevent shoots escaping over the top.

There are dozens of different mints to try. Tashkent mint, *Mentha spicata* 'Tashkent', is an upright plant with heavily textured leaves, while chocolate peppermint, *M.* x *piperita* f. *citrata* 'Chocolate', has dark brown leaves that taste like chocolate creams. *M.* 'Berries and Cream' has a fruity kick and *M. arvensis* 'Banana', as its name suggests, smells of bananas. If you want to grow several different mints, don't plant them side by side or they will lose their individual scent and flavour.

Looking after mint is easy. Grow in a sunny or partly shaded spot and keep plants well watered, especially during hot, dry weather. Top dress twice a year with a handful of bonemeal.

Picking leaves regularly keeps plants compact and encourages them to produce lots of new shoots. When your plants have finished blooming in summer, cut back any flowered shoots to 5cm (2in) above the surface of the compost.

PRESERVING MINT

Mint is best used fresh but you can preserve leaves for use over winter when the plant dies back. Pick shoots, wash well, shake dry, then chop into small pieces and add to an ice-cube mould. Fill with water and freeze. Whenever you need some mint for cooking, simply knock out an ice cube and add it to your recipe.

TOP TIP: NEW PLANTS

When pots of mint become congested you will need to rejuvenate the plant. To do this, upend the container and ease out the root ball. Split it in half, teasing the roots apart, and repot a portion in the same container in fresh compost.

Mint is also easy to propagate from stem cuttings – push 10cm (4in) lengths of stem into small pots of damp compost or stand in water until rooted.

Lemon mint, Mentha x piperita f. citrata 'Lemon', combines peppermint and citrus flavours and works well in both green and fruit salads.

HERBS

Choosing mints

Apple mint, Mentha suaveolens, *has oval leaves and mauve flowers that appear in summer. Good in mint sauce.*

Horse mint, Mentha longifolia, *is a wild form with grey leaves and spires of purple flowers. Used in aromatherapy.*

Ginger mint, Mentha x gracilis, *has oval leaves with a spicy mint scent that goes well with vegetables and fruit.*

Eau de cologne mint, Mentha x piperita f. citrata, *is highly aromatic. Infuse leaves in vinegars.*

Pineapple mint underplanted with violas and bacopa *makes a cottage-style combination for a large rustic container, such as an old chimney pot.*

Calming herbs

Herbs aren't just for flavouring foods, many are also renowned for their calming properties and have foliage or flowers that can be used to make delicately flavoured, soothing teas. Fennel, lemon balm, and chamomile are three such herbs. They thrive in sunny sites and make welcome additions to any container garden.

Fennel *Foeniculum vulgare*

Plants used
Florence fennel
(*Foeniculum vulgare*
var. *azoricum*)
and herb fennel
(*F. vulgare*)

Height
H 2m (6ft)
S 45cm (18in)

Aspect
Full sun

Temperature
Fully hardy

Harvesting period
Leaves from spring
to autumn; seeds
in autumn; harvest
Florence fennel roots
in autumn

Suitable pot size
30cm (12in) or larger

**Suitable container
material**
Plastic, metal

Compost type
Soil-based compost,
eg, John Innes No 3

There are two types of fennel: Florence and the herb. Florence fennel is a biennial grown for its aniseed-flavoured root, which is delicious grated raw into salads or braised, while the feathery leaves of the perennial herb fennel, *F. vulgare*, add an aniseed tang to salads. The pungent seeds of the herb, which follow the yellow flowers, are also used for cooking or to make tea (*see below*). As well as the green-leaved species, try the cultivar 'Smokey' with its bronze leaves and sweet, liquorice flavour.

SOWING AND GROWING
In spring, sow Florence fennel seeds indoors into small pots. After the last frost, transfer seedlings outdoors, spacing them 30cm (12in) apart, and cover plants with fleece until the weather warms up. Grow herb fennel from seed or buy young plants. Both types need a free-draining, soil-based compost with a little slow-release, balanced granular fertilizer mixed into the top layer. Keep plants well watered and mulch the surface with garden compost.

TOP TIP: MAKING FENNEL TEA

Fennel seeds have long been used to make a subtly flavoured tea that is said to aid digestion and relieve stomach cramps. To make a brew, boil 500ml (1 pint) of water, then add one teaspoon of fresh fennel seeds and leave to steep for 10 minutes. Strain and pour into cups. Serve with fresh orange rind.

Florence (centre) and herb fennel *make the perfect combination if you love the taste of aniseed.*

HERBS

Chamomile *Chamaemelum nobile*

Plant used
Chamomile
(*Chamaemelum
nobile*)

Height and spread
H & S 30cm (12in)

Aspect
Full sun

Temperature
Fully hardy

Harvesting period
Summer

Suitable pot size
30cm (12in)

**Suitable container
material**
Terracotta, stone,
plastic

Compost type
Soil-based compost,
eg, John Innes No 3

Chamomile tea is made by adding the fresh or dried flowers of this mat-forming perennial to boiling water. The white, daisy-like flowers appear in summer on long stems above green, feathery foliage, which is highly fragrant when crushed. Roman chamomile (*Chamaemelum nobile*) is the best for flowers – try the form 'Flore Pleno', which reaches 15cm (6in) and produces double flowers. Low-growing types, such as 'Treneague', are used for lawns, but they don't produce the flowers needed for tea.

GROWING GUIDE
Grow chamomile from seed, or buy young plants in spring. Plant in 30cm (12in) pots filled with soil-based compost and stand in full sun. Raise pots up on "feet" to prevent plants rotting in winter, and feed every six weeks in summer with a liquid organic fertilizer. Trim occasionally to prevent stems becoming leggy.

Chamomile soothes frayed nerves.

Lemon balm *Melissa officinalis*

Plant used
Lemon balm
(*Melissa officinalis*
'All Gold')

Height and spread
H 75cm (30in)
S indefinite

Aspect
Full sun

Temperature
Fully hardy

Harvesting period
Late spring to
autumn

**Suitable container
size**
20cm (8in)

**Suitable container
material**
Terracotta, stone,
plastic

Compost type
Soil-based compost,
eg, John Innes No 3

Lemon balm 'All Gold' is ideal for tea.

The essential oil from the leaves of this highly scented perennial herb are widely used in aromatherapy, while lemon balm tea is thought to help relieve tension, aid digestion, and improve memory. The plain green species, *Melissa officinalis*, is rather dull to look at, but the cultivar 'All Gold' is a striking yellow, while variegated 'Aurea' has dazzling green- and yellow-splashed leaves. All three have aromatic leaves that will release their volatile oils at the lightest touch and make soothing teas.

For the best scent, position plants in full sun, and raise containers so they are within easy reach. Trim plants regularly to encourage bushy growth, and remove flower spikes.

WINTER CARE
Lemon balm is a hardy, deciduous, perennial plant but it may suffer during wet winters. Raise containers on pot "feet" and place them in a sheltered position, such as the rainshadow adjacent to the wall of a house or a fence.

Permanent herb displays

Evergreen herbs are valuable plants to grow in the garden. They not only provide colour, structure, and beauty all year round, but during the winter months they're a mainstay when there's very little else to harvest in the herb garden. Bay is an essential ingredient in the classic bouquet garni, together with parsley and thyme, while sage makes the perfect stuffing for roast meats.

Bay *Laurus nobilis*

Plant used
Standard bay
(*Laurus nobilis*)

Height and spread
H 1.8m (6ft)
S 50cm (20in)

Aspect
Full sun

Temperature needs
Hardy, but should be protected in hard winters

Harvesting period
All year round

Suitable pot size
30cm (12in) or larger

Suitable container material
Any

Compost type
Soil-based compost, eg, John Innes No 2

A pair of standard bay lollipops in attractive containers is one of the most elegant ways to frame a front door or entrance. A single plant would also make the perfect centrepiece for a group of pots on the patio, or an accent of green in a colourful annual flower border.

Originally from the Mediterranean, bay needs lots of sun and good drainage. Raise containers on pot feet to improve drainage and prevent roots rotting in soggy compost. If possible, move plants to a frost-free place over winter, or, at the very least, wrap the top in fleece to protect the leaves from wind scorch.

PRUNING BAY
An evergreen shrub with dense-growing leaves, bay is perfect for simple topiary – a cone or pyramid shape is easy to achieve. If left unpruned, plants will soon grow untidy, so clip them with shears in summer. Clear shoots from standard stems by cutting or twisting them off.

TOP TIP: PRESERVING LEAVES

Bay leaves are best used fresh, but stems or individual leaves can be dried in an airing cupboard. Store the leaves whole in airtight bags or containers for up to a year.

Together with parsley and thyme, bay leaves make up the classic flavour of bouquet garni. Gather a handful of herbs and tie them tightly together with string. Use to flavour soups and casseroles.

Feed bay trees in spring *and again in midsummer with a balanced organic fertilizer.*

Sage *Salvia officinalis*

Plants used
Variegated sage
(*Salvia officinalis*
'Tricolor');
Strawberries

Height and spread
H 40cm (16in)
S 1m (3ft)

Aspect
Full sun

Temperature needs
Hardy to frost-
hardy, depending
on variety

Harvesting period
All year round

Suitable pot size
24cm (10in)

**Suitable container
material**
Any

Compost type
Soil-based compost

Sage is a strong-tasting, aromatic herb that combines perfectly with onions in the popular stuffing mix for pork roasts. Common sage (*Salvia officinalis*) has the best taste, but its grey-green leaves make it a fairly nondescript plant for a patio pot. Fortunately, there are many varieties of culinary sage that not only taste good but also have attractive ornamental foliage. Try growing variegated sage, *Salvia officinalis* 'Tricolor', purple sage, *S. officinalis* 'Purpurascens', and *S. officinalis* 'Variegata'.

A native of North Africa and the Mediterranean region, this rough-leaved herb needs a sunny, sheltered spot to set its volatile aromatic oils sizzling. Although it's a shrubby perennial, sage tends to be short-lived, so expect to replace plants every four to five years. Like many perennials, it takes a long time to grow from seed, so either buy young plants from a nursery or take softwood cuttings in spring.

ANNUAL CARE
Common sage is a fairly undemanding plant. Water regularly over summer and keep plants compact by pruning in late spring. Sage doesn't like winter wet, so place pots in a sheltered spot and raise on pot feet. Feed annually in spring with an all-purpose granular fertilizer.

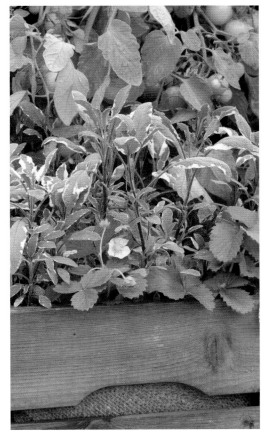

Sage and strawberries *are combined here to create an attractive and aromatic fruit and herb container.*

HERBS

CHOOSING VARIETIES OF SAGE

S. elegans *'Scarlet Pineapple'* *is not a culinary herb, but is worth growing for its pineapple-scented foliage and, in autumn, spires of scarlet flowers.*

S. officinalis *'Tricolor'* *is an attractive form of common sage that looks and tastes good, with cream, green, and pink variegated leaves. Needs winter protection.*

S. officinalis *'Purpurascens'* *is a hardy form, with tactile, deeply textured, pungent leaves. In summer, it is topped by tall spires of pretty mauve flowers.*

S. officinalis, *or the common sage, has aromatic grey-green leaves that are wonderfully useful for cooking. It is fully hardy and will survive outside in winter without any fuss.*

Rich flavours

The aromatic foliage of these flavoursome herbs is at its best on warm, sunny days when the volatile oils they contain fill the air with their pungent scent. Grow thyme and basil in a sunny spot in containers on their own or in combination with other Mediterranean herbs or edible plants for a display that will look as good as it tastes.

Thyme *Thymus vulgaris*

Plants used
Golden thyme; tarragon; chives

Height and spread
H & S 25cm (10in)

Aspect
Full sun

Temperature requirement
Hardy, but protect from winter wet

Harvesting period
All year round

Suitable pot size
15cm (6in) or larger

Suitable container material
Any

Suitable compost
Soil-based compost, eg, John Innes No 3

Position pots or hang baskets of thyme close to the kitchen door, or near your outdoor eating area, so that you can pick fresh leaves to sprinkle over salads or barbecued meats.

Thyme is a tough little evergreen shrub, and extremely drought tolerant. It thrives in a sunny site in well-drained compost, and you can prevent plants from becoming leggy by keeping the compost on the dry side. Over winter, improve drainage by raising pots on "feet". Feed plants fortnightly in summer with a seaweed-based fertilizer, and clip to shape after flowering.

BEST FOR POTS

There are many fabulous ground-cover or spreading thymes, but choose upright types for containers. Among the best for scent, flavour, and good looks are the golden lemon thyme (*Thymus* 'Golden Lemon'), orange-scented thyme (*T.* 'Fragrantissimus'), and *T. pulegioides* 'Archer's Gold'.

TOP TIP: PLANTING PARTNERS

Thyme combines well with other herbs and edible plants. Try growing it alongside red lettuces, chives, and sage for an attractive display in a large container. Apart from culinary uses, thyme makes an excellent companion plant because its pungent smell helps to ward off pests that could damage other crops. Bees also love its pollen- and nectar-rich flowers.

Golden thyme, tarragon, and chives *all love the free-draining conditions of a hanging basket.*

HERBS

Basil *Ocimum basilicum*

Plants used
Basil; French marigolds (*Tagetes*); thyme; tomatoes

Height and spread
H & S 45cm (18in)

Aspect
Full sun

Temperature requirement
Not hardy below 0°C (32°F)

Harvesting period
Spring to early autumn

Suitable pot size
15cm (6in) or larger

Suitable container material
Plastic, terracotta, stone

Suitable compost
Multi-purpose compost

Home-grown basil tastes and looks far superior to those leggy seedlings sold in plastic punnets in supermarkets. Start these half-hardy annuals off from seed sown in late winter or early spring. Fill a 7.5cm (3in) pot with seed compost, firm down and sow a few seeds of your favourite variety over the top. Cover with a thin layer of vermiculite, water carefully and pop it into a propagator. If you don't have one, cover the pot with a small, clear freezer bag and secure with an elastic band. After germination, remove from the propagator or freezer bag. Keep the compost moist, and when the seedlings have four or five leaves, transfer to 7.5cm (3in) pots, placing two or three seedlings in each. Move to larger pots when roots show through the drainage holes at the bottom. Wait until the temperature warms to 10°C (50°F) before moving plants outside.

KEEPING PLANTS PRODUCTIVE

Basil will continue to produce fresh leaves until the end of summer if you transfer plants into larger containers when you see roots through the holes at the bottom of their current pot. Keep plants bushy and productive by pinching out the stem tips regularly, and remove flowers. Feed plants once a month with a balanced liquid fertilizer, and water in the morning.

Basil mixes well with tomatoes, marigolds, and thyme.

HERBS

CHOOSING BASIL VARIETIES

Ocimum basilicum *var. purpurascens 'Dark Opal'* *has purple, oval-shaped, spicy-scented leaves. In summer it produces clusters of small pink flowers.*

O. basilicum *'Horapha Nanum'*, *or Thai basil, is a compact plant with narrow, deeply veined, aniseed-scented leaves that are widely used in Thai cooking.*

O. basilicum *'Well Sweep Purple Miniature'* *is a diminutive type of purple basil that forms a low mound. It has great-tasting, green-edged, tapering leaves.*

O. basilicum *'Minette'* *is a compact basil that forms an attractive rounded mound in a small container. The leaves have a deliciously spicy flavour.*

Cooking essentials

Parsley, rosemary, and oregano are three of the most useful and commonly used herbs in the kitchen, but these culinary delights are not just for eating. All possess handsome foliage, and rosemary and oregano produce pretty flowers that attract beneficial wildlife. Site pots near the kitchen door so they are always close to hand.

Parsley *Petroselinum crispum*

Plant used
Petroselinum crispum

Height and spread
H 30cm (12in)
S 25cm (10in)

Aspect
Partial shade

Temperature needs
Fully hardy

Havesting period
All year round

Suitable pot size
25cm (10in)

Suitable container material
Plastic, stone, terracotta

Compost type
Multi-purpose compost

If you want a herb to add to winter dishes, sow some parsley seeds in autumn and you'll have plenty of tasty leaves to pick over the chilly months ahead. Alternatively, sow in spring for leaves that can be snipped all year. Technically a biennial, parsley is usually grown as an annual, and performs well in pots of multi-purpose compost and a partially shaded site. Water plants regularly and pick leaves frequently, which will encourage more to form. Although curly-leaved parsley looks great and has textured foliage, flat-leaved parsley has a stronger taste and is more useful in the kitchen.

TOP TIP: SOWING PARSLEY SEED

Fill a clean container with compost and sow seeds thinly on top. Cover with a 1cm (½in) layer of compost and water. Leave in a cool spot to germinate, which may take up to a month. When large enough to handle, thin the seedlings so they are 2cm (½in) apart.

Curly-leaved parsley
makes an ornamental
plant for a patio pot,
and produces fresh
leaves all year round.

Rosemary *Rosmarinus officinalis*

Plant used
Rosmarinus officinalis
Prostratus Group

Height and spread
H 15cm (6in) S 30cm
(12in) or more

Aspect
Full sun

Temperature needs
Hardy, but protect
in hard winters

Havesting period
All year round

Suitable pot size
20cm (8in)

Suitable container material
Any

Compost type
Soil-based compost,
eg, John Innes No 3

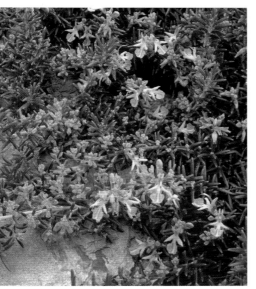

Trailing rosemary is a good option for a stone pot.

Ideal for perking up a patio or terrace all year round, rosemary is an evergreen shrub with pungent, needle-like leaves that release their scent every time you brush past. Plants are perfect for busy gardeners, as they require very little care other than watering and feeding annually in spring with a slow-release granular fertilizer. Rosemary produces pretty blue flowers in spring and summer; cut back stems after the blooms start to fade to keep plants compact.

ROSEMARY CHOICES

There are several rosemaries that make good container plants. 'Miss Jessopp's Upright' is tall and thin, growing to 60cm (24in) in a pot, while Prostratus Group has cascading stems. 'Lady in White' has white flowers, 'Majorca Pink' offers pink blooms, and the sprawling, low-growing 'McConnell's Blue' reaches just 40cm (16in).

Oregano *Origanum vulgare*

Plant used
Origanum vulgare

Height and spread
H & S 30cm (12in)

Aspect
Full sun

Temperature needs
Fully hardy, but
protect from
winter rain

Havesting period
Late spring
to autumn

Suitable pot size
15cm (6in)

Suitable container material
Any

Compost type
Soil-based compost,
eg, John Innes No 3

An essential pizza topping, oregano is easy to grow from seed sown in spring, or you can buy young plants from garden centres. Grow in small pots filled with well-drained, soil-based compost, and site in a sunny place. Although green-leaved oregano is the most popular, there are several showier varieties: 'Gold Tip' has leaves with yellow tips, while 'Aureum Crispum' has yellowish-green wrinkled leaves. 'Kent Beauty' is one of the most ornamental – its small pink flowers are surrounded by deep pink bracts.

PLANT CARE

Water plants regularly, but avoid overwatering as the roots may rot in waterlogged conditions. Stand on pot feet to allow excess moisture to drain away, and in winter, prevent roots from rotting by moving plants to a sheltered spot in the lee of a house wall or into an unheated greenhouse. Trim stems after the flowers fade in summer to keep plants compact, and then give them a boost by applying a liquid fertilizer.

Oregano makes a compact leafy display.

HERBS

Thai herbs and spices

If you enjoy eating Thai food, why not try growing the flavourings for your favourite dishes? Citrussy lemon grass, fresh spicy root ginger, and the seeds and leaves of coriander are considered to be "store-cupboard" ingredients in South-east Asian cooking, and all three will grow well in containers on a sunny, sheltered patio.

Lemon grass *Cymbopogon citratus*

Plant used
Lemon grass

Height and spread
H 90cm (36in)
S 60cm (24in)

Aspect
Full sun

Temperature
Not hardy below 0°C
(32°F)

Harvesting period
All year round

Suitable pot size
20cm (8in)

Suitable container material
Plastic, glazed ceramic

Compost type
Soil-based compost, eg, John Innes No 3

Largely grown for the swollen bases of its edible stems, lemon grass is an exotic grass. It makes a fountain of gently arching, strappy foliage, and can even be grown alongside exotic summer flowers and other ornamentals.

New plants are easily propagated from pieces of stem bought from the supermarket (*see below*), or you can raise them from seed sown indoors in late winter. Sow seeds thinly in pots and germinate in a heated propagator. When seedlings are large enough to handle, transplant three into a small pot and stand on a bright, frost-free windowsill. When roots show through the bottom of the pot, move into a larger one, and continue to pot on as plants grow.

CARING FOR LEMON GRASS
In early summer, stand plants outside in a sunny position, and water frequently. Feed fortnightly with a balanced fertilizer. In late summer, move your plants to a bright area indoors, and reduce watering, allowing the compost to dry out between each application.

Harvest lemon grass when stems are about 30cm (12in). Cut at the base, leaving a 2cm (1in) stump, which will then reshoot.

TOP TIP: PROPAGATING PLANTS FROM STEMS

Buy fresh lemon grass stems and stand them in a jar of water on a sunny windowsill to root. This will take a week or two. Change the water regularly. Once roots have developed, trim the top of the stalks and plant into small pots of moist, soil-based compost. Keep compost damp in summer, but not too wet.

Coriander and ginger *Coriandrum sativum* and *Zingiber officinale*

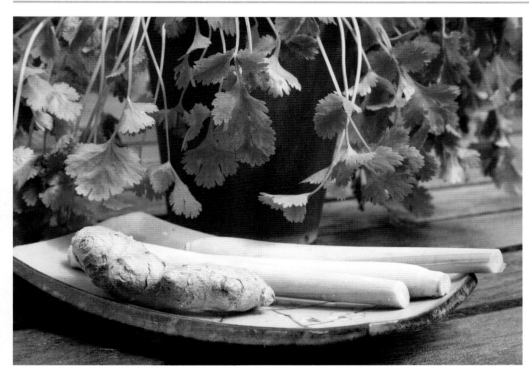

Root ginger, lemon grass, and coriander have exotic looks and flavours, yet they are surprisingly easy to grow in containers.

Plants used
Coriander and ginger

Height and spread
Coriander: H 50cm (20in) S 20cm (8in); ginger: H 90cm (36in) S 40cm (16in)

Aspect
Sun or partial shade

Temperature
Not hardy below 0°C (32°F)

Harvesting period
Coriander: summer to early autumn; ginger: autumn

Suitable pot size
20cm (8in)

Suitable container material
Plastic, placed inside a decorative pot

Compost type
Multi-purpose compost

Coriander makes a pretty clump of decorative foliage in either a sunny or partially shaded position in the garden. Grow the cultivars 'Cilantro' or 'Leisure' if you want to use the leaves; for seeds, choose the species *Coriandrum sativum*. All three grow easily from seed sown in early summer. Sow thinly across the surface of a container filled with multi-purpose compost, and cover over lightly with a sprinkling of compost. If you want to harvest the leaves, thin seedlings to 2.5cm (1in) apart, and for a crop of seeds, thin to 10cm (4in). Keep the compost just damp.

GROWING GINGER
In spring, start plants off from rhizomes, moving them outside in summer (*see right*). Keep the compost moist at all times, and feed every month with a balanced fertilizer. Plants like high humidity, so occasionally mist with a hand-held spray. Ginger needs high light levels and heat to survive winter, so it is best to allow plants to dry out in autumn, and then harvest the roots.

TOP TIP: SPROUTING GINGER

Ginger is easy to grow from rhizomes. In spring, buy fresh, plump, firm roots from the supermarket with lots of knobbly "eyes". Cut roots into 5cm (2in) lengths, making sure that each piece has at least one eye. Bury single lengths, 5cm (2in) deep, in a small pot filled with multi-purpose compost. Water and stand in a bright spot. When shoots appear, move out of direct sun and repot as needed. Feed fortnightly with a liquid fertilizer. Ginger isn't hardy and must come back indoors at the end of summer.

Lemons and limes

Sweetly fragrant flowers, followed by delicious, aromatic fruits make lemon and lime trees highly desirable plants for a cool conservatory in winter, and a warm, sheltered patio throughout summer. Both trees are easy to grow if you can provide the right conditions, and your rewards will be juicy fruits and elegant plants to dress up your home.

CITRUS FRUIT

Lemons

Plant used
Citrus x *meyeri* 'Meyer'

Height and spread
H 1.8m (6ft)
S 1.5m (5ft)

Aspect
Bright and sunny

Temperature needs
Min. 7°C (45°F)

Harvesting period
Varies, depending on type

Suitable pot size
45cm (18in)

Suitable container material
Terracotta, stone, glazed ceramic

Compost type
Specialist citrus compost

Growing your own lemon tree will instantly transport you to the groves of Italy or California, where the scent of these highly fragrant fruits hangs heavy in the air. There are many good varieties to choose from. *Citrus limon* 'Variegata' has two-tone green and yellow leaves and stripy fruit, while 'Meyer' is a compact variety that produces heavy crops of rounded fruit. Ideal for a light, bright, frost-free conservatory or greenhouse, lemons can be moved outside in summer to a warm, sunny patio or terrace.

OVERWINTERING LEMONS
Plant in large pots of specialist citrus compost, water regularly with rain water, and feed monthly in summer with a fertilizer formulated for citrus fruits. Lemons, like all citrus, are frost-tender plants and may suffer at temperatures below 7°C (45°F). However, they can also fail to fruit if they are too warm in winter, so try to maintain a temperature of 10–15°C (50–59°F). Reduce watering and feed less frequently in winter with a specialist winter citrus fertilizer.

TOP TIP: PLANTING PIPS

Although it's easier to buy a plant, it's also fun to try growing your own lemon tree from a pip. Sow seeds from ripe fruit, 1cm (½in) deep, in small pots filled with seed compost. Place in a heated propagator or germinate at 16°C (61°F). Seedlings appear quite quickly but fruit-bearing trees take many years to grow.

Lemons grow happily outside *in summer when given plenty of water. Ensure the root ball is completely soaked.*

Limes

Plant used
Lime

Height and spread
H 1.8m (6ft)
S 1.5m (5ft)

Aspect
Bright

Temperature needs
Min. 7°C (45°F)

Harvesting period
Summer, but can be
all year round

Suitable pot size
45cm (18in)

Suitable container material
Terracotta, stone,
glazed ceramic

Compost type
Specialist citrus
compost

If you fancy home-grown limes to add to your drinks or Asian dishes, you can keep a tree in a large container in a light, bright, sunny area, such as a heated greenhouse or cool conservatory. Before considering a lime, make sure that you will have space to move around the plant, as its stems are armed with vicious spines. Grow and overwinter limes as you would lemon trees (*see opposite*), and water plants regularly, allowing the compost to almost dry out before applying more.

HARVESTING LIMES

It's difficult to know when fruits are ripe just by looking at them, as they don't change colour. However, the fruits do turn a lighter green when they are ready. The skins also feel smooth, and fruits are slightly soft when gently squeezed. To remove, twist the limes carefully from the plant.

Lime trees are armed with sharp spines.

Makrut limes

Plant used
Makrut lime

Height and spread
H 1.8m (6ft)
S 1.5m (5ft)

Aspect
Bright

Temperature needs
Min. 7°C (45°F)

Harvesting period
All year round for
leaves

Suitable pot size
45cm (18in)

Suitable container material
Terracotta, plastic,
glazed ceramic

Compost type
Specialist citrus
compost

While most limes are grown for their fruit, the makrut lime (formerly known as kaffir lime) is mainly grown for its shiny green leaves, which are widely used as a flavouring in Thai cuisine. Apart from providing you with an ingredient that can be difficult to find in all but specialist food shops, the makrut lime is a handsome plant for a large pot. Young shoots are a bronze colour, while each leaf is elongated and comprises two segments. Watch the stems, though, as they are armed with long spines.

GROWING LIMES

Plant up pots as for lemons (*see opposite*) and keep plants in a light conservatory or greenhouse. Ensure that temperatures do not fall below 7°C (45°F) at night and that they are a little higher during the day in winter, although they will enjoy hotter conditions in summer. Limes respond to sudden changes in temperature by dropping their leaves, but can recover when acclimatized. Feed, water, and overwinter plants as for lemons.

Makrut lime leaves and fruits.

Hot-house fruit

You can create your own mini orangery, or grow other citrus fruits, such as mandarins, tangerines, and the weird and wonderful Buddha's hand, if you have a frost-free greenhouse or conservatory. Provide trees with sufficient light and heat, and you can produce a range of jewel-like fruits.

CITRUS FRUIT

Plant used
Calamondin orange

Height and spread
Standard tree:
H 1.5m (5ft)
S 1m (3ft)

Aspect
Bright indoors; full sun outside

Temperature needs
Not hardy below 0°C (32°F); min. 14°C (57°F) when fruiting

Harvesting period
Summer to autumn

Suitable pot size
45cm (18in)

Suitable container material
Terracotta, stone, glazed ceramic, plastic

Compost type
Special citrus compost or soil-based compost, eg, John Innes No 3, with extra grit

Living in a cool climate, it is hard to imagine plucking citrus fruits from the branches of your own tree, but it is quite possible in the warmth of a heated greenhouse or conservatory.

Plants are widely available from specialist nurseries, most of which offer mail-order services. The trees require large, sturdy containers filled with specialist citrus or soil-based compost, and a bright position, as they will perform badly in poor light. They can be placed outside during the summer months, but ensure plants are moved back indoors before night-time temperatures start to fall at the end of summer or beginning of autumn.

CARING FOR CITRUS PLANTS

Plants need regular watering, especially when the fruits are developing because dry compost at this stage can cause them to drop prematurely. Citrus trees do not like hard, calcium-rich water, so try to use rainwater if possible, and feed every month in spring and summer with a special liquid fertilizer formulated for citrus plants in active growth. Reduce watering and feeding in winter – when you do water, add a half-strength solution of fertilizer designed for citrus plants in winter.

To fruit well citrus plants need a temperature of at least 14°C (57°F) for the six months after flowering, and they may become dormant if temperatures fall below this. It can also take up to 11 months for fruit to ripen after the flowers have been pollinated.

*Centre: **Calamondin is a dwarf orange** that produces sweet fruits and can tolerate lower temperatures than many citruses.*

TOP TIP: PRUNING CITRUS

Citrus plants do not require any major pruning. Simply remove any dead, diseased, or damaged branches as you notice them, along with any crossing stems that may rub and create wounds. Then reduce the sideshoots to maintain an attractive rounded shape. Pruning is best carried out between winter and early spring.

Citrus choices

Orange trees *are widely available and some are hardy to -5°C (23°F). They have dark green, glossy leaves and white, scented flowers, followed by fruits in late spring and early summer. Choose a compact form for a pot.*

Citrus medica *var*. digitata, *known as Buddha's hand, is one of the most surprising fruits you're ever likely to see. Plants need heat to thrive. The inedible fruits are used in the Far East for their amazing fragrance.*

Mandarine trees *often bear fruits from spring until autumn. There are many cultivars to choose from, with plants in a range of sizes and fruits with different flavours. The branches are quite brittle and may need supporting.*

Kumquat *is a slow-growing tree that produces orange, egg-shaped fruits with a sweet skin and slightly bitter flesh. Fruits are ready to harvest between late autumn and midwinter, and follow white, scented flowers.*

Tangerine trees *are part of the mandarin family and produce small, sweet, easy-to-peel fruits. Look out for tangelo plants, too, which are crosses between tangerines and grapefruits or oranges.*

Clementine trees *are often sold as standards with bushy heads of dark, evergreen leaves. Grown for their small, sweet fruits, clementines can be harvested between autumn and midwinter, depending on the variety.*

Currant trends

Easy to grow, packed with vitamins, and delicious in puddings, pies, sauces, and juices, currants are suitable for new and more experienced gardeners alike. The jewel-like, sharp-flavoured fruits of white- and redcurrants will add sparkle to patio pots in summer, while new varieties of blackcurrant produce large, sweet, and juicy fruits on tough bushes.

PUDDING FRUIT

Redcurrants

Plant used
Redcurrant 'Rovada'

Height and spread
H up to 2m (6ft)
S 60cm (24in)

Aspect
Sun or partial shade

Temperature needs
Fully hardy

Fruiting period
Summer

Suitable pot size
Min. 30cm (12in)

Suitable container material
Terracotta, stone, plastic

Compost type
Multi-purpose and soil-based compost

Although redcurrants are closely related to blackcurrants, they are, in fact, grown more like gooseberries. These cool-climate plants do well in northern regions and will happily tolerate partial shade, although the fruits will ripen more quickly and taste sweeter if given some direct sun. You can buy container-grown bush and ready-trained cordon plants at any time of the year, but the best time to plant them is in early autumn. Choose a sheltered site out of strong winds and avoid frost pockets.

PLANTING IN POTS
Redcurrants will thrive in pots of multi-purpose compost mixed with some soil-based compost. Keep plants well watered when fruiting but avoid waterlogging – place containers on pot "feet" to allow excess water to drain away.

Keep an eye out for gooseberry sawfly caterpillars, which will quickly strip the foliage. Check regularly and either pick pests off by hand or spray with a suitable pesticide. Feed and prune as for whitecurrants (*see opposite*).

Redcurrant 'Rovada' is a heavy cropper; when fruits start to form, move plants to a sunny spot to boost their sweetness.

TOP TIP: CHOOSING REDCURRANTS

There are a number of new varieties of redcurrant that grow well in containers. Try 'Stanza', a late-flowering variety and good choice for frost-prone areas; 'Junifer', which fruits very early and produces a heavy crop; and 'Rovada' and 'Red Lake', which are both disease-resistant and heavy croppers.

Blackcurrants

Plant used
Blackcurrant 'Ben Lomond'

Height and spread
H 1.2m (4ft)
S 1m (3ft)

Aspect
Sun or partial shade

Temperature needs
Fully hardy

Fruiting period
Summer

Suitable pot size
Min. 45cm (18in)

Suitable container material
Terracotta, stone, plastic

Compost type
Multi-purpose compost

Tough and resilient, blackcurrant bushes are relatively low maintenance and will fruit with very little effort. New varieties, with 'Ben' in their names, produce large fruits that can be eaten fresh as well as cooked. Plant them in big pots of multi-purpose compost and site in a sheltered place, out of strong winds. Plant bushes a little deeper than the original soil mark on the stem; this will encourage new underground stems to form. Feed as for whitecurrants (*see below*).

PRUNING BLACKCURRANTS
After planting in spring, cut stems back to one bud. The new stems will then produce fruit in the coming summer. Each year in late winter, cut the old fruiting stems back to one bud. If frost is forecast, bring pots inside or cover with fleece.

Blackcurrant 'Ben Lomond' has large fruits.

Whitecurrants

Plant used
Whitecurrant 'Blanka'

Height and spread
H 1.5m (5ft)
S 60cm (24in)

Aspect
Sun or partial shade

Temperature needs
Fully hardy

Fruiting period
Summer

Suitable pot size
Min. 30cm (12in)

Suitable container material
Terracotta, stone, plastic

Compost type
Multi-purpose and soil-based compost

Whitecurrant 'Blanka' produces sweet berries.

Sweeter than redcurrants, whitecurrants are cool-climate plants that fruit well in northern countries. 'Blanka' and 'Versailles Blanche' are particularly good varieties. Like redcurrants, they are shallow-rooted and grow well in large pots. Stand containers on pot "feet" to boost drainage. In dry weather water regularly, ensuring the compost never dries out.

In late winter, scrape off the top layer of compost from the pot and replace with fresh compost mixed with a handful of slow-release fertilizer granules. After feeding, water well and apply a mulch of well-rotted manure to aid water retention and reduce weed growth.

PRUNING WHITECURRANTS
Prune plants in late winter or early spring. Remove a quarter of the old stems, cutting them down to the base. Reduce remaining stems by a half, cutting to an outward-facing bud. Prune sideshoots back to one bud.

PUDDING FRUIT

Tart flavours

The stems of rhubarb and plump, juicy fruits of gooseberries make wonderful summer treats when sweetened with sugar and turned into pies, tarts, crumbles, and fools. Both plants produce fruit year after year with very little fuss or bother, and they not only taste delicious, but make attractive patio plants into the bargain.

Rhubarb

Plant used
Rhubarb 'Timperley Early'

Height and spread
H & S 45cm (18in)

Aspect
Sun or partial shade

Temperature
Fully hardy

Harvesting period
Spring to summer; late winter if forced

Suitable pot size
45cm (18in) or larger

Suitable container material
Stone, terracotta, plastic, glazed ceramic

Compost type
Soil-based compost, eg, John Innes No 3

Thanks to its massive plate-like leaves, rhubarb injects a dramatic note into a patio or garden display. The pink, red, or greenish leafstalks also taste great when cooked and added to pies and crumbles. Plants are happy in full sun, although they will also tolerate partial shade, and need a big pot and copious amounts of water to thrive. Buy young plants in spring, and repot them into larger containers several times until they reach their final size. If plants start to get too big for their designated position, snip off a leaf or two from around the outside. Rhubarb is generally harvested in spring, although "forcing" produces an earlier crop. Remove old growth when the plant dies back in autumn.

FORCING RHUBARB

To produce an early crop of tender pink stems, put a handful of straw over dormant plants in late winter, then exclude light by covering them with a terracotta forcing pot or a bucket with a solid base. The stems will develop in the dark and be ready to cut after about four weeks.

TOP TIP: HARVESTING RHUBARB

Avoid cutting off stems of rhubarb with a knife as this will leave a wound that could become diseased and infect the plant. Instead, hold the stalk at the base and ease it out of the compost or carefully twist it off; try not to snap it off. You can harvest rhubarb stems between spring and summer.

Feed rhubarb plants in early spring with a slow-release granular fertilizer, and keep the compost moist at all times.

Gooseberries

Plant used
Gooseberry
'Hinnonmäki Röd'

Height and spread
H & S up to 1m (3ft)

Aspect
Sun or partial shade

Temperature
Fully hardy

Harvesting period
Summer

Suitable pot size
45cm (18in)

Suitable container material
Stone, terracotta, plastic, glazed ceramic

Compost type
Soil-based compost, eg, John Innes No 3

Forget the sour fruits you may have bought in supermarkets, home-grown gooseberries are remarkably sweet, with tender skins and melt-in-the-mouth flesh. Producing fruits in midsummer, gooseberries are usually cultivated as bushes in the ground, but you can easily grow a lollipop-shaped half-standard in a large container. As well as taking up less space, the area around the stem of a standard can be used for growing other edibles, such as herbs.

YEAR-ROUND CARE
Buy container-grown plants at any time, but you may find they get off to the best start in autumn. Pot them up in soil-based compost in sturdy containers that will not topple over as the plant matures. Standards may also need staking.

Water gooseberry plants regularly, especially in hot weather, as dry conditions can result in split fruit. Also work a slow-release granular fertilizer into the top layer of compost in late winter or early spring. When in flower, cover plants with fleece if frost threatens. Half-standards often send suckers up from the base, so either pull them off or cut them back to just beneath the compost. To ensure a bumper crop and to maintain an attractive rounded head, prune stems after picking all the fruit, cutting sideshoots back to around five leaves.

Net gooseberry plants to keep birds off the fruits.

PUDDING FRUIT

CHOOSING GOOSEBERRY VARIETIES

'Invicta' is a very popular and vigorous variety, producing heavy crops of large, smooth-skinned berries with a good flavour from early to midsummer.

'Hinnonmäki Gul', like its sister 'Hinnonmäki Röd' (see main picture) produces mildew-resistant fruits in early summer. The berries are large, sweet, and aromatic.

'Xenia' is laden with large, red-skinned fruits that are ready to pick in early summer, and add an ornamental touch to gardens. Plants are also mildew-resistant.

'Leveller' has smooth, light green fruits with one of the sweetest flavours on offer. However, plants may succumb to mildew, and growth is not as vigorous as others.

Juicy fruits

Biting into a sweet, juicy peach or apricot that has ripened to perfection is a real treat. These days you don't need a heated greenhouse to enjoy such home-grown delights, as there are many new cultivars that will crop well in cooler climates. Grow them as a free-standing tree or fan-train the branches against a south- or west-facing wall for speedy ripening.

Peaches

MEDITERRANEAN FRUIT

Plant used
Dwarf peach

Height and spread
H 1.5m (5ft)
S 1m (3ft)

Aspect
Full sun

Temperature
Fully hardy

Harvesting period
Summer

Suitable pot size
Min. 45cm (18in)

Suitable container material
Any

Compost type
Soil-based compost, eg, John Innes No 3

Choose a peach tree on dwarfing rootstock (*see below*) and grow as a free-standing tree, or buy a partially trained fan to grow against a wall or fence. You can plant bare-root trees in late autumn or early spring, while container-grown trees can be planted all year round.

For maximum flavour and quick ripening, peaches require a sunny, sheltered site. Your tree will also need regular watering and feeding. In spring, remove the top layer of compost in the pot and replace with fresh. Add a slow-release, granular fertilizer and top-dress with well-rotted manure. When fruiting, give trees a weekly boost with tomato fertilizer. Protect plants from rainfall in late winter and early spring to avoid problems with leaf curl, and bring blossoming trees under cover or wrap in fleece if frost threatens.

BUMPER HARVEST
When your peach tree starts to blossom, spend a few minutes pressing the bristles of a small, soft paintbrush into every flower. This will improve pollination and boost your crops.

TOP TIP: DWARF ROOTSTOCKS
Trees grown on the dwarfing rootstock 'Saint Julien A' are ideal for containers; their size is naturally limited to 1.2–1.5m (4–5ft) without the need for heavy pruning. 'Duke of York' has delicious, pale juicy flesh; 'Peregrine' is an old favourite with excellent flavour; 'Garden Lady' has sweet, juicy, yellow-fleshed fruit; yellow-fleshed 'Bonanza' is a heavy cropper. Fruit trees often need other trees close by to aid pollination, but these peaches are all self-fertile.

Pot-grown peaches *often carry bumper crops, and you will need to thin out the fruits to stop the branches snapping.*

Apricots

Plant used
Apricot

Height and spread
H 1.5m (5ft)
S 1m (3ft)

Aspect
Full sun

Temperature
Fully hardy

Harvesting period
Summer

Suitable container size
Min. 45cm (18in)

Suitable container material
Terracotta, glazed ceramic, stone

Compost type
Soil-based compost, eg, John Innes No 3

A warm, sunny, sheltered patio is the perfect site for this succulent, juicy fruit. Grow as a bush, or if you're tight for space, fan-train the tree on a framework of canes against a south- or west-facing wall or fence.

Apricots are hardy, but because they flower early in the year the blossom and young buds are vulnerable to spring frosts – lose them and you won't get any fruit. If the temperature threatens to dip below zero, protect your tree by wrapping it in horticultural fleece or bringing it under cover. Some of the new varieties, bred in North America and France, flower later, reducing the risk of frost damage.

When the baby fruits are about the size of a fingernail, thin them to a spacing of 10cm (4in). Water regularly, feed, and boost pollination as for peaches (*see opposite*). Net developing fruits to protect them from birds and squirrels. Despite all your efforts, though, it has to be said that a bumper crop is dependent on a long, hot summer.

ROOTSTOCK CHOICE
Like peaches, apricots are available on dwarfing rootstocks, including 'Saint Julien A' (*see opposite*). Trees suitable for container growing are also available on 'Torinel' rootstock, which is termed "semi-vigorous". They are slightly taller, but still manageable, and produce heavy crops.

Apricots need heat to ripen.

CHOOSING APRICOT VARIETIES

Flavorcot ('Boyoto') is a Canadian-bred variety that is a very heavy cropper. It produces large, orange-red fruits with a firm texture and intense flavour. Self-fertile.

'Petit Muscat' produces an abundance of walnut-sized, yellow and red fruits. The apricots are deliciously fragrant with an intense, juicy sweetness. Self-fertile.

'Tomcot' is the earliest cropping apricot. Its red-flushed fruits, which look pretty on the tree, are ready to pick in midsummer. It is self-fertile and a heavy cropper.

'Alfred' has large, oval-shaped fruits with attractive orange-blushed skins and juicy orange flesh. Trees are self-fertile and have good disease resistance.

Mediterranean treats

Transport yourself to holidays in the sun by growing a fig or olive tree on your patio. Evocative of Mediterranean landscapes, they can still produce a good crop in cooler climates, given a little care and attention, and even if yours don't bear fruit, both figs and olives are worth growing for their ornamental foliage and graceful forms.

Figs

Plant used
Ficus carica 'Brown Turkey'

Aspect
Full sun

Temperature
Fully hardy

Harvesting period
Summer

Suitable pot size
45cm (18in)

Suitable container material
Terracotta, stone

Compost type
Soil-based compost, eg, John Innes No 3

Although figs are grown primarily for their fruit, their large, deeply lobed leaves make them stand out from the crowd. They grow quite happily in large pots, and restricting their roots helps to prevent them forming too much top growth at the expense of fruit. More compact plants are also easier to prune.

Buy fig plants in spring and pot up into large containers filled with soil-based compost. Water them regularly and feed with a liquid tomato fertilizer while the fruits develop. Give plants a boost in early spring by mixing some slow-release fertilizer granules into the compost.

FRUITING SEASON

Figs first appear in early spring as tiny round growths, the size of peas, on the bare branches. These swell over spring and summer, and are generally ready to pick in late summer. A second crop of embryonic figs appears around the same time as the first are being picked. In warm countries these will grow fat and juicy, but they need care over winter to ripen in cooler climes.

TOP TIP: OVERWINTERING FIGS

Young figs that formed in the summer won't ripen outdoors in cooler climes, so move the pot to a greenhouse or cool conservatory where the fruits can continue to ripen. If you don't have space inside, strip the stems, removing all the young fruits to prevent them from rotting over winter and infecting the plant.

The fig 'Brown Turkey' is a popular variety and will grow and fruit well in a large container on a sunny, sheltered patio.

Olives

Plant used
Olea europaea

Height and spread
Olives are available
in many sizes.
A half-standard is:
H 2m (6ft)
S 60cm (24in)

Aspect
Full sun

Temperature
Some are hardy
to -10°C (14°F)

Harvesting period
Autumn

Suitable pot size
30cm (12in) or larger

Suitable container material
Terracotta, stone,
wooden Versailles
planter

Compost type
Soil-based compost,
eg, John Innes No 3

Olives are drought-tolerant plants that love to bask in warm, sunny, sheltered sites. Grow one in a large decorative container and enjoy its shimmering silvery foliage, tiny white flowers, which are often scented, and attractive fruits. Water well in the growing season, and set pots on "feet" to ensure good drainage. Feed monthly with a balanced liquid fertilizer to encourage a good crop of olives, and maintain an attractive shape by pruning in midsummer. Remove any dead or diseased branches when you see them.

WINTER CARE
Many olives are hardy, but branches can still be damaged by severe frosts. Bring plants inside, or cover the branches with several layers of horticultural fleece and wrap the pots in bubble plastic. Reduce watering if placed under cover.

TOP TIP: PREPARING OLIVES TO EAT

Olives are too hard and bitter to eat directly from the tree and need preparing to make them edible. There are several methods you can use. Either dry-cure them in salt for several weeks, or soak in salted water for several days. Alternatively, cover them in oil for a few months. Specialist nurseries should be able to advise you on the best method for your olives.

Prune olive trees
in summer to allow
time for the wounds
to heal before their
winter dormancy.

Fruit medley

These three fascinating fruits will tantalize your taste buds and are guaranteed to create a talking point. Pineapples and guavas are fun to grow but both are tropical fruits and need the protection of a warm, bright conservatory, while quinces make striking specimens for outdoor containers, and the fruits are prized ingredients for pickles and jellies.

Pineapple *Ananas comosus*

Plant used
Ananas comosus

Height and spread
H & S 1m (3ft)

Aspect
Full sun, in a warm, bright conservatory

Temperature
Min. 15°C (59°F)

Harvesting period
When fruit is fully ripened

Suitable pot size
20cm (8in)

Suitable container material
Plastic, place inside a decorative pot holder

Compost type
Soil-based compost, eg, John Innes No 3 with added grit

A member of the tropical bromeliad family, the pineapple is an attractive plant with strappy, spiny leaves and spiky-topped fruit. For something so exotic, pineapples are surprisingly easy to grow. Either buy ready-grown plants or start your own in spring from shop-bought fruit. Cut a thick slice off the top of the pineapple and remove the lower leaves. Scoop out any soft flesh and leave this to dry for a few days before planting, scoop-side down, in a pot of soil-based compost. A sunny conservatory is essential as pineapples need six hours of bright sun a day and a minimum temperature of 18°C (64°F).

TOP TIP: ENCOURAGING FRUITING

Pineapples grow slowly and won't fruit until they are at least three years old. They need a bright, sunny spot. Keep the "well" between the leaf rosettes full of water, and mist plants now and then. When in growth, feed once a month with a liquid tomato fertilizer.

Tropical pineapples make striking plants for a conservatory, where the bright light and warmth will suit their needs.

Guava *Psidium guajava*

Plant used
Psidium guajava

Height and spread
H & S 2m (8ft)

Aspect
Full sun

Temperature
Min. 3°C (37°F)

Harvesting period
Late spring

Suitable pot size
30cm (12in) or larger

Suitable container material
Terracotta, stone, glazed ceramic

Compost type
Soil-based compost, eg, John Innes No 3

Small, green guava fruit is rarely seen in shops, and plants will be the star attraction when grown in a conservatory in cooler climates. They can be grown from seed, but it's easier to start with a young plant. Guavas need plenty of space and lots of light, so plant them in large containers filled with soil-based compost and set in a warm, bright conservatory. Trees can go outside in summer in a sheltered area next to a warm, south-facing wall, but both the early blossom and ripening fruits must be protected from frost. Plants will only fruit after a long, hot summer.

CARING FOR YOUR TREES
Ensure the compost doesn't dry out, but avoid overwatering. Give guavas a boost in spring by working a slow-release, balanced fertilizer into the top layer of compost. Keep plants bushy and within bounds by pruning shoot tips in spring.

Guavas have a sweet, pineapple-mint flavour.

Quince *Cydonia oblonga*

Plant used
Cydonia oblonga

Height and spread
Standard plants:
H 1.5m (5ft)
S 1m (3ft)

Aspect
Full sun

Temperature
Hardy, but avoid frost pockets

Harvesting period
Autumn

Suitable pot size
Min. 45cm (18in)

Suitable container material
Terracotta, stone

Compost type
Soil-based compost, eg, John Innes No 3

Quince fruits are aromatic as well as ornamental.

The aromatic, pear-shaped, yellow fruits of *Cydonia* are used to make a sweet jelly to serve with meats and cheese, and are a world away from the far less palatable fruits that appear on the ornamental Japanese quince.

Grow trees in large containers of soil-based compost and stand in the sunniest, warmest spot possible outside to ensure the fruits ripen. Keep plants well watered and raise containers on "feet" to aid drainage. In late winter, remove the top layer of compost in the pot and replace with fresh, mixed with a slow-release, balanced granular fertilizer. Quinces can become quite large, but standard plants are more compact. Pruning the shoot tips also limits their sprawl.

HARVESTING FRUIT
Fruits are ready to harvest when they turn golden in late autumn. Pick before they get hit by frost. Store quinces, unwrapped, in a cool, dry, dark place and, because they are highly scented, store them separately from other fruits.

Strawberry basket

The quintessential summer fruit, nothing compares with the taste of fresh strawberries ripened to perfection in the sun. Grow these glistening beauties in large baskets, and choose a selection of early and late-fruiting types, or those that produce a continuous supply of delicious berries all summer.

SUMMER BERRIES

Plant used
Everbearing strawberry

Height and spread
H 15cm (6in)
S 30cm (12in)

Aspect
Full sun

Temperature needs
Hardy

Harvesting period
From summer to early autumn

Suitable pot size
30cm (12in) hanging basket or container

Suitable container material
Large baskets

Compost type
Multi-purpose compost with added soil-based compost, eg, John Innes No 2

Growing strawberries in baskets has several advantages. Not only are fruits raised up to head height, making picking easy, but they are also out of reach of many pests and should not rot, as they have no direct contact with the soil. There are many strawberry varieties to choose from, and they are split into two groups based on when they fruit. Most are classed as summer-fruiting varieties, and usually have a single, heavy flush of fruit between early and late summer, depending on the variety. The second group, known as "everbearers" or perpetual strawberries, produce berries throughout summer and into the autumn.

Strawberries are generally planted in autumn or spring. In spring, plant them in baskets filled with a mixture of soil-based John Innes No 2 and multi-purpose compost, then hang in a sunny, sheltered spot. In autumn, plant up baskets in the same way and store in frost-free place until spring. Strawberries need plenty of water and a weekly dose of tomato fertilizer. Protect fruits from birds by covering plants with anti-bird netting.

OVERWINTERING PLANTS
Everbearers run out of steam after harvesting and are best replaced annually, but summer-fruiting plants will reward you with crops for about four years. After harvesting, cut back tatty foliage, and in autumn place baskets in a cool, light room, or a frost-free greenhouse to protect plants from poor weather.

Centre: **Plant a large hanging basket** *with perpetual berries for a continuous supply of sweet fruits from midsummer until the middle of autumn.*

TOP TIP: GROWING ALPINES IN WALL POTS

Alpine or wild strawberries are valued for their intensely flavoured, tiny berries. Plants produce a light crop of fruit over a long period, but you can ensure a larger yield by growing several plants in a windowbox or raised trough, where they will be easy to pick. Alpine strawberries also grow well in dappled shade.

Strawberry choices

'Cambridge Favourite' *produces sweet berries that can be left on the plant longer than most without rotting.*

'Albion' *is an everbearing disease-resistant variety with bright red, cone-shaped, sweet, tasty fruits.*

'Mara des Bois' *is an everbearer, with aromatic, sweetly flavoured fruits borne from midsummer to autumn.*

'Domanil' *is a vigorous, leafy plant, and produces masses of large, dark red berries in midsummer.*

'Flamenco' *is a perpetual variety that produces a heavy crop of large, sweet, and juicy fruits from midsummer.*

'Elsanta' *is a very popular variety with large, orangey-red, tasty berries that are borne in great profusion in midsummer.*

'Sonata' *bears heavy crops of very sweet, light red berries with firm flesh in the middle of the summer.*

Alpine strawberries *may be a fraction of the size of named varieties, but they are aromatic and deliciously sweet.*

SUMMER BERRIES

Juicy fruits

Grown for their large juicy fruits, blackberries, tayberries, and loganberries offer a taste of summer. Many are too vigorous for pots, but some new plants have been developed in recent years that do well in confined spaces. All plants are grown in a similar way, and it's quite easy to produce a bumper crop of berries.

SUMMER BERRIES

Blackberry

Plant used
Blackberry 'Loch Maree'

Height and spread
H 1.8m (6ft)
S 1m (3ft)

Aspect
Sun or partial shade

Temperature needs
Fully hardy

Harvesting period
Summer to early autumn

Suitable pot size
30cm (12in) or larger

Suitable container material
Terracotta, stone, plastic

Compost type
Soil-based compost, eg, John Innes No 3

Many blackberries are unruly thugs that need to be tamed by training against a system of horizontal wires. However, there are varieties that make perfectly well-behaved plants for pots, including 'Loch Maree', which produces double pink flowers in spring followed by sweet, juicy berries, and 'Loch Ness' with its single white flowers. Both have thornless stems.

Grow blackberries in a sunny spot, although they will also tolerate partial shade, and plant in a large container. Stake the flexible stems with canes, and water plants well, especially during dry spells. Set pots on "feet" to aid drainage, as blackberries dislike waterlogged soil.

PRUNING PLANTS
After planting, tie in shoots regularly to ensure the plant doesn't grow beyond its bounds. In its first winter, cut back sideshoots made on the main canes to 5cm (2in) to encourage fruiting spurs to form that will carry the berries. After that, each winter cut back to the base the old canes that carried that season's fruit.

TOP TIP: FEEDING BLACKBERRIES

Blackberries perform well if given a feed in spring when they start to come into growth. Get plants off to a flying start when planting by mixing a balanced granular fertilizer into the compost, following the application rates on the packet. In following years, apply a slow-release granular fertilizer in spring.

The blackberry 'Loch Maree' is a thornless variety, bred specifically for large containers and small gardens.

Tayberry

Plant used
Tayberry

Height and spread
H: 1.8m (6ft)
S: 1m (3ft)

Aspect
Full sun

Temperature needs
Fully hardy

Harvesting period
Summer

Suitable pot size
45cm (18in)

Suitable container material
Plastic, terracotta

Compost type
Soil-based compost, eg, John Innes No 3

Although tayberries taste much like blackberries and are grown in a similar way, they actually look more like raspberries. Borne in dense clusters from mid- to late summer, the 5cm- (2in-) long red fruits are sweet and fairly aromatic. In the past it was a struggle to raise tayberries in pots because of their vicious spiny canes, but the advent of thornless varieties, such as 'Buckingham', has made it possible to grow these beautiful berries on a patio or terrace.

GROWING TAYBERRIES
Place a piece of trellis in a container or move your pot against a wired-up wall and train the stems onto the wires. Water plants well during the growing season, but provide good drainage over winter by raising pots up on "feet". Prune canes as for blackberries.

The tayberry 'Buckingham' has thornless stems.

Loganberry

Plant used
Loganberry

Height and spread
H: 1.8m (6ft)
S: 1m (3ft)

Aspect
Full sun

Temperature needs
Fully hardy

Harvesting period
Late summer to early autumn

Suitable pot size
45cm (18in)

Suitable container material
Plastic, terracotta

Compost type
Soil based compost, eg. John Innes No 3

Choose a less vigorous variety of loganberry for a pot.

Thornless loganberries bear heavy crops of fruit when grown in large containers, but remember that some forms are vigorous, so choose a slower-growing, thornless variety such as 'Ly 654'. A cross between a raspberry and a blackberry, loganberries produce long, dark red fruits, which are usually ready to harvest between late summer and early autumn. Apart from their delicious fruits, plants are magnets for wildlife, attracting bees and butterflies into the garden with their nectar-rich, white flowers.

CARING FOR LOGANBERRIES
Place containers in a sunny, open, sheltered site with protection from the wind. To keep plants cropping well, water regularly, especially during the summer, and feed plants with a balanced granular fertilizer in spring.

Train plants against a sturdy support, as for tayberries (*see above*). In autumn, after the plants have cropped, cut down to the base all the stems that produced fruit.

Berries blue
Blueberry and honeyberry

Known as "superfoods" due to their high vitamin content, these delicious berries are produced on compact shrubs that grow happily in patio pots. Apart from the beautiful blue fruits, many offer a long season of interest, boasting attractive flowers and foliage, and fiery autumn colours.

SUMMER BERRIES

Plants used
Blueberry and honeyberry

Height and spread
Blueberry: H & S 1m (3ft); Honeyberry: H & S up to 1.5m (5ft)

Aspect
Sun or partial shade

Temperature needs
Fully hardy

Harvesting period
Summer

Suitable pot size
45cm (18in)

Suitable container material
Any non-porous material

Compost type
Blueberry: soil-based ericaceous compost; Honeyberry: soil-based compost

GROWING BLUEBERRIES
Healthy blueberries are the perfect fruits for a small garden or patio, providing a wealth of interest. In spring, plants bear a profusion of tiny white flowers, followed by the blue summer berries, and, in some varieties, fiery scarlet autumn foliage.

Grow blueberries in pots of soil-based ericaceous compost, and water using rainwater from a water butt – only use tap water as a last resort during periods of drought. While in growth, give them a fortnightly dose of balanced feed formulated for acid-loving plants, and site pots in full sun or partial shade.

Select a plant, from the many varieties on offer, that is naturally compact and suited to a pot. Some are not self-fertile, and so you will need to buy two plants. In a large pot, you could team them with cranberries, which like the same ericaceous growing conditions and will extend the fruiting season until autumn.

GROWING HONEYBERRIES
Native to Siberia, honeyberry plants are extremely hardy. They are grown for their large fruits that look and taste like blueberries, and the best results are achieved by growing two plants together. Honeyberries also do well in pots of soil-based compost and you can use water straight from the tap. Apply a slow-release granular feed in spring, and tomato fertilizer every two weeks after the flowers appear.

TOP TIP: PRESERVING

When they are ripe, remove berries from plants by gently pulling them from the stems. They are best eaten fresh or cooked in desserts. However, berries will keep fresh for several weeks in the refrigerator. Place them in a single layer in a storage container, ensuring that they do not rest on top of one another or the weight could cause bruising and result in rotting. If you end up with a glut, berries can also be frozen.

Blueberries need acid soil but you can grow them easily in pots if your garden conditions are alkaline.

Berry selections

Blueberry 'Brigitta' has richly flavoured fruits that ripen at the end of summer. Grow another variety with it.

Blueberry 'Earliblue' makes a vigorous bush that is covered with large, juicy berries in midsummer.

Blueberry 'Toro' produces a bumper crop of berries over the summer, and has bright red autumn foliage.

Honeyberry bears long, oval berries in early summer with a blueberry flavour and honey aftertaste.

Delicious plump berries are produced in abundance in summer, but birds also enjoy these juicy fruits. To prevent your crop disappearing, cover plants with anti-bird netting.

Late-summer delights

Once considered only suitable as orchard trees because of their size, cherries and plums are now available on dwarfing rootstocks. Plant one of these fruiting favourites in a warm, sunny, sheltered spot and enjoy a confection of beautiful spring blossom, followed by a heavy crop of sweet, juicy fruits from mid- to late summer.

Cherries

Plant used
Dwarf cherry

Height and spread
H 2.5m (8ft)
S 1m (3ft)

Aspect
Full sun

Temperature needs
Fully hardy

Harvesting period
Summer

Suitable pot size
Min. 45cm (18in)

Suitable container material
Terracotta, plastic, glazed ceramic

Compost type
Soil-based compost, eg, John Innes No 3

With breathtaking spring blossom followed by glossy fruits in summer, cherries make attractive trees for a garden or patio. They are available as free-standing bushes or space-saving, columnar minarettes, which bear fruit on short spurs along a single upright trunk, rather than on spreading branches. You can also train a tree as a fan or cordon against a wall or fence.

Grow cherries in large containers of soil-based compost in a sunny, sheltered site. They flower early in spring and the buds are vulnerable to frost damage, so if a severe frost threatens, bring the tree under cover or wrap it in fleece.

ANNUAL CARE
Keep trees well watered, especially when fruits are swelling and during dry periods. In late winter, give them a good feed by removing the top layer of compost and replacing it with fresh, mixed with a balanced slow-release granular fertilizer. Raise the container on pot "feet" to improve drainage. When fruits are ripening, cover trees with netting to deter hungry birds.

Modern varieties of cherry will grow happily and produce a good crop of fruits within the confines of a container.

TOP TIP: SELECTING DWARF CHERRIES

Only recently has it been possible to grow cherries successfully in containers. Old-fashioned varieties were too vigorous to have their roots confined, but self-fertile trees grown on modern rootstocks, such as Gisela 5, remain compact. Among the best cherries to try are 'Sunburst', 'Crown Morello', and 'Stella' (*left*).

Plums

Plant used
Plum 'Stanley'

Height and spread
H 2.2m (7ft)
S 1m (3ft)

Aspect
Full sun

Temperature needs
Hardy

Harvesting period
Late summer

Suitable pot size
Min. 45cm (18in)

Suitable container material
Plastic, terracotta, glazed ceramic

Compost type
Soil-based compost, eg, John Innes No 3

Plums were once the preserve of large kitchen gardens, where mature spreading trees would take up a huge amount of ground space. But plums on a full-sized tree are difficult to pick and protect from bird damage – as with cherries, you need to cover them with netting to ensure you get your fair share of fruits. Modern dwarf trees are much more garden friendly, and plums are now available as small pyramids, minarettes – which bear fruits on short spurs along a single, main trunk – or as fans or cordons trained against a wall or fence.

For the heaviest crops, position your tree in a sunny, sheltered position and water regularly, ensuring the compost in the pot never dries out, especially when the fruits are developing. Feed plants in late winter with a balanced granular fertilizer, and protect them from severe frosts (*for details, see cherries, opposite*). Plums can be heavy croppers, so check branches regularly for signs of imminent snapping, and have a supply of canes and ties ready for extra support.

CHOOSING ROOTSTOCKS
There are three rootstocks available: semi-dwarfing 'Pixy', which restricts growth to around 2.2m (7ft); the new 'VVA1' rootstock for trees that reach around 2.5m (8ft); and 'Saint Julien A', which produces slightly more vigorous 2.7m (9ft) plants.

Plum 'Stanley' is a self-fertile tree that produces masses of blossom followed by deep blue plums.

TREE FRUIT

CHOOSING VARIETIES OF PLUM

'Victoria' is an old favourite dating back to the 1840s. This self-fertile plum produces masses of sweet, juicy, red fruit in late summer. A delicious dessert or cooked fruit.

'Warwickshire Drooper' has an attractive weeping habit. Its yellow plums are sweet and juicy and cascade from the branches. Self-fertile, it crops in early autumn.

'Marjorie's Seedling' has good disease tolerance and is partially self fertile. In late summer, its sweet, purple-blue fruits are ready to pick; enjoy them fresh or cooked.

'Giant Prune' is an American heirloom plum with very sweet oval fruits that are ready for picking in early autumn. It has good frost and disease resistance.

Orchard on a patio

With hundreds of apple varieties to choose from, in an assortment of shapes, sizes, colours, and flavours, it's well worth growing your own. Many favourites are grafted onto dwarf rootstocks, which means they produce full-size fruit on compact plants that are happy growing in large patio containers.

TREE FRUIT

Plant used
Malus 'Fiesta'

Height and spread
H 1.8m (6ft)
S 1m (3ft)

Aspect
Full sun

Temperature needs
Fully hardy

Harvesting period
Late summer
to autumn

Suitable pot size
45cm (18in)

Suitable container material
Terracotta, stone,
heavy-duty plastic

Compost type
Soil-based compost,
eg, John Innes No 3

You may not have space to plant up an orchard in your garden, but you can still enjoy your own home-grown apples. Compact trees are ideal for large pots on a sunny, sheltered patio, as long as they are not placed in a frost pocket or wind tunnel. Apples generally flower in late spring, and are pollinated by insects that will be discouraged by strong winds.

The overall height and spread of an apple is largely governed by its rootstock. If grown on their own roots, apples become too large or produce disappointing crops. To overcome this, they are grafted onto a rootstock, which controls the growth rate and size of the tree. Plants suitable for pots are grafted onto 'M26' rootstocks, which produce trees 2.5–3m (8–10ft) tall, or you can opt for an 'M9' rootstock for a slighter smaller tree. To ensure good pollination, grow a few varieties in separate pots, or buy a family tree, which has several varieties grafted onto one rootstock.

BOOSTING FRUIT PRODUCTION

Water trees regularly during the growing season and give plants a boost in early spring with a slow-release granular fertilizer. Maintain the shape by pruning in winter, removing vigorous shoots and thinning congested stems. Large clusters of fruit result in small apples, as they don't have sufficient space to grow. Although trees naturally drop some fruit in summer, give them a hand by thinning them out. Remove the low-quality large central "king", along with any diseased or misshapen apples.

TOP TIP: STORING APPLES

Harvest apples when they come away from the tree with a gentle twist. Wrap in tissue paper and put in a single layer in wooden trays. Or store without wrapping in slatted plastic trays, ensuring that fruits do not touch. Store apples in a frost-free garage or shed, and check fruit regularly for signs of rot.

'Fiesta' apple trees
are widely available
on dwarf rootstocks,
and produce sweet
apples in autumn.

Apple choices

'Discovery' *produces clusters of pretty white blossom in spring, followed by medium-sized, red-skinned apples that are usually ready to be picked between midsummer and early autumn. The fruits are crisp and juicy.*

'Red Falstaff' *produces attractive round fruits that are ready to pick in the middle of autumn. Renowned for their superior flavour, these crisp apples store incredibly well, so you may still be eating them in spring.*

'Egremont Russet' *is a highly popular apple with slightly rough, browny-yellow skin and a sweet, nutty flavour when you bite into the creamy flesh. Harvested in early autumn, fruits will keep until midwinter if stored well.*

'Pixie' *produces medium-sized, sweet fruits with greenish-yellow skins that are flushed red. They look very pretty on the tree and are produced in abundance on small plants. They are ready for picking in mid-autumn.*

'Improved Ashmead's Kernel' *is a heritage variety that produces highly aromatic fruits with pale yellow skins and a peardrop flavour. The sweet, juicy apples can be eaten raw or cooked, and they are ready in mid-autumn.*

'Ellison's Orange' *is an old variety and many nurseries offer it on a dwarf rootstock. It produces apples with crisp, juicy flesh, and a slight aniseed taste. The red-flushed, yellowy-green fruits are ready for picking in early autumn.*

Pears for pots

The wonders of modern, dwarfing rootstocks have made even the most vigorous of fruit trees, the pear, available to container gardeners. As easy to grow as apples, pears just need a little more warmth, sunshine, and frost and wind protection. That said, if you get the site right, your diminutive tree will reward you with bumper crops of sweet fruit.

TREE FRUIT

Plant used
Pear 'Terrace Pearl'

Height and spread
H 1.2m (4ft)
S 1m (3ft)

Aspect
Full sun

Temperature needs
Fully hardy

Harvesting period
Late summer to autumn

Suitable pot size
Min. 45cm (18in)

Suitable container material
Plastic, terracotta, stone

Compost type
Soil-based compost, eg, John Innes No 3

Dwarf pear trees may only grow to just above waist height, but they produces masses of foamy white blossom in spring followed by a heavy crop of delicious pears. Perfect for a big container, the dwarf 'Terrace Pearl' is one of the smallest available. You can restrict the growth of others by training them as cordons, espaliers, or fans. Another option is to grow a duo-minarette, which bears two varieties of pear on short spurs up the trunk rather than on spreading branches.

Plant trees in large containers of soil-based compost, and water them regularly. Feed in spring with a slow-release, balanced, granular fertilizer, and remove any suckers from the base.

THINNING FRUIT

Pears naturally drop some of their developing fruit but will need further thinning. In summer, remove deformed or damaged fruits to give those remaining more space to develop. Fruit will be ready to pick between late summer and early autumn. Gently twist off ripe pears from the tree.

The dwarf pear 'Terrace Pearl' *produces a veil of white spring blossom, and a good crop of juicy fruits on a tiny tree.*

TOP TIP: PRUNING DWARF PEAR TREES

Encourage trees to produce more fruit with careful pruning. In summer, cut side branches to leave 5 or 6 leaves of the summer's new growth. Prune sideshoots growing from these branches to 3 leaves beyond the basal cluster (closely spaced leaves at the base of the shoot), and new sideshoots to one leaf beyond the basal cluster. Also prune in winter to shape the tree.

Choosing patio pears

'Concorde' *is a heavy cropping pear renowned for its slender but juicy, smooth-skinned fruits.*

'Doyenné du Comice' *bears large fruits in mid-autumn with pale russet, yellow-green skins. Grow in a warm area.*

'Humbug' *has green, yellow, and pink striped skin. The tear-drop-shaped fruits are very sweet and juicy. Stores well.*

'Williams' Bon Chrétien' *has large, pale green fruits with delicious, juicy flesh. Ready to pick in early autumn.*

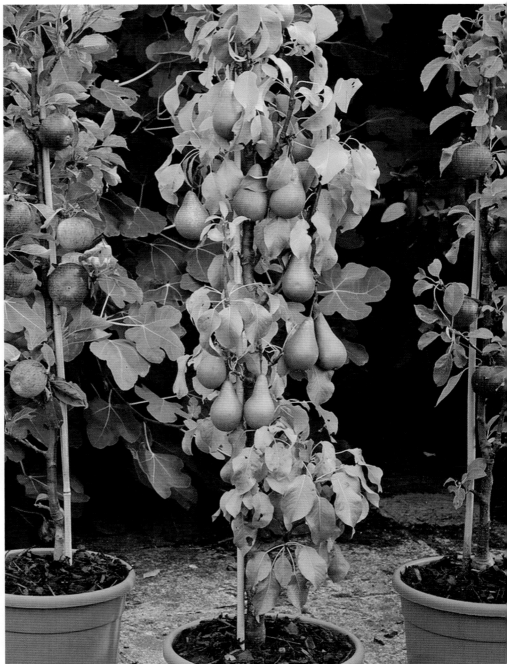

Upright cordon pears *are perfect for patio pots, producing a crop of fruits close to the stem on short spurs, rather than on wide, spreading branches.*

Exotic fruits

It's surprising what you can grow in containers on a warm patio. If you love Mexican food you could be harvesting your own home-grown tomatilloes, which are a key ingredient in the classic salsa verde. Or, for the health conscious, save a small fortune by growing your own "superfoods". High in antioxidants, the jewel-like goji and aronia berries are easy to grow and make attractive plants.

Goji berry

UNUSUAL FRUIT

Plant used
Goji berry

Height and spread
H & S 1.2m (4ft)

Aspect
Sun or partial shade

Temperature
Fully hardy

Harvesting period
Autumn

Suitable pot size
30cm (12in)

Suitable container material
Terracotta, stone, glazed ceramic

Compost type
Soil-based compost, eg, John Innes No 3, with extra grit

The red, oval fruits of the goji or wolfberry are displayed like jewels on the branches of this hardy shrub. As well as their aesthetic appeal, the berries are also crammed with antioxidants, vitamins, and minerals. Young plants are available in spring, ready to plant out into pots of soil-based compost. To improve drainage, add extra grit and raise pots on "feet", and boost plant growth by mixing a slow-release, balanced fertilizer into the compost. Water regularly, and lightly prune plants in spring. The purple or pink flowers produced in summer are followed by autumn fruits, but remember that plants won't crop until their second year. Shake berries from the branches rather than picking them off.

TOP TIP: DRYING BERRIES

Berries can be used fresh or dried. To dry them, spread the fruits in a single layer on a wire rack and allow to dry naturally in a warm and light place. Alternatively, dry the berries on a rack in an oven set on a low temperature. Avoid touching the fruits as their skins will discolour your hands.

Ripe goji berries *are full of health-giving properties. Enjoy them fresh or dried.*

Aronia berry

Plant used
Aronia berry

Height and spread
H & S 1.2m (4ft)

Aspect
Sun or partial shade

Temperature
Fully hardy

Harvesting period
Autumn

Suitable pot size
30cm (12in)

Suitable container material
Terracotta, stone, glazed ceramic

Compost type
Soil-based compost, eg, John Innes No 3

The nutrient-rich, blackcurrant-like berries of aronia or chokeberries can be juiced or made into jam. In spring and summer, this deciduous shrub forms a mound of glossy green foliage, but in autumn the leaves turn a fiery red, which is even brighter if plants are placed in full sun. The small, white, spring flowers are followed by dark purple autumn berries.

In their native habitat, aronias are found growing in damp, acid soil, but they will thrive in a range of soil conditions. Plant in pots of soil-based compost, such as John Innes No 3, and keep plants well watered.

WHAT TO GROW
The wild species produces prolific crops of berries, but more compact cultivars, such as Iroquois Beauty ('Morton') and 'Hugin', are better suited to the cramped conditions in a container.

Aronia berries contain high levels of antioxidants.

Tomatillo

Plant used
Tomatillo 'Toma Verde'

Height and spread
H & S 1m (3ft)

Aspect
Full sun

Temperature
Not hardy below 0°C (32°F)

Harvesting period
Late summer

Suitable pot size
20cm (8in)

Suitable container material
Plastic

Compost type
Soil-based compost, eg, John Innes No 3

Tomatilloes are related to Cape gooseberries.

Related to the Cape gooseberry, tomatilloes have plump fruit hidden inside a papery husk, only in this case they are green. These vigorous, tender plants produce masses of large, yellow flowers, followed in late summer by the fruits, which are used in Mexican cooking.

STARTING FROM SEED
Sow seed thinly in small pots in late winter and early spring, transplanting the seedlings into individual pots when they are big enough to handle. Plants can go outdoors in a sunny, sheltered area after the last frost, but they will crop better in a conservatory or greenhouse. Tomatilloes aren't self-fertile, so you will need more than one for pollination. Like cordon tomatoes (another relation), their stems need to be tied to canes to support the weight of the fruits. Don't overwater or you'll ruin their flavour, and feed occasionally with a balanced liquid fertilizer. Harvest in late summer, when the husks spilt and the tomatilloes are still green.

UNUSUAL FRUIT

PLANTING GUIDE

In this chapter you will find advice on some of the best methods for planting and growing ornamentals, such as trees, shrubs, and perennials, as well as techniques for sowing vegetable seeds in containers. Pests and diseases can undo all your hard work and ruin your plants and crops, so check out ways to prevent attacks and tackle any problems should they arise.

Sow vegetable seeds carefully to reap the rewards, and keep all your containers well watered to produce healthy plants. Recognise common pests and diseases, and help to conserve moisture in pots with a mulch.

Planting up shrubs and perennials

Planting up beautiful containers of flowers and shrubs is surprisingly easy
if you follow this tried-and-tested method. The key is to choose your pots
and compost carefully, and check that they will suit the final size of your
plants and the conditions they enjoy. And unless the temperature falls
below freezing, it's a job you can tackle at any time of year.

1 Choose containers with drainage holes in the bottom. Then, to prevent the compost clogging them up, cover over the holes with some pieces of broken clay pot or polystyrene packaging.

2 Add a deep layer of compost, choosing the type your plants prefer. If you are using terracotta pots, you can line them first with bubble plastic to help protect them during freezing conditions.

3 Add some slow-release fertilizer granules to the compost. Check the instructions on the packaging for application rates. These granules will sustain most perennials and shrubs for a full growing season.

4 Give your plants a good soak. Stand them in their pots in a bucket of water; wait until bubbles stop rising to the surface before lifting them out to drain. Arrange them, still in their pots, in the container.

5 Once you're happy with the arrangement, remove the plastic pots and reposition your plants, packing compost around their root balls. Plants should go in at the same depth as when they were in their original pots.

6 When planting, ensure that there is a 5cm (2in) gap between the compost's surface and the rim of the container to allow space for watering. Position your pots in a site appropriate to the plants' needs, and water regularly, aiming the spout of your can or hose at the compost, rather than spraying the foliage and flowers.

Planting bulbs in pots

Pots brimming with spring bulbs lift the spirits after the long dark days of winter. Plan ahead and plant up pots in autumn, and for a truly dazzling display, combine a collection of different flowers in one large container.

1 Prepare your container as for shrubs and perennials (*see step 1, opposite*). Add a layer of compost and arrange the largest bulbs, such as daffodils, on top. Plant them twice as deep as the height of the bulb.

2 Cover the bulbs with a layer of compost, then plant slightly smaller bulbs, such as tulips. Ensure the pointed tips of your bulbs are uppermost, and space them closer than recommended on the packet.

3 Cover these bulbs with a layer of compost, then plant small bulbs, such as grape hyacinths (*Muscari*) on top. Cover with compost and set the pot on "feet" to prevent waterlogging. Place in a sunny spot to flower.

Choose bulbs *that flower simultaneously for a dramatic burst of colour in spring. This display blooms in mid-spring.*

Planting trees in containers

Small trees make elegant features when grown in large containers on a patio, or as a focal point in a garden. Choose a small or compact type, or one grafted onto a dwarf rootstock, and plant with care. Remember that you will need to feed your tree each year in spring, and you must ensure that the compost never dries out.

1 Buy a large container with drainage holes in the base. Place pieces of broken clay pot or polystyrene packaging over the holes. Stand your tree in a bucket of water to soak the root ball.

2 Add a deep layer of soil-based compost, such as John Innes No 3, to the bottom of the container and mix in some slow-release fertilizer granules, at the rate specified on the packaging.

3 Leave the tree soaking until bubbles have stopped rising to the surface of the water. Lift out to drain; slip off its pot and gently tease out the roots. Stand the tree in its new container, ensuring the stem is upright.

4 Check that when the tree is planted its root ball will sit at the same depth as it was in its pot. Fill in around the root ball with compost mixed with slow-release fertilizer, firming it with your fingers as you go.

5 Leave a gap of at least 5cm (2in) between the top of the compost and the rim of the container to allow space for watering. Firm the compost around the root ball, checking once again that the stem is upright. Water the tree well, and keep the compost moist at all times. Feed annually in spring by carefully removing the top layer of compost and replacing it with fresh, mixed with a slow-release granular fertilizer.

Planting a hanging basket

Plant up a large hanging basket with a medley of different colours and textures for interest all year round. In summer, you can create glorious spheres of flowers and foliage (*as shown here*); for the colder months, replace tender plants with hardy types, such as grasses, bulbs, and violas. Hang your basket at head height on a patio, terrace, or balcony on a sturdy metal bracket.

1 Sit the basket in a pot while you work. Position your chosen liner in the basket. To help retain moisture, lay a small circle of polythene, punched with a few holes, over the bottom and cover with gravel.

2 Cut slits in the shape of a cross in the liner, just above the polythene. Add a layer of compost. Wrap the leaves of trailing plants with polythene and thread them through the liner, one plant per slit.

The plants used here are *Verbena* 'Derby' and *Verbena* 'Peaches 'n' Cream', together with trailing blue lobelia, *Lotus berthelotii*, *Dichondra argentea* 'Silver Falls' and a pink-coloured diascia. A summer basket like this will need watering every day, even if it has been raining. In autumn, remove the plants and compost them, and plant up the basket with some evergreen grasses, spring bulbs, and dainty violas for an autumn to early spring display.

3 Fill the basket to just below the rim with compost, then add the rest of your plants. Work from the centre out, with the tallest plant in the middle, and small or trailing plants set evenly around the edge.

4 Fill in around the plants with more compost mixed with some slow-release fertilizer granules. Water the basket well, and add a layer of gravel over the compost to help retain moisture and suppress weeds.

TOP TIP: FIXING BRACKETS TO A WALL

To fix a hanging basket bracket securely to the wall, place it in position and use a spirit level to check that it is perpendicular. Mark the positions of the screw holes, then remove the bracket and use an electric drill with a masonry bit to drill holes through the centre of your pencil marks. Push a wallplug into each hole, and line up the bracket with the holes on the wall. Insert a washer and coach bolt and screw it into the wall. Repeat for the second hole, and tighten up both bolts.

Caring for container plants

Plants in hanging baskets, pots, and planters require more hands-on care than those grown in the ground, where their roots have greater access to soil moisture and nutrients. Plants confined to containers require you to supply all their water and food needs, but there are some useful tips that you can follow to make these jobs a little easier and to save time.

Watering

Keeping thirsty plants supplied with water is essential if you want to maintain their health and vigour. If you don't have time to water every day in summer and during dry spells, choose large containers, which hold more compost and, therefore, correspondingly larger volumes of water. Small terracotta pots need watering the most frequently, while tall containers made from plastic or other man-made materials will require less attention. Covering the compost with a layer of mulch will also help to seal in moisture (*see opposite*).

When planting up, ensure that you leave a gap of 5cm (2in) between the top of the compost and the rim of the pot to allow space for water to accumulate and filter down to the plants' roots. Aim your watering can or hose onto the compost, where it's needed, rather than the leaves.

Top: *A good soaking* once or twice a week, making sure the water reaches the roots at the bottom of the pot, is more effective than a light sprinkling every day.

Right: *Hanging baskets* need watering once or twice a day in summer. Use a long-handled hose to make the job easier.

Automatic irrigation

If you work long hours, are going on holiday, or have lots of patio containers to look after, consider installing an automatic watering system. Most systems come in kit form, consisting of a timer, which you attach to an outside tap (there are also kits available to fit rainwater barrels), and a network of tubes into which you insert feeder pipes and small drip nozzles that deliver water directly to your pots.

Some systems are a little fiddly to install and you will need to read the instructions carefully. If you are finding it difficult to attach the feeder pipes or drip nozzles, soak the tubes in hot water for a few minutes to soften the plastic. Also, check your plants every few days to ensure that they are not being over- or under-watered and adjust the flow or watering period accordingly.

Top left: *Run a main pipe* alongside your containers, cut it where it meets each pot, and attach a feeder pipe at that point with a connector.

Top: *Attach drip nozzles* to the feeder pipes and lay them on the surface of the compost.

Left: *Fit the timer* on your tap, and set it to water early in the morning or in the evening when it is cooler and evaporation rates are low.

Feeding plants

There are three basic nutrients that plants require to maintain good health. These are nitrogen (N), which is needed for leaf and shoot growth; phosphorous (P), required for good root development; and potassium (K), which helps flowers and fruits to form. All-purpose fertilizers usually contain a balance of all three nutrients, but those that are formulated to promote good fruit or flower production will have a high potassium content, while fertilizers for leafy crops or foliage plants contain high levels of nitrogen.

CHOOSING FERTILIZERS

Trees, shrubs, and perennials that will live in their pots for a few years benefit from an annual application of all-purpose fertilizer in spring. Granular fertilizers labelled "slow-release" or "controlled" are best, as these are easy to apply and will continue to feed plants over the whole growing season. If you want to boost flower or fruit production, give your plants additional doses of a potassium-rich liquid fertilizer as soon as the flowers start to form. Tomato fertilizers are a good choice for any flowering or fruiting plants. If you are growing plants with specific needs, such as orchids or citrus trees, buy a fertilizer formulated for that particular plant.

Mulching

A mulch is an organic or inorganic material (*see options, below*) that you spread over the top of your compost to seal in moisture and lower the rate of evaporation from the surface. Before applying your chosen mulch, water your containers thoroughly to soak the compost.

A layer of mulch that is thick enough to exclude light will also help to inhibit weed growth. On an aesthetic level, mulches add a decorative finish to containers, particularly where a single-stemmed plant, such as a tree, is surrounded by bare compost.

MULCHING OPTIONS

The best mulches for containers are both practical and beautiful. Good choices include washed gravel, colourful crushed glass that has been milled to take off the sharp edges, or dyed and crushed sea shells, which are a by-product of the seafood industry. For larger containers, try using smooth pebbles, slate chips, or finely shredded bark. Mulches are excellent for all plants, but are especially effective for those, such as alpines and drought-lovers, whose stems must be kept dry.

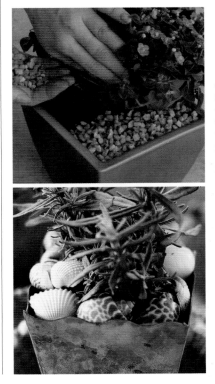

Apply a layer of gravel around summer bedding or alpines. As water runs off it into the compost below, it will help to keep the plants' stems dry, preventing them from rotting.

Decorative mulches, such as sea shells, add to the aesthetic appeal of your container displays. You can use almost any material as a mulch, including nut shells, glass beads, or even buttons.

Sowing vegetable seeds

If you thought seed sowing was just for the experts, think again. Most vegetables germinate quickly and easily, requiring only a little care and attention to get them off to a good start. The technique shown here is for sowing seed directly into containers outside; to sow tender crops, such as tomatoes, see specific plant entries (*see pp.156–191*).

1 Prepare your container as for shrubs and perennials (*see Step 1, p.234*). Fill it to within 5cm (2in) of the rim with an equal mix of multi-purpose and soil-based composts. Sow seeds as specified on the packet.

2 Water the container with a watering can fitted with a fine rose to avoid disturbing the seeds. Place in a sunny, sheltered spot, and keep the compost moist. Most seedlings will appear within a week or two.

3 When the seedlings have produced four leaves or more, remove the weakest to allow the others sufficient space to develop. Check packets for spacings; you can usually grow plants a little closer in pots.

4 Keep your seedlings well watered; if they are allowed to dry out, their growth will be inhibited. At the other extreme, you must also safeguard against waterlogging, so stand seed pots on "feet" or pebbles.

5 When crops are mature and ready to harvest, gently remove them from their pots with a hand fork; for plants such as lettuces or chard, simply cut off their stems with sharp scissors. For quick-maturing crops, such as radishes, sow some seeds every few weeks to maintain your supply throughout the summer.

Growing tomatoes in growing bags

The compost in vegetable growing bags is specially formulated for optimum growth, but it can dry out quickly. To overcome this problem, increase the volume by inserting open-ended pots into the holes in the top of the bags and then fill them with good-quality multi-purpose compost. The extra compost gives the plant roots more space to develop and holds more water.

1 Using a knife, make drainage holes in the base of the bag, and cut three large circles in the top. Insert bottomless plastic pots (make your own or buy ready-made) into the openings and fill with extra compost.

2 Transfer your tomato plants to the growing bag when their first flowers are about to open. Plant one tomato per pot, positioning the root ball just below the top of the compost, and water them in well.

3 Add canes for support, and pinch out all fast-growing sideshoots that appear between the leaves and the main stem, as they divert energy away from fruit production. Apply a weekly dose of liquid tomato fertilizer.

4 As the main stems grow, tie them to the canes with soft twine. Prevent the plants from growing too tall by removing the uppermost tip, two or three leaves beyond the last cluster of fruit on the stem.

5 Keep your tomato plants well watered throughout the growing season, as the fruits may either split or succumb to disease if they do not receive sufficient moisture. If you are growing tomatoes in a greenhouse, or you have a number of containers to care for, consider installing an automatic watering system (*see p.238*).

Keeping pests and diseases at bay

The risk to plants from pests and diseases can be reduced by growing
them in the conditions they enjoy, and checking them at regular intervals
so that you can nip any problems in the bud. In addition, where a plant
is particularly prone to a disease, choose a resistant variety, and if pests
are causing problems, encourage predators in to track them down.

Reduce the risks

Healthy plants will often shrug off attacks from pests and
diseases, so ensure yours are not under stress by growing
them in appropriate conditions and watering regularly.
Feed plants according to their needs, but avoid
overfeeding, as aphids love the resulting soft growth.

Inspect your plants regularly for signs of attack.
Shrivelled or distorted leaves and shoots are often a sign
of aphid infestation, while holes in leaves will be most
likely due to slugs and snails. Check flower buds and the
undersides of leaves, and either pick off the culprits, in
the case of slugs and snails, or, with a gloved hand, wipe
off aphids or use a spray hose to wash them off. Prevent
diseases by sterilizing pots and tools when growing seeds,
and pick off and bin any infected leaves, flowers, or stems.

Drought-stressed plants are growing below par and are at risk from
pest attacks. Keeping plants well watered will help prevent problems.

Choose healthy plants

Above: **Rosa 'Graham Thomas'
('Ausmas')** is prized for its blooms
and disease-resistant foliage.

Right: **'Sungold' tomatoes** have
been bred for their sweet fruits and
resistance to diseases and viruses.

To ensure that pests and diseases are not unwittingly
brought into your garden, check plants carefully before
you buy them. Reject any that are wilting, have yellow
or marked foliage, or have weeds that may be carrying
diseases growing on the compost surface.

In addition, where possible, select disease-resistant
plants. Roses, for example, suffer from several diseases,
including black spot, mildew, and rust, but scan through
catalogues and plant labels and you will find many that
offer resistance to these infections. Many new selections
of tomatoes and other vegetables also provide resistance
to viruses and blight.

An easy way to spot exceptional plants is to look out
for the Royal Horticultural Society's Award of Garden Merit
cup logo. Plants that receive this accolade are
recommended, "tried-and-tested" choices.

Encourage pest predators

Both the adults and larvae of ladybirds, and lacewing and hoverfly larvae, will all help to gobble up aphids, while frogs and toads like nothing better than a slug feast. To lure these useful creatures into your garden and encourage them to stay, plant nectar-rich flowers, and install a pond or a barrel pool on your patio. Leafy ground-cover plants will provide a hiding place for amphibians.

Top: **Ladybirds** *have a voracious appetite for aphids and will actively seek out infested plants.*

Above: **Frogs and toads** *eat slugs and flies, and will visit your garden if you have a small pond or pool.*

Use physical barriers

They may not be the most attractive additions to your patio display, but if you are growing crops you may need to cover them with bird- or insect-proof netting at key times to guard against pests. To deter slugs and snails, wrap copper tape around containers – it gives the pests a nasty electric shock.

Net strawberries *and other fruit before birds eat them; wrap a strip of copper tape around containers to ward off molluscs.*

House plant problems

Protected from most outdoor pests, house plants still succumb to a few that find their way inside. Many are brought in on new plants, so carefully inspect potential acquisitions before buying. Diseases and other problems increase when plant care and hygiene are neglected.

Mealybug is a sap-sucking insect with a protective waxy coating that attacks cacti, succulents, and other house plants. It causes leaf and stem distortion. Use the biocontrol, *Cryptolaemus*, or spray with thiacloprid, acetamiprid, fatty acids, or plant oils.

Whitefly and their whitish-green nymphs suck sap from indoor plants and greenhouse vegetables. They excrete sugary honeydew, which attracts sooty mould. Use the parasitic wasp, *Encarsia*, as a biocontrol, or spray with an appropriate insecticide.

Scale insects affect many house plants. The adults, which are covered with protective, flat, circular scales, suck plant sap. A bad infestation can seriously weaken plants. Spray with thiacloprid, acetamiprid, fatty acids, or plant oils.

Grey mould rots plant tissue, and covers plants with a grey, fluffy fungus. Flower petals may also develop small brown spots. Keep your home well ventilated and water plants in the morning to reduce humid conditions, which the fungus loves.

Ornamental plant diseases and pests

Coral spot is commonly seen on the dead twigs of trees and shrubs, or woody debris. In damp weather, small pink or red eruptions appear on infected bark. The fungus can infect through open wounds and, once established, kills branches rapidly. *Acer*, *Elaeagnus*, figs, currants, and gooseberries are often affected. Cut out diseased wood promptly.

Powdery mildew causes a powdery white coat to appear on any part of a wide range of plants, distorting the infected tissue. The leaves may drop, buds die, or stems die back. Watering during dry periods and improving air circulation by pruning or ventilation will help, as will spraying with an appropriate fungicide.

Rust affects a wide range of plants and causes pustules of powdery spores to appear on the underside of leaves and stems, with corresponding pale spots on the upper surface. Plants such as rhododendrons, roses, and fuchsias develop orange-brown spores. Leaves often fall prematurely. Destroy these and do not compost, to help prevent the disease spreading.

Rusts spread by rain splash, wind, or animals. Spores need a moist environment to germinate and infect, and so rust infections are generally at their most severe in damp conditions. Spray infected plants with an appropriate fungicide; some plants, such as fuchsias, are sensitive to sprays, so check the labels of fungicides carefully.

Rose black spot causes dark brown or black blotches to appear on leaves from late spring onwards. The affected leaves will fall prematurely, which can weaken the plant, but encouraging vigorous growth will help. Initial infection is mainly from spots on stems in which the fungus *Diplocarpon rosae* has overwintered. Severe spring pruning helps to remove this tissue, as does thorough leaf clearance in autumn and mulching in spring.

Various fungicides are available to help kill black spot, and alternating applications of different active ingredients will allow you to find the most effective product. Spray plants immediately after spring pruning, and then spray once again when the leaves open.

Camellia yellow mottle virus causes bright yellow or creamy-white blotches or speckling on the dark green leaves. The virus may also cause flower discolouration. The plant's vigour is not affected, but prune out affected branches to help prevent the virus from spreading. The virus is spread by the grafting of infected nursery stock.

Leaf miners are usually fly or moth larvae, but there are also leaf-mining sawflies and beetles. All eat through leaf tissue leaving distinctive coloured lines or blotches in the foliage where they have tunnelled. Leaf miners do not seriously harm plants, but you can cover them with horticultural fleece to shield them from attack.

Ornamental plant pests

Lily beetle eats the foliage of lilies, giant lillies, and fritillaries, as well as damaging the flowers and seedpods. The adult beetle is 8mm (¾in) long and bright red, with a black head and legs. The grubs are often completely covered with their own wet, black excrement. Damage occurs from spring to early autumn. Remove the beetles by hand.

Rose leafhopper causes a coarse, pale mottling to develop on the upper leaf surfaces of rose leaves. The insects suck sap from the underside of leaves, especially on roses grown in sheltered places. Adult rose leafhoppers are pale yellow and 3mm (⅛in) long, and jump off the plant when disturbed. Control them with insecticide.

Aphids suck sap from most garden plants using their needle-like mouthparts. Heavy infestations stunt growth and soil the plant with their sticky excrement and resulting sooty mould. When they need to move on to another host plant, winged aphids develop. Control aphids with a biological control or an appropriate insecticide.

Earwigs hide in dark places during the day. At night, they emerge to eat the soft foliage and petals of flowers such as dahlias, chrysanthemums, and clematis. In some years earwigs can be particularly abundant and damaging. Trap them in pots loosely stuffed with grass, or spray plants with an appropriate insecticide.

Flea beetles eat small, round holes in the upper leaf surfaces, and attack brassicas as well as ornamentals. Heavy attacks can kill seedlings and check the growth of older plants, so protect seedlings by sowing when weather and soil conditions will allow rapid germination and growth through the vulnerable seedling stage.

Sawflies are caterpillar-like larvae with seven or more pairs of clasping legs on their abdomens. The larvae often feed together in groups and can quickly devour the foliage of certain trees, shrubs, and herbaceous plants. Other sawfly feed as larvae inside developing fruits or as leaf miners. Remove the larvae by hand.

Slugs and snails feed by rasping the surface of leaves, stems, and flowers with their "tongues". They prefer cool, dark conditions, and do most of their feeding at night or after rain. Seedlings and soft young growth are particularly vulnerable. Pick off by hand, use slug pellets, or deter with copper tape (*see also p.98*).

Vine weevil grubs are up to 10mm (½in) in length, creamy-white, and legless (the adults look like black wingless beetles). They eat plant roots and bore into begonia and cyclamen tubers from autumn to spring, and can kill plants, especially those in pots and containers. Use a biological control or an appropriate insecticide.

Vegetable diseases, disorders, and pests

Blossom end rot in tomatoes is caused by calcium deficiency and is often seen in acid soils or inadequately watered soil, which prevents the plant taking up calcium. A sunken, leathery, dark brown to black patch appears at the fruit's flower end. If blossom end rot does develop, pick off affected fruits and improve the watering routine.

Clubroot is usually introduced on seedlings brought into the garden. It causes vegetable roots to thicken and distort into a swollen mess; plants become stunted and leaves may wilt on hot days, recovering overnight. Improving drainage and using good-quality soil-based compost in your vegetable containers will help to prevent clubroot.

Tomato blight causes fruit to discolour and rot rapidly, with brown patches developing on the leaves. Outdoor plants are particularly at risk. If fruit is picked from diseased plants, keep for five days to see if rot develops. If nothing happens, it is safe to eat. Prevent by spraying with a copper-based fungicide or one based on mancozeb.

Potato common scab causes scabby spots to develop on the skin. The tubers are unsightly, but the damage is not serious. It occurs on light soils that lack organic matter and is worse in dry years. Use a good-quality, soil-based compost and water plants regularly when the tubers are forming. Resistant varieties of potato are available.

Potato blight causes dead patches to appear at the tip of leaflets, which enlarge to kill the leaf; the rot is a hard, reddish-brown patch. It spreads rapidly in wet conditions, and airborne spores can infect plants even when no diseased material is present. Affected tubers will not store. Spray foliage with fungicide before blight appears.

Brassica downy mildew is usually most severe in seedlings, and the seeds may be infected. Yellow patches appear on the upper leaf surfaces with white fungal growth underneath the lesions. Improve ventilation by giving plants more space. Buy resistant cultivars and use fresh compost each year, as the fungus can survive in the soil.

Tomato viruses typically cause mottling and distortion of leaves, stunting, and poor fruit yields. Tomato mosaic virus (TMV) is highly contagious and serious: fruit can fail to set and young fruit is "bronzed" or streaked. If symptoms are seen, destroy plants immediately. Tools and hands should be cleaned well, and pest control is important.

Tomato moth caterpillars are brown or pale green with a thin yellow line along the sides. They are up to 40mm (1½in) long and between mid- and late summer they eat the foliage and fruits of tomatoes. When fully fed, the caterpillars go into the soil to pupate. Remove the caterpillars by hand or spray with pyrethrum or bifenthrin.

Vegetable pests

Cabbage whites are most dangerous to crops at the larval stage, when the yellow and black caterpillars devour the outer leaves. Prevent the butterflies from laying eggs by growing cabbages under fine mesh netting. Pick off caterpillars or control with pyrethrum or bifenthrin, but not those feeding inside cabbage heads.

Carrot fly larvae are slender, pale yellow, and up to 10mm (½in) long, and they tunnel into carrots, parsnips, and parsley roots. No effective insecticide is available. Protect plants by growing under horticultural fleece or in tall pots (the pest flies close to the ground). Some cultivars, such as 'Flyaway', and 'Resistafly' are less susceptible.

Brassica flea beetles can attack all brassicas, as well as allied plants such as turnip, swede, radishes, and rocket. These tiny, mostly black, beetles eat small holes in foliage and can kill seedlings. Encourage seedling growth by watering well. If necessary, spray crops with bifenthrin, thiacloprid, or pyrethrum to control the pests.

Cutworms are brownish-white caterpillars of various moth species. They live in the surface layers of the soil and eat cavities in root crops and potato tubers. They also kill seedlings and lettuce by eating through the roots. There is no effective treatment – if a plant wilts, search through the soil around the base, and remove the pest.

Wireworms are mainly a problem in new gardens. The slender, orange-yellow grubs are up to 25mm (1in) long, with three pairs of short legs at the head end. They kill seedlings and bore into potato tubers, onion bulbs, and other root vegetables. There is no insecticide available for their control, but numbers decline after a year or two.

Leek moth caterpillars are whitish green and up to 11mm (½in) long. They live as leaf miners and also tunnel into the stems and bulbs of leeks and onions. Small plants develop secondary rots and may be killed. There is no effective insecticide available; protect plants from the pests by growing them under horticultural fleece.

Pea moth eggs are laid on pea plants from early to midsummer. The caterpillars bore into pods and feed on the developing pea seeds. Early or late sowings of quick-maturing pea cultivars that flower outside the moth's flight period avoid damage. Mid-season peas can be protected with bifenthrin a week after the onset of flowering.

Pigeons devour the foliage of peas, cabbages, and other brassicas. Damage can occur at any time of year, but often increases in winter. Growing vulnerable vegetables under netting will keep pigeons away from the foliage. Scaring devices are likely to give only temporary protection against the ravages of this bird.

Fruit and herb diseases and disorders

Brown rot affects many fruit trees. Spots of soft rot appear on fruits and rapidly enlarge. Rings of buff spores appear on this tissue and initiate more infections. Rotten fruits remain on the tree, and the fungus can then grow back into the branches. Prune out the diseased wood, and remove all rotten fruits from the tree to prevent infection from spreading.

Pear scab causes blackish-brown, scabby patches to appear on the skin of fruits, and greenish-grey spots on the leaves. The fruits are often small and misshapen and are prone to splitting and then spoiling. Rake up and destroy infected leaves and fruits. Prune out cracked and scabby shoots, and apply an appropriate fungicide.

Canker grows on apple and pear trees near buds or wounds, which become elliptical with concentric rings of shrunken bark. Spores enter through wounds. Prune out small cankered branches; on larger limbs, chisel back to green wood and apply wound paint. Spray with a copper fungicide after harvest and again after half the leaves fall.

Peach leaf curl affects peaches and apricots. Red or pale green blisters develop on new leaves, which swell and curl, and are later covered in white spores, some of which overwinter on dormant shoots. Remove diseased tissue and apply copper fungicide as buds begin to swell in midwinter, and a fortnight later. Also buy resistant cultivars.

Apple bitter pit causes brown spots to appear within the flesh, or sometimes on the skin of apples, giving a bitter taste. The spots on the skin are usually slightly sunken, but otherwise the fruits are normal in shape and size. Feed, water, and mulch trees to prevent the disease, and spray developing fruits with calcium nitrate solution.

Strawberry grey mould enters through flowers and remains dormant until fruits mature, where it can be seen as greyish growth. It spreads by contact or air-borne spores, surviving on plant debris or in the soil. Remove infected plant parts and debris promptly. Mulch around plants with straw and remove weeds, which may carry spores.

Strawberry leaf spot is caused by a fungus that creates white spots ringed with purple. It is spread by rain splash, and lesions occur on flowers, fruits, and stems. Its effect on plant growth is not severe, although it spoils the appearance of foliage. To control it, remove plant debris on which the fungus overwinters and use resistant cultivars.

Pear rust causes bright orange spots to appear on the upper surface of leaves in summer. Fruits and twigs can also be infected. The fungus causes perennial swellings on juniper bushes, which release spores in spring. Removal of affected junipers may help, but spores can still travel. Treating for pear scab can help to control rust too.

Fruit and herb pests

Mice eat the developing corms and seeds of germinating peas, beans, and sweetcorn. They also eat crocus corms and orchard fruits, both in gardens and when produce is being stored. They can be controlled by setting mouse traps. If traps are set in gardens, place under a log or brick shelter to reduce the danger to birds and pets. Rats cause similar damage.

Apple sawfly larvae feed inside apples at the fruitlet stage, causing them to fall in early summer. Those that stay on the tree develop a long, brown-yellow scar by late summer. Remove damaged fruitlets. If the tree was heavily attacked the previous year, spray with bifenthrin at petal fall to control the hatching larvae.

Plum moth caterpillars feed inside the fruits of plums, damsons, and greengages in late summer. Choose varieties that ripen later in the season, as moths tend to attack early fruits. This pest is hard to control as effective insecticides are not available, but pheromone traps can be used in early summer to capture male moths.

Gooseberry sawfly larvae feed on gooseberry and redcurrant foliage, and can cause complete defoliation. The caterpillar-like larvae are up to 20mm (¾in) long and pale green, often marked with black dots. Two or three generations occur between spring and the end of summer. Search for the larvae and spray with an appropriate insecticide.

Rosemary beetle and their greyish-white grubs eat the foliage of rosemary, lavender, thyme, and sage. Damage occurs from late summer until the following spring. The adults are 7–8mm (¼–⅜in) long, with purple- and green-striped wing cases. Remove by shaking the plant over a sheet of newspaper, or spray with insecticide.

Bay sucker nymphs suck sap from the underside of leaves, causing them to curl over and become yellow and thickened; damaged parts will dry up and turn brown. Two generations occur during the summer. The adults resemble aphids, have wings and are 2mm (¹⁄₁₂in) long. Pick off infested leaves or spray with an appropriate insecticide.

Cuckoo spit is a white frothy liquid created by immature froghopper nymphs. These sap-sucking insects surround themselves with cuckoo spit, feeding on the stems of herbs and garden flowers; the nymphs are especially attracted to lavender. Little harm is done to the plant, so insecticide treatment is not required.

Apple codling moth caterpillars feed in the cores of ripening apples and pears. By the time the fruit is ready for picking, the caterpillar has usually left by an exit tunnel. Pheromone traps may catch enough male moths to reduce the mating success of females on isolated apple trees, and so may reduce the number of maggoty apples.

Index

A

Abelia x *grandiflora* 'Kaleidoscope' 139
Abutilon x *hybridum* 139
Acer (maple) 10, 68–9, 145
  A. palmatum 8–9, 68–9
  A. p. 'Bloodgood' 69
  A. p. 'Chitose-yama' 69
  A. p. var. *dissectum* 'Filigree' 69
  A. p. var. *d.* 'Garnet' 69
  A. p. 'Katsura' 69
  A. p. 'Linearilobum' 69
  A. p. 'Nicholsonii' 69
  A. p. 'Sango-kaku' 69
acid soils 63, 122, 128
acid-loving plants 63, 122–3, 124,
  222, 231
Acorus 146
  A. gramineus 'Ogon' 147
Adiantum 30
  A. venustum 97
Aechmea fasciata 62, 63
Aeonium 78–9
  A. arboreum 79
  A. 'Ballerina' 79
  A. haworthii 79
  A. h. 'Variegatum' 79
  A. 'Zwartkop' 79
Aeschynanthus 30
African violet *see Saintpaulia*
Agastache 67
Agave 67, 80
  A. americana 80
  A. a. 'Mediopicta Alba' 80
  A. parryi var. *truncata* 80
  A. schidigera 80
  A. stricta 80
  A. victoriae-reginae 80
Alocasia 34, 64
  A. x *amazonica* (elephant's ear)
    30, 60
  A. sanderiana 64, 65
Aloe 3, 81, 84
  A. arborescens 'Variegata' 81
  A. ferox 81
  A. variegata 81
  A. vera 81
alpines 12, 13, 24, 121, 134–5, 239
amaryllis *see Hippeastrum*
Ananas comosus var. *variegatus* 77
Androsace villosa var. *jacquemontii* 121
Anemanthele 27
angel's trumpet *see Brugmansia*
annuals 20, 21, 106–7
Anthurium 13
  A. andraeanum 62, 63
apples 24, 226–7, 248, 249
  'Improved Ashmead's Kernel' 227
  'Discovery' 227
  'Egremont Russet' 227

'Ellison's Orange' 227
'Fiesta' 226–7
'Pixie' 227
'Red Falstaff' 227
apricots 213, 248
  'Alfred' 213
  Flavorcot ('Boyoto') 213
  'Petit Muscat' 213
  'Tomcot' 213
aquatics 136–7
Aralia elata 'Variegata' 23
ariona berries 230, 231
  'Hugin' 231
  Iroquois Beauty ('Morton') 231
Arisaema 52, 53
  A. candidissimum 53
Armoracia rusticana (horseradish) 184
  A. r. 'Variegata' 184
artichokes 21
Asplenium scolopendrium 97
  A. s. Cristatum Group 96–7
Aster 144
  A. amellus 144
  A. novi-belgii 144
Astilbe 71
Astilboides tabularis 71
Athyrium niponicum var. *pictum* 96–7
Atriplex (orach) 161
  A. hortensis var. *rubra* 161
  A. h. 'Scarlet Emperor' 161
aubergines 18, 166
  'Fairy Tale' 18
  'Listada de Gandia' 18
  'Pingtung Long' 18
  'Pinstripe' 166
Aubrieta 34, 121
  A. 'Silberrand' 120
autumn colour 68, 69, 119, 144–5,
  222, 223, 231
azalea *see Rhododendron*

B

Bacopa 19, 144, 126–7, 193
balconies 11, 24–5, 26–7, 67, 80
bamboos 10, 23, 26–7, 54–5, 68
bananas 48–9, 50
bark 48, 173, 239
basil 28, 30, 159, 199
  Greek 168–9
baskets 12, 13, 19, 30, 31, 144, 158
  for bulbs 31, 36, 114
  see also hanging baskets
bat flower *see Tacca chantrieri*
bay *see Laurus nobilis*
beans 249
  French 107, 176–7
  runner 178–9
bedding 16, 22
bedding aster *see Callistephus*

bees 38, 129, 188, 198, 221
beet spinach 175
beetroot 21, 159, 184, 185
  'Boltardy' 185
  'Chioggia Pink' 185
  'Forono' 185
  'Red Ace' 185
Begonia 19, 100–1, 245
  B. aconitifolia 101
  B. benichoma 101
  B. 'Fire Flush' 101
  B. Hiemalis Group 30
  B. masoniana 101
  B. 'Merry Christmas' 101
  B. 'Plum Rose' 101
  B. rex hybrids 100–1
  B. serratipetala 101
  B. 'Silver Queen' 101
Bidens 9
biological controls 99, 243, 245
birch 23
birds 145, 181, 213, 249
  deterring 174, 181, 211, 218, 223,
  224, 225, 243, 247
black-eyed Susan see
  Thunbergia alata
black-stemmed bamboo see
  Phyllostachys nigra
blackberries 152, 220
  'Loch Maree' 220
  'Loch Ness' 220
blackcurrants 209
  'Ben Lomond' 209
blanket flower *see Gaillardia*
Blechnum gibbum 103
blood grass 20
blueberries 222, 223
  'Brigitta' 223
  'Earliblue' 223
  'Toro' 223
bog plants 70–1
bok choy 172, 173
bolting 156, 158, 173, 175, 185, 191
borders, containers in 6, 18, 19, 52, 53
Bougainvillea 112, 113
  B. x *buttiana* 113
  B. x *b.* 'Enid Lancaster' 113
  B. x *b.* 'Raspberry Ice' 113
  B. Camarilla Fiesta ('Monle') 113
  B. glabra 113
box *see Buxus*
Brachyscombe 9
brassicas 173, 174, 191, 245, 247
bromeliads 31, 77, 216
Brugmansia x *candida* 'Grand
  Marnier' 47
bubble plastic 11, 13, 48, 66, 68, 72,
  215, 234
buckets 137

bulbs 16, 20, 22, 28, 29, 36, 121, 150,
  235, 237
  forcing 150–1
  planting 42, 116, 148, 150, 235
bush lily *see Clivia*
busy Lizzies 20, 22, 50–1, 94
butterflies 38, 129, 159, 174, 191, 221,
  246–7
Buxus sempervirens (box) 10, 17, 20,
  24, 28, 29, 142–3

C

cabbage palm *see Cordyline australis*
cabbages 18, 21, 191, 247
  'January King 3' 191
  'Jewel' 191
  'Siberia' 191
  'Tarvoy' 191
cacti 15, 82–3, 235, 243
Calamagrostis 27
Calamondin orange 206–7
Calathea makoyana (peacock plant) 61
Calendula (pot marigold) 21, 158
Callicarpa bodinieri var. *giraldii*
  'Profusion' 145
Callistephus (bedding aster) 144
Caltha palustris 137
Camellia 122, 244
campanulas 28
Canna 13, 20, 50–1
  C. 'Assaut' 51
  C. 'Black Knight' 50, 51
  C. 'Cleopatra' 51
  C. 'Durban' 50–1, 51
  C. 'Richard Wallace' 51
  C. 'Rosemond Coles' 51
  C. speciosa 'Tropical Rose' 51
  C. 'Striata' 51
Cape jasmine see *Gardenia augusta*
Cape primrose see *Streptocarpus*
Carex 26, 146
  C. comans bronze form 13
  C. c. 'Bronze Perfection' 147
  C. dipsacea 15
  C. flagellifera 147
  C. 'Ice Dance' 147
carrots 186–7, 247
  'Amsterdam Forcing 3' 187
  'Autumn King 2' 187
  'Bangor' 187
  'Carson' 187
  'Chantenay Red Cored 2' 187
  'Infinity' 187
  'Mini Finger' 186–7
  'Parmex' 187
  'Volcano' 187
Celosia argentea Plumosa Group 49
Cercis canadensis 'Forest Pansy' 145
Cerinthe major var. *purpurascens* 106

Chamaedorea elegans 56
Chamaemelum nobile (chamomile)
　195
　C. n. 'Flore Pleno' 195
　C. n. 'Treneague' 195
Chamaerops humilis 73
chard 152, 159, 172, 240
　'Bright Lights' 172
　'Lucullus' 172
　'Ruby Chard' 172
Cheiranthus cheiri see Erysimum
Chenopodium giganteum 174, 175
cherries (fruit trees) 224
　'Crown Morello' 224
　'Stella' 224
　'Sunburst' 224
cherry (flowering) *see Prunus*
cherry pie *see Heliotropium*
chicory 160
　'Treviso Precoce Mesola' 160
chilli peppers *see* peppers
chives 14, 18, 154, 162, 163, 198
Chlorophytum (spider plant)
　C. comosum 94, 95
　C. laxum 30
chokeberries *see* aronia berries
Christmas cherry *see Solanum*
　pseudocapsicum
Chrysanthemum 26, 245
Chusan palm *see Trachycarpus*
　fortunei
cineraria *see Pericallis* x *hybrida*
Citrus medica var. *digitata*
　206, 207
citrus fruit 204-7
city gardens 23, 55
Clematis 104-5, 107, 245
　C. 'Arabella' 105
　C. Chantilly Evipo 105
　C. 'Fireworks' 105
　C. Fleuri 105
　C. florida var. *florida* 'Sieboldii'
　　105
　C. Ice Blue 104
　C. Kingfisher 104
　C. 'Niobe' 105
　C. Ooh La La 104-5
　C. 'The President' 105
　C. 'Vyvyan Pennell' 105
clementines 207
climbers 20, 104-13
Clivia 148, 149
　C. miniata 149
cloches 155, 162, 172, 175, 186, 191
coastal gardens, plants for 67, 73
Codiaeum (croton) 61
　C. variegatum var. *pictum*
　'Excellent' 61
　C. v. var. *p.* 'Gold Star' 61
　C. v. var. *p.* 'Petra' 61
coleus *see Solenostemon*
Colocasia 50
companion plants 198
compost 194, 234, 235, 236, 246

aquatic compost 136, 137, 235
citrus compost 204, 206
ericaceous compost 122, 124, 128,
　222, 231, 235
orchid compost 77, 90, 235
renewing top layer 68, 119, 209,
　217, 224, 236
see also growing bags
conifers 24, 26
conservatories 48, 57, 62, 90, 112-13,
　139, 166
fruit in 204-7, 214, 216, 231
containers 6-13, 234
for alpines 134
contemporary 8, 10-11, 12, 17, 30,
　31, 33, 55, 72, 73, 100, 124, 125
grouping 14-15, 21, 121, 147
for houseplants 30-1
recycled 8, 9, 19, 21, 30, 31
rustic 8, 12-13, 16, 144, 171
for urban gardens 23, 55
wall-mounted 26, 81, 85, 103
contemporary schemes 6, 8, 10-11,
　17, 25, 32
Convolvulus 19
　C. tricolor 107
copper tape 71, 181, 243
coral pea *see Hardenbergia*
Cordyline australis 65
　C. a. Purpurea Group 67
coriander 159, 202, 203
　'Cilantro' 203
　'Leisure' 203
Corydalis 114
Cosmos 15
Cotinus coggygria 'Young Lady' 145
Cotoneaster salicifolius 'Gnom' 145
cottage garden style 12, 14, 19, 28
country garden style 6, 8, 12-13, 30,
　32, 126
courgettes 166, 167
　'De Nice A Fruit Rond' 167
　'Defender' 167
　'Golden Delight' 167
　'Parador' 167
　'Venus' 167
crab apple *see Malus*
cranberries 222
Crassula 82-3, 84
Crocosmia 50
Crocus 114, 249
croton *see Codiaeum*
Cuphea 50-1
cuttings 192, 197
Cycas revoluta 57
Cyclamen 22, 124, 245
　C. persicum 125
Cymbidium 90-1
　C. Golden Elf 91
　C. hookerianum 91
　C. Lisa Rose 90
　C. Pontac 'Mont Millais' 91
　C. Portelet Bay 91
　C. Showgirl 91

D
daffodils 9, 29, 32, 36, 114, 116, 121,
　150-1, 235
　see also Narcissus
Dahlia 6, 15, 20, 23, 130-1, 245
　D. 'David Howard' 131
　D. Gallery Series 130, 131
　D. 'Gallery Art Deco' 130-1
　D. 'Pink Giraffe' 131
　D. 'Purple Gem' 131
　D. 'Roxy' 131
　D. 'Small World' 131
　D. 'Tally Ho' 131
　D. 'Yellow Hammer' 131
Daphne x *burkwoodii* 37
　D. tangutica 37
Dasylirion longissimum 14
Delosperma 135
Dendrobium 88, 89
　D. fimbriatum 89
　D. Momozono 'Princess' 89
　D. nobile 89
　D. Sonia 89
　D. Sweet Dawn 89
devil's ivy *see Epipremnum aureum*
Dianthus (pink) 21, 22, 28, 40, 41
　D. 'Devon Flores' (syn. 'Starry
　　Night') 41
Diascia 237
Dichondra argentea 'Silver Falls' 237
disease-resistant plants 175, 208,
　211, 213, 242, 246, 247, 248
diseases 52, 242, 244, 246, 248
　fruit 211, 248
　house plants 243
　ornamental plants 52, 242, 244
　vegetables 157, 163, 167, 175, 242, 246
dividing plants 50, 54, 77, 92, 98, 102,
　146, 163, 192
donkey's tail *see Sedum*
　morganianum
Doritaenopsis 86
　D. Taida Sweet Berry 86
Doritis 86
drainage 44, 121, 134, 234, 236, 246
Dryopteris affinis 97
　D. erythrosora 97
dwarf fan palm *see Chamaerops*
　humilis
dwarfing rootstocks 212, 213, 224,
　225, 226, 227, 228, 236

E
Echeveria. 15, 25, 31, 78-9, 84
　E. agavoides 79
　E. 'Duchess of Nuremberg' 14
　E. gibbiflora var. *metallica* 79
　E. secunda var. *glauca* 79
Echinocereus 83
edibles 10, 18, 20, 24, 25, 26, 28
　see also fruit; herbs; vegetables
Elaeagnus ebbingei 26
elephant's ear *see Alocasia* x
　amazonica

endive 191
Ensete ventricosum (banana) 48, 49
　E. v. 'Maurellii' 49
　E. v. 'Tandarra Red' 49
Epipremnum aureum (devil's ivy) 103
Equisetum hyemale 137
Eragrostis elliotii 147
Eriobotrya japonica (loquat) 65
Erysimum (wallflower) 34, 116-17, 120
　E. 'Poem Lavender' 120
Euonymus alatus 'Compactus' 145
　E. fortunei 'Emerald 'n' Gold' 15
Euphorbia characias Silver Swan 12
　E. mellifera 37
　E. trigona 82-3
exposed sites 35, 154

F
fan palm *see Rhapis excelsa*
Fargesia (bamboo) 54
　F. murielae 55
Fatsia japonica 34, 64, 65
fennel *see Foeniculum*
ferns 11, 13, 30, 71, 96-7, 103, 148
fertilizers 239
Festuca 146
　F. glauca 11, 146
Ficus carica 'Brown Turkey' 214
　F. elastica (rubber plant) 76
　F. e. 'Decora' 76
　F. e. 'Doescheri' 76
　F. e. 'Tineke' 76
　F. pumila 'Sonny' 58
figs 214, 244
flame nettle *see Solenostemon*
flamingo flower *see Anthurium*
fleece 64, 128, 129, 155, 186, 194,
　209, 211, 212, 213, 215, 224
　for deterring pests 244, 247
　for overwintering 64, 66, 78, 80,
　　172, 175, 191, 196
focal points 14, 16, 32, 60, 68, 72,
　74, 104
Foeniculum (fennel) 28, 259
　F. vulgare 194
　F. v. var. *azoricum* 194
　F. v. 'Smokey' 194
forcing
　bulbs 150-1
　rhubarb 210
forget-me-not *see Myosotis*
fountain grass 15
Frankenia thymifolia 41
French beans 107, 176-7
　'Blue Lake' 177
　'Cobra' 177
　'Delinel' 177
　'French Rocquencourt' 177
　'Purple Tepee' 177
　'The Prince' 177
French marigold *see Tagetes*
frost protection 42, 64, 70, 78, 155, 234
　fruit 206, 209, 211, 212, 213, 224, 225
　herbs 194, 195, 196, 197

see also fleece
fruit 21, 28, 204–31
  pests and diseases 248–9
fruit trees 18, 21, 204–7, 212–14, 224–9
Fuchsia 18, 94–5, 244
  F. 'Alice Hoffman' 94
  F. 'Genii' 94, 95
  F. 'Lady Thumb' 94, 95
  F. 'Lena' 95
  F. magellanica var. *molinae* 95
  F. 'Mrs Popple' 94, 95
  F. 'Riccartonii' 94
  F. 'Tom Thumb' 94

G

Gaillardia. x *grandiflora* 132, 133
  G. x *g.* 'Dazzler' 133
  G. x *g.* 'Goldkobold' 133
  G. x *g.* 'Kobold' 133
Galanthus (snowdrop) 115
  G. nivalis 115
garden styles 8–13
Gardenia augusta 47
garlic 170, 171
Gaura 22
Gentiana acaulis 121
Gerbera 23, 132
  G. 'Everglades' 132
  G. Everlast Series 132
  G. Garvinea 132
  G. Garvinea 'Nikki' 42–3
  G. 'Klondike' 132
  G. (Landscape Series)
    'Mount Rushmore' 132
ginger 202, 203
Gloriosa (glory lily) 112
  G. superba 'Rothschildiana' 112
goji berries 230
gooseberries 210, 211, 249
  'Hinnonmäki Röd' 211
  'Hinnonmäki Gul' 211
  'Invicta' 211
  'Leveller' 211
  'Xenia' 211
goosefoot plant *see Syngonium*
grape hyacinth *see Muscari*
Graptopetalum bellum 84
  G. paraguayense 84
  G. rusbyi 84
grasses 22, 26, 27, 68, 120, 146–7, 237
  contemporary schemes 17, 20,23, 25
  pots for 10–11, 12, 20
gravel 78, 121, 134, 137, 173, 237, 239
Greek basil 168–9
greenhouses 62, 109, 162, 166, 243
  fruit in 204–7, 214, 231
  overwintering in 48, 50, 52, 67, 78,
    90, 155, 201, 218
  tomatoes in 165, 241
grouping containers 14–15, 21, 121, 147
growing bags 154, 164, 165, 167, 186, 241
guavas 216, 217
Gunnera manicata 70
  G. tinctoria 70

H

Hakonechloa macra 'Aureola' 22
half barrels 13, 21, 136, 145
Hamamelis (witch hazel) 44–5
  H. 'Arnold Promise' 45
  H. x *intermedia* 'Jelena' 45
  H. x i. 'Pallida' 45
  H. mollis 44
  H. virginiana 45
hanging baskets 81, 85, 103, 237, 238
  crops 21, 164–5, 176–7, 198, 218–19
Hardenbergia violacea 112, 113
heathers 22
Hebe 23, 129
  H. 'Johnny Day' 129
  H. 'Rosie' 129
  H. 'Silver Queen' 129
  H. topiaria 129
  H. 'Watson's Pink' 129
Hedera helix (ivy) 10, 16, 25, 29, 31,
  37, 94, 95, 118, 143
Hedychium densiflorum 64, 65
Helianthemum 'Rhodanthe
  Carneum' 135
Helichrysum italicum 22
  H. petiolare 22
Heliotropium (cherry pie) 41
  H. arborescens 41
  H. 'Dwarf Marine' 41
  H. 'Marine Hybrid' 41
herbs 6, 18, 24, 30, 155, 159,
  192–203, 211
  containers for 10, 28
  on patios 20, 21, 23, 196
  pests and diseases 248–9
hessian 48, 64, 72
Heuchera 10, 40, 94, 95, 98, 99
  H. 'Amber Waves' 99
  H. brizoides 99
  H. 'Can-can' 99
  H. 'Plum Pudding' 99
  H. 'Silver Scrolls' 15, 99
Hibiscus 129
  H. rosa-sinensis (rose of China) 138
  H. r. 'Athene' 138
  H. r. 'Cooperi' 138
  H. syriacus Blue Bird (syn. 'Oiseau
    Bleu') 129
Hippeastrum (amaryllis) 148
holly *see Ilex*
honeyberries 222, 223
honeysuckle *see Lonicera*
horseradish 184
horticultural fleece *see* fleece
Hosta 25, 26, 71, 98
  H. 'August Moon' 98
  H. fortunei var. *albopicta* f. *aurea* 98
  H. 'Francee' 98
  H. 'Krossa Regal' 98
house plants 24, 30–1, 35
  pests and diseases 243
  see also under plant names
houseleek *see Sempervivum*
Hoya carnosa 46

H. lanceolata subsp. *bella* 46
Hyacinthus (hyacinth) 36, 116, 150–1
  H. orientalis 'Blue Jacket' 151
  H. o. 'City of Haarlem' 151
  H. o. 'Ostara' 151
  H. o. 'Pink Pearl' 31, 151
Hydrangea 128
  H. macrophylla 128
  H. m. Endless Summer Twist-n-Shout
    128
  H. paniculata 128
  H. quercifolia 145
Hypericum 'Magical Red' 145

I

Ilex (holly) 142
  I. crenata 'Mariesii' 143
Imperata cylindrica 'Rubra' 10–11
Indian azalea *see Rhododendron simsii*
informal gardens 8, 12–13, 19, 22
insects 34, 154, 226
  see also bees; butterflies; pests
Ipomoea 49, 107
  I. batatas 'Margarita' 42–3, 107
Iris 17
  I. danfordiae 115
  I. 'Edward' 115
  I. laevigata 137
  I. reticulata 115
  I. r. 'Cantab' 115
  I. r. 'J.S. Dijt' 115
  I. winogradowii 115
irrigation systems 54, 71, 119, 238, 241
ivy *see Hedera helix*

J

Japanese-inspired gardens 10, 68–9
jasmine *see Jasminum; Stephanotis;
  Trachelospermum*
Jasminum polyanthum 111
Juncus effusus f. *spiralis* 99
  J. ensifolius 137
junipers 248

K

kaffir limes 205
Kalanchoe 84, 85
  K. blossfeldiana 85
  K. b. 'Calandra Monroe' 85
  K. b. Pink Form 85
  K. manginii 85
  K. pumila 85
  K. 'Tessa' 85
  K. 'Wendy' 85
kale 21, 174
  'Black Tuscany' 174
  'Dwarf Green Curled' 174
  'Red Curled' 174
  'Red Russian' 174
  'Redbor' 174
kohl rabi 172, 173
  'Olivia' 173
  'Violetta' 173
kumquats 207

L

Lantana camara 'Feston Rose' 139
  L. c. 'Mine d'Or' 139
  L. c. 'Sunkiss' 139
Lathyrus odoratus (sweet pea) 19,
  109, 176
  L. o. 'Blue Ripple' 109
  L. o. Heirloom Mixed 109
  L. o. 'Jayne Amanda' 109
  L. o. 'Matucana' 109
laurel 142
Laurus nobilis (bay) 17, 18, 21, 142,
  143, 196
Lavandula (lavender)18, 22, 23, 28,
  67, 249
  L. angustifolia 38
  L. a. 'Hidcote' 38–9
  L. a. 'Loddon Pink' 39
  L. a. 'Munstead' 39
  L. a. 'Nana Alba' 39
  L. x *chaytoriae* 'Sawyers' 39
  L. pinnata 39
  L. stoechas 'Kew Red' 39
  L. 'Willow Vale' 39
leeks 14, 190, 247
lemon balm *see Melissa officinalis*
lemon grass 202
lemons 204
  'Meyer' 204
  'Variegata' 204
Leontopodium alpinum (edelweiss)
  121
lettuces 21, 24, 156–7, 198, 240, 247
  'Bubbles' 157
  Dazzle 156–7
  Green Frills 156–7
  'Little Gem' 157
  'Lollo Rosso' 157
  'Nymans' 157
  'Pandero' 157
  'Salad Bowl' 157
  'Tintin' 157
  'Winter Density' 157
Leymus arenarius 22
Ligularia 8
lilac *see Syringa*
Lilium (lily) 42–3, 71, 245
  L. formosanum var. *pricei* 42–3
  L. 'Journey's End' 43
  L. martagon 43
  L. medeoloides 43
  L. nepalense 43
  L .pyrenaicum 43
  L. speciosum var. *rubrum* 43
  L. 'Star Gazer' 43
  L. 'Sterling Star' 43
limes 205
Liquidambar styraciflua 'Gumball' 145
Lobelia 15, 237
  L. cardinalis 137
  L. siphilitica 137
loganberries 220, 221
  'Ly 654' 221
Lonicera (honeysuckle) 142

L. fragrantissima 44, 45
 L. nitida 142
 L. n. 'Baggeson's Gold' 143
loquat *see Eriobotrya japonica*
Lotus berthelotii 52, 53, 168–9, 237
Lysimachia nummularia 'Goldilocks'
 122–3
Lythrum salicaria 71

M
magnolias 122
Mahonia 12
makrut limes 205
Malus (crab apple) 119
 M. 'Adirondack' 119
 M. 'Butterball' 119
 M. 'Red Sentinel' 119
 M. transitoria 119
Mammillaria zeilmanniana 83
mandarins 206, 207
mangetouts 180, 181
 'Carouby de Mausanne' 181
 'Oregon Sugar Pod' 181
manure 209, 212
maple *see Acer*
maple (flowering) *see Abutilon* x
 hybridum
marigold *see Calendula; Tagetes*
marjoram 23
Matteuccia struthiopteris 96, 97
Medinilla magnifica 62
Melianthus major 64, 65
Melissa officinalis (lemon balm)
 195
 M. o. 'All Gold' 195
 M. o. 'Aurea' 195
Mentha (mint) 18, 154, 192–3
 M. arvensis 'Banana' 192
 M. 'Berries and Cream' 192
 M. x *gracilis* 193
 M. longifolia 193
 M. x *piperata* f. *citrata* 193
 M. x *p.* f. *c.* 'Chocolate' 192
 M. x *p.* f. *c.* 'Lemon' 192
 M. spicata 'Tashkent' 192
 M. suaveolens 193
 M. s. 'Variegata' 193
metal containers 11, 14, 17, 19, 21, 23,
 25, 26–7, 29
Mexican tree spinach 174, 175
micro greens 159
mind-your-own-business *see*
 Soleirolia soleirolii
mint *see Mentha*
Miscanthus 26, 27
 M. sinensis 'Morning Light' 25
mizuna 158
modern schemes 6, 8, 10–11, 17, 25, 32
Monstera deliciosa (Swiss cheese
 plant) 58, 59
morning glory *see Convolvulus;*
 ipomoea
moth orchid *see Phalaenopsis*
mother-in-law's tongue *see*

Sansevieria
mulches 15, 173, 194, 209, 239, 248
 gravel 121, 134, 173, 239
 ornamental 54, 55, 78, 84, 239
mulching 44, 68, 173, 232, 238,
 239, 244
Musa basjoo (bamboo) 49
Muscari (grape hyacinth) 36, 114, 235
 M. macrocarpum 'Golden
 Fragrance' 36
Musella 48
mustard 158, 159
 'Red Giant' 158
Myosotis (forget-me-not) 114
 M. scorpioides 114
 M. s. 'Royal Blue' 116–17

N
Narcissus (daffodil) 9, 29, 32, 36, 114,
 116, 121, 150–1, 235
Narcissus 'Acropolis' 114
 N. 'Avalanche' 151
 N. 'Carlton' 114
 N. 'Cheerfulness' 151
 N. 'Hawera' 114
 N. 'Ice Follies' 114, 151
 N. 'Inbal' 31
 N. 'Jack Snipe' 114
 N. 'Pipit' 114
 N. 'Salome' 114, 151
 N. 'Tête à Tête' 114
nasturtiums 21, 107
New Zealand flax *see Phormium*
New Zealand spinach 175
Nicotiana (tobacco plant) 22, 35, 40
Notocactus magnifica (syn. *Parodia
 magnifica*) 83
nutrients 133, 164, 235, 239
Nymphaea (water lily) 136
 N. odorata var. *minor* 136
 N. 'Pygmaea Helvola' 136
 N. 'Pygmaea Rubra' 136
 N. tetragona 136

O
obelisks 19, 107, 108, 112, 113
Ocimum basilicum (basil) 28, 30,
 159, 199
 O. b. 'Horapha Nanum' 199
 O. b. 'Minette' 199
 O. b. var. *purpurascens* 'Dark Opal'
 199
 O. b. 'Well-Sweep Purple Miniature'
 199
olives 11, 214, 215
Oncidium 88
 O. Sharry Baby 88
 O. Sweet Sugar 88
onions 152, 170, 171, 247
 Red Baron 171
Ophiopogon 12, 15, 27, 146
 O. planiscapus 'Nigrescens' 147
Opuntia 82–3
 O. microdasys var. *albispina* 83

orach 160, 161
oranges 206–7
orchids 32, 86–93, 235
oregano *see Origanum vulgare*
oriental leaves 158–9
Origanum vulgare (oregano) 200, 201
 O. v. 'Aureum Crispum' 201
 O. v. 'Gold Tip' 201
 O. v. 'Kent Beauty' 201
Oscularia 134
 O. deltoides 135
Osmanthus delavayi 37

P
Pachyphytum 134, 135
Pachypodium 82–3
pak choi 172, 173
palms 56–7, 72–3
pansies *see Viola*
Paphiopedilum (slipper orchid) 92–3
 P. callosum 93
 P. Clair de Lune 93
 P. fairrieanum 93
 P. hybrids 92–3
 P. insigne 93
 P. Maudiae 'Coloratum' 93
 P. Pinocchio 93
 P. venustum 93
 P. villosum 93
parlour palm *see Chamaedorea
 elegans*
parrot's beak *see Lotus berthelotii*
parsley 18, 28, 30, 154, 196, 200, 247
parsnips 247
partial shade, plants for 34, 35
patios 10–11, 14, 22, 23, 67, 73, 80, 104
 containers for 13, 20–1, 22
 edibles on 18, 20, 21, 152–3, 166–7
peace lily *see Spathiphyllum*
peaches 212, 248
 'Bonanza' 212
 'Duke of York' 212
 'Garden Lady' 212
 'Peregrine' 212
peacock plant *see Calathea
 makoyana*
pears 228–9, 248
 'Concorde' 229
 'Doyenné du Comice' 229
 'Dwarf Pearl' 228
 'Humbug' 229
 'Williams' Bon Chrétien' 229
peas 180, 247, 249
 'Blauwschokker' 180
 'Purple Podded' 180
 see also mangetouts; sugar snaps
Pelargonium 16, 19, 28, 29, 64, 132, 133
 P. 'Lady Plymouth' 34, 64, 65
 P. 'Trend Scarlet Red' 133
Penstemon 8
peppers 14, 21, 168–9
 'Aji Amarillo' 169
 'Alma Paprika' 169
 'California Wonder' 169

 'Cherry Bomb' 169
 'Cheyenne' 168–9
 'Gourmet' 169
 'Hungarian Hot Wax' 18
 'Medusa' 24
 'Numex Twilight' 169
 'Pepper Gypsy' 169
 'Prairie Fire' 169
perennials *see also plant names* 33
 planting 234
Pericallis x *hybrida* 124
 P. x *h.* Senetti Series 125
perpetual spinach 175
pests 38, 78, 99, 140, 232, 242–3,
 244–5, 246–7
 animals 114, 116, 213, 249
 on fruit 208, 249
 on vegetables 159, 174, 181, 186,
 191, 198, 246–7
 see also birds; slugs; snails
Petunia 16, 22, 29, 35, 40, 107, 130
 P. Million Bells 168–9
Phalaenopsis (moth orchid) 86–7
 P. Brother Little Amaglad 87
 P. Brother Pico Sweetheart 87
 P. cornu-cervi 87
 P. Doris 87
 P. I-Hsin Black Tulip 87
 P. Lundy 87
 P. stuartiana 87
 P. violacea 87
Phalaris arundinacea 'Dwarf Garters' 37
Phillyrea 142
Philodendron 58
 P. angustisectum 59
 P. bipinnatifidum 59
 P. hederaceum 59
 P. melanochrysum 59
Phlox subulata 'Lilacina' 135
Phormium (New Zealand flax) 11, 17,
 25, 66
 P. cookianum 66
 P. 'Jester' 66
 P. 'Pink Panther' 66
 P. 'Platt's Black' 66
 P. tenax 66
Phygelius 23
Phyllostachys (bamboo) 26, 54
 P. bambusoides 'Castillonis' 54
 P. nigra 26–7
 P. vivax 'Aureocaulis' 55
Pieris 122
Pilea depressa 100–1
pineapple plant *see Ananas comosus*
pineapples 216
pinks *see Dianthus*
Pinus (pine) 26
plants
 care 238–9
 choosing 34–5, 242
Plectranthus zatarhendii 106
Pleioblastus variegatus 55
plums 224, 225, 249
 'Giant Prune' 225

'Marjorie's Seedling' 225
'Stanley' 225
'Victoria' 225
'Warwickshire Drooper' 225
Polypodium vulgare
'Cornubiense' 97
Polystichum makinoi 96-7
P. polyblepharum 97
P. setiferum Divisilobum Group 97
potatoes 182-3, 246, 247
'Accent' 183
'Belle de Fontenay' 183
'Charlotte' 183
'Foremost' 183
'Pink Fir Apple' 183
'Ratte' 183
'Red Duke of York' 183
'Yukon Gold' 183
pots
terracotta 12, 13, 16, 19, 22, 26, 28, 54, 114, 234, 238
see also containers
predators 242, 243
primulas 30, 31, 37
privet 20, 143
propagation *see* cuttings; dividing
propagators 74, 163, 164, 166, 167, 168, 188, 199, 202
Prunus 119
P. 'Beni Yutaka' 119
P. 'Fukubana' 119
P. 'Kiku-shidare-zakura' (syn. 'Cheal's weeping') 119
P. laurocerasus 26
P. 'Pink Perfection' 119
see also apricots; cherries; peaches; plums
Pseudosasa japonica 54, 55
pumpkins 188, 189
purple coral pea *see Hardenbergia violacea*

Q

quinces 216, 217

R

radicchio 160
radishes 159, 162, 240, 247
'Cherry Belle' 162
'China Rose' 162
'French Breakfast' 162
'Scarlet Globe' 162
Rebutia krainziana 83
recycled containers 8, 9, 19, 21, 30, 31
redcurrants 208, 249
'Junifer' 208
'Red Lake' 208
'Rovada' 208
'Stanza' 208
Rhapis excelsa 57
R. e. 'Taiheinishiki' 57
R. e. 'Variegata' 57
R. e. 'Zuikonishiki' 57

Rhodochiton 106
R. atrosanguineus 106
Rhododendron 26, 122-3, 244
R. augustinii 123
R. 'Dopey' 122
R. 'Dreamland' 122
R. 'Fragrantissima' 123
R. 'Gunborg' 122-3
R. 'Lemon Dream' 122
R. 'Louise Dowdle' 123
R. luteum 123
R. 'Palestrina' 123
R. simsii 124
R. 'Temple Belle' 123
R. yakushimanum 24, 123
R. 'Yellow Hammer' 123
rhubarb 154, 210
'Timperley Early' 210
Ribes odoratum 37
rocket 159, 247
Rodgersia pinnata 'Superba' 71
roof terraces 11, 24-7
root vegetables 184-7, 247
rootstocks, dwarfing 212, 213, 224, 225, 226, 227, 228, 236
Rosa (rose) 126-7
R. Anna Ford 127
R. Baby Love 127
R. Baby Masquerade 127
R. Chatsworth 127
R. Drummer Boy 127
R. Graham Thomas 242
R. Queen Mother 127
R. Regensberg 126-7
R. Stacey Sue 127
R. Sweet Dream 127
rose of China *see Hibiscus rosa-sinensis*
rosemary *see Rosmarinus*
roses 126-7, 242, 244, 245
see also Rosa
Rosmarinus (rosemary) 10
R. officinalis 23, 28, 200, 201, 249
R. o. 'Lady in White' 201
R. o. 'McConnell's Blue' 201
R. o. 'Majorca Pink' 201
R. o. 'Miss Jessopp's Upright' 201
R. o. Prostratus Group 201
rubber plant *see Ficus elastica*
Rumex (sorrel) 160, 161
R. sanguineus 161
R. scutatus 161
runner beans 178-9
'Hestia' 179
'Lady Di' 179
'Painted Lady' 179
'Polestar' 179
'White Lady' 179
rustic style 8, 12-13, 16, 144, 171, 180

S

sage *see Salvia officinalis*
sago palm *see Cycas revoluta*
Saintpaulia (African violet) 30, 140, 141

S. 'Delft' 141
S. 'Fancy Pants' 141
S. 'Kristi Marie' 141
S. 'Rococo Anna' 141
S. Spectra-Color Series 141
salads 9, 18, 28, 156-63
Salvia 15, 26
S. elegans 'Scarlet Pineapple' 197
S. officinalis (sage) 21, 28, 196, 197, 198, 249
S. o. 'Purpurascens' 197
S. o. 'Purpurascens Variegata' 197
S. o. 'Tricolor' 197
Sansevieria trifasciata 'Laurentii' 102
Sasa (bamboo) 54
S. veitchii 55
saving seed 106
Saxifraga (saxifrage) 12, 121
S. x *arendsii* 13
S. sancta 121
S. 'Southside Seedling' 121
S. stribrnyi 121
Schefflera arboricola 'Gold Capella' 58
Schlumbergera truncata 83
sedges 34, 146-7
Sedum 26, 142-3
S. morganianum 81
S. rupestre 135
S. sedoides 135
seed, saving 106
seedlings 240, 245, 247
thinning 156, 158, 161, 175, 186, 200, 240
seeds, sowing 240, 245
Sempervivum (houseleek) 24
S. arachnoideum 134
S. tectorum 35, 135
shade 53, 64, 71, 96-7, 121
plants for 35, 154
shallots 170
'Mikor' 171
'Red Sun' 171
sheltered sites, plants needing 35
shrubs 13, 22, 25, 28, 33, 128-9
planting 44, 234
sinks 121, 134
Skimmia 122
S. japonica 'Rubella' 15
slipper orchid *see Paphiopedilum*
slugs 71, 98, 181, 242, 243, 245
Smithiantha (temple bells) 75
S. cinnabarina 75
S. 'Extra Sassy' 75
S. 'Little One' 75
smoke bush *see Cotinus coggygria*
snails 71, 98, 181, 242, 243, 245
snapdragons 15
snowdrop *see Galanthus*
Solanum pseudocapsicum 148, 149
Soleirolia soleirolii 30, 31, 141
Solenostemon 40, 52
S. scutellarioides 52
sorrel 160, 161
sowing seeds 156, 175, 186, 240, 245

Spathiphyllum (peace lily) 30
spider plant *see Chlorophytum comosum*
spinach 174, 175
'Galaxy' 175
'Medania' 175
Mexican tree spinach 174, 175
New Zealand 175
perpetual 175
spring onions 162, 163
'North Holland Blood Red' 163
'Vigour King' 163
'White Lisbon' 163
squashes 188-9
'Crown Prince' 189
'Jack Be Little' 189
'Sweet Dumpling' 189
'Turk's Turban' 189
Stachys byzantina 25
star jasmine *see Trachelospermum jasminoides*
Stephanotis floribunda 110
Stipa 26, 146
S. tenuissima 147
strawberries 14, 18, 21, 24, 27, 152, 197, 218-19, 248
'Albion' 219
Alpine 218, 219
'Cambridge Favourite' 219
'Domanil' 219
'Elsanta' 219
'Flamenco' 219
'Mara des Bois' 219
'Sonata' 219
Streptocarpus (Cape primrose) 140
S. 'Gwen' 140
S. 'Katie' 140
Stromanthe sanguinea 'Triostar' 77
successional sowing 156, 175, 186
succulents 10, 30, 78-85, 134, 135, 243
sugar snaps 180, 181
'Cascadia' 181
'Sugar Ann' 181
sunny sites, plants for 34
Sutera cordata see *Bacopa*
sweet peas *see Lathyrus odoratus*
Swiss cheese plant *see Monstera deliciosa*
Syngonium podophyllum 148
Syringa (lilac)
S. x *laciniata* 118
S. meyeri 'Palibin' 118
S. pubescens subsp. *patula* 'Miss Kim' 118
S. vulgaris 'Andenken an Ludwig Späth' 118

T

Tacca chantrieri 74
Tagetes (French marigold) 21, 199
tangelos 207
tangerines 206, 207
tarragon 28, 198

Taxus baccata (yew) 142, 143
tayberries 220, 221
    'Buckingham' 221
temple bells *see Smithiantha*
terraces 14, 20, 21, 22, 23, 80
    see also patios
terracotta pots 12, 13, 16, 19, 22, 26, 28, 54, 114, 234, 238
Tetrapanax 64, 65
    T. papyrifer 'Rex' 65
Teucrium scorodonia 'Crispum' 99
Thai herbs and spices 202–3
thinning
    fruit 213, 226, 228
    seedlings 156, 158, 161, 175, 186, 200, 240
Thunbergia alata (black-eyed Susan) 29, 107, 176–7
Thymus (thyme) 23, 116, 130, 196, 198, 199, 249
    T. 'Golden Lemon' 198
    T. 'Fragrantissimus' 198
    T. pulegioides 'Archer's Gold' 198
    T. 'Silver Posie' 130
    T. vulgaris 198
Tiarella 'Snow Blanket' 122–3
Tillandsia 31
tobacco plant *see Nicotiana*
tomatilloes 230, 231
    'Toma Verde' 231
tomatoes 14, 21, 24, 28, 154, 164–5, 199, 231, 246
    'Balconi Red' 28
    in growing bags 241
    'Minibel' 18, 24
    'Moneymaker' 165

'Primabel' 24
'Sungold' 165, 242
'Sweet Olive' 165
'Tigerella' 165
'Totem' 165
'Tumbling Tom Red' 164–5
'Tumbling Tom Yellow' 165
topiary 10, 20, 24, 28, 142–3, 196
Trachelospermum asiaticum 108
    T. jasminoides 20, 108
Trachycarpus fortunei 72, 73
traditional designs 12–13, 16
trees 10, 13, 19, 23, 26, 32, 68–9
    planting 212, 236
    see also fruit trees
trellis 27, 107, 108, 113, 221
troughs 21, 26, 121, 134, 191, 218
Tulipa (tulip) 116–17
    T. 'Abu Hassan' 116–17
    T. 'Angélique' 116–17
    T. 'Artist' 117
    T. 'Ballerina' 117
    T. 'China Pink' 117
    T. clusiana 117
    T. 'Estelle Rijnveld' 117
    T. 'Queen of Night' 117
    T. species 121
    T. 'Spring Green' 117
    T. 'West Point' 117
Turk's cap lily *see Lilium martagon*

U

umbrella plant *see Schefflera arboricola*
underplanting 18, 37, 52, 67, 114, 139, 211
urban gardens 23, 55

V

variegation, retaining 58
vase plant *see Aechmea*
vegetable gardens 18
vegetables 10, 14, 21, 28, 154–91
    pests and diseases 246–7
    sowing and planting guide 155
Verbena 'Derby' 237
    V. 'Peaches 'n' Cream' 237
Viburnum 142
    V. x *burkwoodii* 37
    V. carlesii 37
    V. farreri 37
    V. x *juddii* 37
    V. opulus 'Xanthocarpum' 145
    V. tinus 26
    V. t. 'Variegatum' 143
Vinca minor 22
Viola 10, 16, 21, 22, 29, 34, 237
    as underplanting 114, 116, 168–9, 193
    V. cornuta 118
    V. c. 'Gem Apricot Antique' 19
    V. c. 'Sorbet Coconut Duet' 31
    V. 'Etain' 120, 122–3

W

wall-mounted pots 26, 81, 85, 103
wallflower *see Erysimum*
walls 17, 19, 20, 23, 26, 27
water features 136–7
water lily *see Nymphaea*
watering 232, 234, 236, 238, 242, 243
    hanging baskets 237, 238
    with rainwater 63, 124, 137, 206, 222
    seedlings 240, 247
    tomatoes 28, 164, 241, 246
    see also irrigation systems

wax flower *see Hoya*
whitecurrants 209
    'Blanka' 209
    'Versailles Blanche' 209
wind 24, 26, 27, 154, 174, 208, 209, 226
windowboxes 24, 28, 29, 146, 159, 162, 165, 218
windowsills 20, 28–9, 30, 31, 159, 166
witch hazel *see Hamamelis*
wooden containers 10, 12, 13, 22, 26, 30
    crates 8, 19, 152, 170, 171, 190

Y

yew *see Taxus baccata*
Yucca 67
    Y. filamentosa 'Bright Edge' 67

Z

Zantedeschia hybrid 137

Acknowledgments

Martyn Cox would like to thank Alis, Louis, and Lily.

Dorling Kindersley would like to thank the following:
Helena Caldon for proofreading; Jane Coulter for indexing; Brian North for additional photography; Becky Shackleton for editorial assistance; Mel Watson for the use of her home and garden; Steve Crozier for assistance with image retouching

The publisher would like to thank the following for their kind permission to reproduce their photographs:
(Key: a-above; b-below/bottom; c-centre; f-far; l-left; r-right; t-top)

9 GAP Photos: Tim Gainey (br); Graham Strong (bc). **10 Marianne Majerus Garden Images:** Marianne Majerus (br). **Photolibrary:** Ken Hayden (c). **10-11 Photolibrary:** Pernilla Bergdahl. **11 The Garden Collection:** Nicola Stocken Tomkins (bl). **Photolibrary:** Clive Nichols (cb). **12 GAP Photos:** Richard Bloom (r). **The Garden Collection:** Derek Harris (bl). **13 GAP Photos:** Jonathan Buckley - Design: John Massey, Location: Ashwood Nurseries (c); Friedrich Strauss (bl); Visions (tl). **14 GAP Photos:** J S Sira - Design Suzan Slater HCFS 2005 (bc). **15 GAP Photos:** Richard Bloom (bc). **The Garden Collection:** Marie O' Hara, Designer: Paul Williams (bl). **Photolibrary:** Flora Press (cl). **16 GAP Photos:** Suzie Gibbons, Design: David Letham (r). **Marianne Majerus Garden Images:** Marianne Majerus (clb). **17 Photolibrary:** A S Milton (t); Ron Sutherland (b). **18 GAP Photos:** Graham Strong (cra) (cla). **Marianne Majerus Garden Images:** Marianne Majerus (b). **19 GAP Photos:** Friedrich Strauss (bl) (t). **20 GAP Photos:** Heather Edwards (cr). **Marianne Majerus Garden Images:** Marianne Majerus (br). **21 GAP Photos:** J S Sira (cr). **Marianne Majerus Garden Images:** Marianne Majerus (bc). **22 GAP Photos:** Friedrich Strauss (br) (bc). **Getty Images:** Janet Kimber (tr). **23 GAP Photos:** Jonathan Buckley, Design: Robin Green and Ralph Cade (bc). **Marianne Majerus Garden Images:** Marianne Majerus (r). **24 GAP Photos:** Friedrich Strauss (r). **Photolibrary:** Friedrich Strauss (bl). **25 GAP Photos:** Nicola Browne - Design: Jinny Blom (t); J S Sira, Design: Foundation Degree Course and Landscape Design Students (Year 3) Warwickshire College (br); Rob Whitworth, Design: Jo Ward-Ellison & Janette Dollamore (bl). **26 GAP Photos:** Jerry Harpur, Design: Van Oordt (bl). **Harpur Garden Library:** Jerry Harpur (br). **26-27 Marianne Majerus Garden Images:** Marianne Majerus. **27 GAP Photos:** Jerry Harpur - Design Christopher Bradley-Hole (b). **28 GAP Photos:** John Glover (bl). **Photolibrary:** Lynne Brotchie (br). **29 GAP Photos:** Tim Gainey (bl). **Getty Images:** redcover.com (c). **Marianne Majerus Garden Images:** Marianne Majerus (bc). **Photolibrary:** Suzie Gibbons (cr); Ellen Rooney (t). **30 GAP Photos:** Clive Nichols (bl); Friedrich Strauss (bc) (br). **31 GAP Photos:** (tr); Lynn Keddie (bl); Friedrich Strauss (br) (cl). **Photolibrary:** Flora Press (tl). **34 GAP Photos:** Friedrich Strauss (bl). **35 GAP Photos:** Jerry Harpur/Design Nancy Heckler - Oyster Point (tr). **36 The Garden Collection:** Michelle Garrett (cr). **37 GAP Photos:** Friedrich Strauss (b). **38-39 GAP Photos:** Jerry Harpur/Design Geoffrey Whiten. **40 GAP Photos:** Jerry Harpur/Design Nancy Heckler - Oyster Point (r). **45 GAP Photos:** Neil Holmes (r). **48 GAP Photos:**

Jonathan Buckley, Design: Christopher Lloyd (r). **49 GAP Photos:** BBC Magazines Ltd (cla); Visions (clb). **50-51 The Garden Collection:** Andrew Lawson. **51 Getty Images:** Martin Page (br). **53 GAP Photos:** Rob Whitworth (b). **Getty Images:** GAP Photos (t). **55 Clive Nichols:** (r). **62 GAP Photos:** Friedrich Strauss. **65 Getty Images:** GAP Photos RM (br). **70 GAP Photos:** Mark Bolton/Design Bob Purnell. **73 GAP Photos:** Friedrich Strauss (b). **74 GAP Photos:** Heather Edwards (r). **82-83 GAP Photos:** Friedrich Strauss. **87 Clive Nichols:** (bc). **89 Photolibrary:** Maria Mosolova (br). **92-93 Photolibrary:** Pernilla Bergdahl. **105 Raymond Evison:** www.raymondevisonclematis.com (tr) (bc). **108 GAP Photos:** Claire Davies. **109 Clive Nichols:** (t). **Thompson & Morgan:** (br/'Matacuana') www.thompson-morgan.com (bl) (fbl). **110 GAP Photos:** Jerry Harpur. **113 GAP Photos:** Brian North (bl). **114 GAP Photos:** Visions (r). **115 GAP Photos:** Friedrich Strauss (t) (b). **116-117 Marianne Majerus Garden Images:** Marianne Majerus/Susan Bennett. **118 GAP Photos:** Friedrich Strauss (r). **119 GAP Photos:** Friedrich Strauss (t). **120 GAP Photos:** Friedrich Strauss (b). **122-123 GAP Photos:** Friedrich Strauss. **129 GAP Photos:** Neil Holmes (br). **136 GAP Photos:** John Glover (b). **139 GAP Photos:** Friedrich Strauss (tr). **142-143 GAP Photos:** Juliette Wade. **143 GAP Photos:** Visions (tc). **145 GAP Photos:** Friedrich Strauss (t); Visions (b). **148 GAP Photos:** Friedrich Strauss (r). **152 GAP Photos:** Friedrich Strauss (bl). **154 GAP Photos:** Friedrich Strauss (bl). **155 Getty Images:** Kathy Collins (br). **160 Photoshot:** Photos Horticultural (cr). **162 GAP Photos:** John Glover (br). **163 Dorling Kindersley:** Airedale (b). **171 GAP Photos:** Friedrich Strauss (r). **179 GAP Photos:** Lynn Keddie (r). **180 GAP Photos:** FhF Greenmedia (r). **184 GAP Photos:** Howard Rice (r). **185 Brian North (tr). 186 Brian North (c). 189 Garden World Images:** Martin Hughes-Jones (bl). **190 GAP Photos:** Friedrich Strauss (b). **204 Photolibrary:** (r). **205 Getty Images:** StockFood (t). **206-207 GAP Photos:** Heather Edwards. **207 Getty Images:** Tim Hawley (cr). **Photolibrary:** Martin Page (tr). **210 Marianne Majerus Garden Images:** Marianne Majerus (r) (bl/Petit Muscat). **213 Blackmoor Nurseries:** www.blackmoor.co.uk (br/Tomcot). **Getty Images:** Inga Spence (t). **214 Marianne Majerus Garden Images:** Marianne Majerus (r). **215 Photolibrary:** Richard Bloom (b). **216 GAP Photos:** Friedrich Strauss (b). **217 GAP Photos:** FhF Greenmedia (r). **Photolibrary:** Photos Lamontagne (tr). **221 Getty Images:** Zara Napier (b). **223 Garden World Images:** Francoise Davis (r). **224 The Garden Collection:** Marie O' Hara (r). **225 GAP Photos:** Rob Whitworth (tr). **226-227 Getty Images:** Paul Debois. **229 Photolibrary:** Claire Higgins (cr). **230 Alamy Images:** Lou-Foto (b). **Getty Images:** Brand X (cr). **232 GAP Photos:** Sarah Cuttle (bc). **241 The Garden Collection:** Andrew Lawson (cr). **243 Royal Horticultural Society, Wisley:** (bc). **244 Getty Images:** Nigel Cattlin/Visuals Unlimited, Inc. (tr); Mark Turner (tc). **Royal Horticultural Society, Wisley:** (bc). **245 GAP Photos:** Sarah Cuttle (bl). **Royal Horticultural Society, Wisley:** (tl). **246 FLPA:** Nigel Cattlin (bl) (br). **GAP Photos:** Dave Bevan (fbl). **Royal Horticultural Society, Wisley:** (fbr). **247 GAP Photos:** Dave Bevan (ftr); FhF Greenmedia (fbl). **248 FLPA:** Nigel Cattlin (bl) (br). **Royal Horticultural Society, Wisley:** (fbr)

All other images © Dorling Kindersley
For further information see: www.dkimages.com